Engagements with Close Reading

What should we *do* with a literary work? Is it best to become immersed in a novel or poem, or is our job to objectively dissect it? Should we consult literature as a source of knowledge or wisdom, or keenly interrogate its designs upon us? Do we excavate the text as an historical artifact, or surrender to its aesthetic qualities?

Balancing foundational topics with new developments, *Engagements with Close Reading* offers an accessible introduction to how prominent critics have approached the task of literary reading. This book will help students:

- learn different methods for close reading
- perform a close analysis of an unfamiliar text
- articulate meaningful responses.

Beginning with the New Critics and recent arguments for a return to formalism, the book tracks the reactions of reader-response critics and phenomenologists, and concludes with ethical criticism's claim for the value of literary reading to our moral lives. Rich in literary examples, most reprinted in full, each chapter models practical ways for students to debate the pros and cons of objective and subjective criticism. In the final chapter, five distinguished critics shed light on the pleasures and difficulties of close reading in their engagements with poetry and fiction.

In the wake of cultural studies and historicism, *Engagements with Close Reading* encourages us to bring our eyes back to the words on the page, inviting students and instructors to puzzle out the motives, high stakes, limitations, and rewards of the literary encounter.

Annette Federico is Professor of English at James Madison University, USA.

Routledge Engagements with Literature

This series presents engagement as discovery. It aims to encourage ways to read seriously and to help readers hone and develop new habits of thinking critically and creatively about what they read—before, during, and after doing it. Each book in the series actively involves its readers by encouraging them to find their own insights, to develop their own judgments, and to inspire them to enter ongoing debates. Moreover, each *Engagements* volume:

- Provides essential information about its topic as well as alternative views and approaches;
- Covers the classic scholarship on its topic as well as the newest approaches and suggests new directions for study and research;
- Includes innovative "Engagements" sections that demonstrate practices for engaging with literature or that provide suggestions for further independent engagement;
- Provides an array of fresh, stimulating, and effective catalysts to reading, thinking, writing, and research.

Above all, *Routledge Engagements with Literature* shows that actively engaging with literature rewards the effort and that any reader can make new discoveries. My hope is the books in this series will help readers discover new, better, and more exciting and enjoyable ways of doing what we do when we read.

Series Editor
Daniel A. Robinson

Available in this series:

Engagements with Close Reading
Annette Federico

Engagements with Narrative
Janine Utell

Engagements with Close Reading

Annette Federico

 Routledge
Taylor & Francis Group

LONDON AND NEW YORK

First published 2016
by Routledge
2 Park Square, Milton Park, Abingdon, Oxon OX14 4RN

and by Routledge
711 Third Avenue, New York, NY 10017

Routledge is an imprint of the Taylor & Francis Group, an informa business

British Library Cataloguing-in-Publication Data
A catalogue record for this book is available from the British Library

Library of Congress Cataloging-in-Publication Data
Federico, Annette, 1960–
Engagements with close reading / Annette Federico.
    pages cm. – (Routledge engagements with literature)
    Includes bibliographical references and index.
    1. Discourse analysis, Literary. 2. Reading, Psychology of.
    3. Literature–History and criticism. 4. Criticism. I. Title.
    P302.5.F43 2016
    808.001'4-dc23   2015014368

ISBN: 978-0-415-74801-8 (hbk)
ISBN: 978-0-415-74802-5 (pbk)
ISBN: 978-1-315-75775-9 (ebk)

Typeset in Sabon
by Wearset Ltd, Boldon, Tyne and Wear

FSC
www.fsc.org
MIX
Paper from
responsible sources
FSC® C013604

Printed and bound by CPI Group (UK) Ltd, Croydon, CR0 4YY

Contents

Contributors to Chapter 5

Charles Altieri grew up in the Bronx and earned his Ph.D. at the University of North Carolina, Chapel Hill, in 1969. He holds the Rachael Anderson Stageberg Endowed Chair of English at the University of California, Berkeley.

Heather Dubrow was raised in New York City and received her Ph.D. from Harvard University. After teaching for many years at Carleton College in Northfield, Minnesota, and at the University of Wisconsin, Madison, she currently holds the John D. Boyd, SJ, Chair in the Poetic Imagination at Fordham University.

Sandra M. Gilbert, Distinguished Professor of English Emerita at the University of California, Davis, was educated at Cornell University, New York University, and Columbia University, where she received her Ph.D. in 1968. With Susan Gubar, she is co-author of the groundbreaking work of feminist criticism *The Madwoman in the Attic: The Woman Writer and the Nineteenth-century Literary Imagination* (1979).

James Phelan, born in Flushing, New York, in 1951, studied at Boston College and at the University of Chicago where he worked with Sheldon Sacks and Wayne C. Booth. He is Distinguished University Professor at The Ohio State University where he teaches and writes about the English and American novel, nonfiction narrative, and narrative theory.

Herbert Tucker grew up in New England and was educated at Moses Brown School, Amherst College, and Yale University. He has served on the faculty at Northwestern University, the University of Michigan and, since 1986, the University of Virginia, where in 2003 he was named to the John C. Coleman Chair in English.

Preface

There is a growing sense that models of literary critique that have been current for the past three decades have run out of steam, and that we are approaching a turning point in the practice of literary criticism and English pedagogy. At the center of this debate is reading, and the conversation has diverse participants.

In the mainstream media and within academia, a new book or article on the fate of reading in the digital age appears every month. There has been an explosion of interest in reading and the brain, cognitive theory, and neuroaesthetics. The history of reading and readers are huge topics, generating electronic research communities, major seminars, and new textbooks, anthologies, monographs, and collected editions in all areas of specialization. The field of textual studies discusses reading as a complex interface with material culture, embracing a range of disciplines from computer science and cinema to lexicography and linguistics. In response to these revolutionary developments, some English departments are being rebranded as departments of "Literature, Criticism, and Textual Studies," "English and the Digital Humanities," or "English, Modern Languages, and Mass Communication," and many offer institutes or specialized degrees in digitization, editorial theory, and book history and design.

These are all vital components of the discussion that's taking place about the past, present, and future of reading. Scholars who have oriented their pursuits toward media and cultural studies continue to reshape English departments across the United States and Great Britain in spectacular and very positive ways. Yet there has been some noticeable discomfort within the academy to the decentering of English study, what one scholar has called our "intellectual laissez-faire." To imply that the salient meaning of a literary work is discovered in its periodization and mode of production, in its resistance to or complicity with ideology, or in its materiality and historical reception may run the risk of ignoring the text's independence as a work of art, its unpredictable power and energy. These methodologies may also require students to follow their professors into the archives as amateur historians, or else draw them into specialized fields before they are intellectually prepared. As a result, students are trained to imitate their professors in pursuing a comparatively narrow theoretical path, instead of being encouraged to delve into a literary work on their own.

In response, some scholars have urged a return to aesthetic matters, a New Formalism that would more fully take into account the distinctive literary features of a text. Others have wanted to reconnect reading and affect, or discuss reading in light of the reader's response. And some of our most established critics have passionately testified to the importance of literary reading to human situations and our lives as moral and ethical agents. Each of these critical strands, *form, feeling,* and *ethics,* implicitly asks that we bring our eyes back to the words on the page, to account for the beauty and strangeness of language, chart the emotional resonance of our literary encounters, or affirm literature's real-world relevance and unpredictable social consequences.

This book is designed as a resource for those who want to balance sociological models for approaching literature with something closer to the formal, experiential, and ethical standpoints that are currently making a comeback. It is not a manifesto for formalism in opposition to cultural and historical critique, and it is not about a return to the canon (although, because of copyright restrictions, many of my examples are from older, canonical works). I also do not want to instruct anyone on how he or she should read literature by supplying a set of rules or a back-to-basics treatise, as so many handbooks have done, from Mortimer Adler's *How to Read a Book,* published in 1940, to Harold Bloom's *How to Read and Why,* half a century later. Instead, *Engagements with Close Reading* condenses the story of objective versus subjective criticism and distills current arguments through the presentation of many concrete examples. For although I accept the opinion of specialists in educational theory, as well as of scholars in the humanities, that there has been a generational shift in cognitive styles, and that many young people learn best when they can switch focus among tasks and access multiple information streams, I want to keep alive the practice of reading complete sentences and whole paragraphs. So I have avoided the snapshot approach used in some literary handbooks (boxes, bullet points, keywords, etc.), and instead produce small chunks of criticism along with the literature. We can only appreciate the labors of the creative imagination, as well as the perseverance and insight of good literary critics, by encountering texts directly and on our own terms. I felt that a book on close reading must be written under the assumption that it would be read through, the ideas debated, the examples discussed in class along with other texts chosen by the instructor. Overall, I have wanted to validate and quicken the impulse that makes people gravitate to reading and studying literature in the first place.

The central mission of an English department should be to help students develop the cognitive attention, emotional awareness, and ethical judgment that reading literature requires, and to model for them why reading literature matters. When we teach close reading, whatever our theoretical bent or specialization, we take as a matter of faith that literature has a human value, and carry the hope that immersive reading and appreciative criticism still have the potential to reveal meaningful knowledge of the world and of ourselves, as well as meaningful change.

Acknowledgments

This project received support from the Program of Grants for Faculty Educational Leaves, the Department of English, and the College of Arts and Letters at James Madison University.

Charles Altieri, Heather Dubrow, Sandra M. Gilbert, James Phelan, and Herbert Tucker responded to my invitation to contribute to this book—a fan letter in academic dress—with kindness and optimism. I am so grateful to them, and honored to have such distinguished critics associated with so small a foray into the world of literary reading.

Amanda Freeman allowed me to include a portion of her superb seminar paper on Gerard Manley Hopkins in Chapter 3. She and the students in English 640—Julian Dean, Michael Harper, Krista Sarraf, Alan Stauffer, Jana Zevnik, and Doug Zimmerman—entertained my queries and claims about reading with wonderful stamina and bonhomie.

I also must thank the indefatigable Daniel Robinson for inviting me to contribute to *Engagements with literature* and for encouraging me to follow my own path.

Finally, this book is for Chuck Dotas. Whenever the blues become my only song, I concentrate on you.

1 Close reading, critical reading

Criticism must be sincere, simple, flexible, ardent, ever widening its knowledge.

(Arnold 1970a: 157)

A critic must be emotionally alive in every fibre, intellectually capable and skillful in essential logic, and then morally very honest.

(Lawrence, 1973: 119)

In an essay called "The Perfect Critic," from 1921, T. S. Eliot complains that contemporary literary criticism has become confused and degenerate. Information *about* literature is swallowing up knowledge *of* literature. The world has changed so drastically in the last hundred years, he observes, that people who supposedly devote their lives to reading and criticizing poetry, drama, and fiction don't quite know what they are about anymore. There is so much "information ... so many fields of knowledge in which the same words are used with different meanings" that it is difficult to judge whether or not a critic really knows what she is talking about (Eliot 2011: 7). In fact, an ordinary intelligent person, a scientist or a stockbroker, who takes an interest in literature may form judgments based on nothing more than personal inclination—whether or not she likes the emotions expressed in a poem, or if she can relate to a character in a novel. For T. S. Eliot, this will not do. There must be some kind of critical methodology, some meaningful equilibrium, and so he sets out accordingly to examine "how far criticism is 'feeling' and how far 'thought,' and what sort of 'thought' is permitted" (2011: 5).

The fact that Eliot has to place the words *feeling* and *thought* in quotation marks suggests there's something delicate or slippery about the entire question for him, or that maybe these two modes of experiencing literature are so intricately entangled that it is a bit ingenuous to treat subjectivity and objectivity as separate things. (That they *have* been treated as separate things, from the Enlightenment on, Eliot knew very well.) What exactly, Eliot wants to know, is the critic's job in the twentieth century? Should he cultivate objectivity, delineate standards, analyze a poem stanza by stanza to detect verbal subtleties? Or must a critic, above all, develop a sensitive mind, learn to isolate feelings and impressions, transform criticism into a creative act? Should a critic introduce elements of the author's biography and historical data into her reading? Or must she concentrate only on her direct experience with the literary work, disregarding other kinds of knowledge as irrelevant?

Eliot concludes that since around the nineteenth century, criticism has taken two wrong turns. It is either so scientific or abstract in spirit that it loses its way in generalities, or else it is too cozily impressionistic, an accident of personal feeling rather than a deliberate judgment. Criticism of the first kind uses language that cannot appeal to our senses, and so offers us nothing meaningful about the work being studied. Not only is it too "technical," he says, but the worst practitioners keep getting in the reader's way, trying to coerce or expound a lesson rather than simply "elucidate" the work and let the reader form her own opinions. Another danger is that such criticism has a tendency to be overly methodical and codified because it tries to come across as a science. This kind of criticism runs the risk of slipping from "understanding to mere explanation" (Eliot 1957: 131).

Yet the second kind of criticism is just as bad—in fact, for Eliot, it was probably worse. For when a literary critic explains a work of art in terms of her personal impressions and emotional responses, she distorts both the work and her responses: as soon as she tries to explain her emotions, she has begun to analyze them, and in the process something new gets created—it certainly may turn into a fine bit of writing, but it is definitely *not* a work of criticism. No, the perfect critic should leave his messy personal associations at the door, and have "no emotions except those immediately provoked by the work of art" (Eliot 2011: 8). Pernicious distortions take place when a critic allows his own feelings to take the place of objective inquiry. On the other hand, knowledge always begins in perception, Eliot says, and critics who replace acute literary sensitivity with "historical" or "philosophical" analysis are also on the wrong road. There is, Eliot concludes, "no method except to be very intelligent" (2011: 7).

Why begin with the concerns of literary criticism in a book about close reading? Because, in a positive sense, good readers and good critics share the same problems. Indeed, almost everything that's said about the difficulties of literary criticism is applicable to the enterprise of literary reading, and not only because both are demanding intellectual activities. The good reader, like the good critic, has to take his personal experience of life and his limited knowledge of the world into a formal and self-contained space created in another person's mind. How would the ideal reader enter that space? How might she balance emotional and subjective responses to it—identifying with the heroine, being swept away by a beautiful line of verse, discovering a buried memory—with objective or evaluative criteria? Does the reader who loses sight of things such as style, structure, the choice of figurative language, or the work's situation in literary history really know or appreciate what she is reading? Or is it better to become so absorbed by the literary work that the technicalities of writing just don't register? Perhaps the perfect reader, like Eliot's perfect critic, should try to become someone who exquisitely manages both—a discriminating observer who can turn her knowledge and attention to the details of the literary work, and a responsive individual with a unique personal history and emotional self-awareness.

It seems many important critics in the first half of the twentieth century were cognizant of this objective–subjective problem for critical reading. In 1951, for example, Harvard professor Reuben Brower wrote that a good literary critic must always pay attention to the specific literary features of the work, but that it would be a mistake to overlook the value of our intuitions. "Hunches about how experience hangs together are necessary to any successful intellectual activity," he argued, "whether in science or poetry, or in criticism, which lies somewhere between the other two" (2013: 15). Brower calls descending to details and honoring one's hunches the Scylla and Charybdis of literary criticism, this being almost by definition the kind of work that straddles analysis and self-expression, science and art. As the critic Allen Tate wrote, also in 1951, what makes literary criticism so difficult to master is its exasperating "middle position between imagination and philosophy" (2008: 71). Indeed, for the contemporary cultural historian Peter de Bolla, this state of "in-between-ness" is a defining aspect of our experience with all works of art, the "thinking-feeling" response, as he puts it, which is "part physical and part mental, in the orbit of the emotive yet also clearly articulated ... within the higher orders of mental activity" (2001: 3). We might say that criticism is the art of calibrating a response (and a judgment) about something that is designed to discombobulate us—to provoke the head and the heart.

Today, after half a century of pioneering critical explorations and all the challenges brought by postmodern philosophy, literary scholars are again debating criticism's perplexing intermediary position, the epistemological tightrope that criticism extends between subjective and objective forms of knowing. They are asking again basic questions about how we should read, write, and talk about literature in ways that will address the fullness of the literary encounter.[1] Some are insisting that we should return to the fundamental activity of English departments, which has always been the reading of literature and the practice of literary criticism.[2] Others want to re-examine the notion of a group of core works in the study of literature, or draw stricter boundaries between literature and other textual media. Most important, and as I will explain later in this chapter, many scholars have lately been asking about the value and substance of the kind of historical, political, and cultural approaches to literary study that have dominated English departments for the last thirty years. They're urging a return to the work itself, and especially to the broadly descriptive practice long known as *close reading*.[3] As a consequence, three venerable and influential critical approaches that were sidelined by historicism and cultural studies are finding fresh iterations in different strands of criticism focused on the relationship between the reader and the text. They are *formalism*, *reader-response criticism*, and *ethical criticism*.

Although these three approaches often argue from opposite sides of the objective–subjective divide, acting and reacting to swings of the critical pendulum, they are harmonious in their fundamental concern with the primacy of the reading experience. In different ways, each circles back to Eliot's problem: how does a good reader find the ideal middle position between feeling and thought, hold the equipoise between imagination and philosophy, poetry and science? Can "sensibility, intelligence, and capacity for wisdom," to quote Eliot again, be turned into a methodology (1957: 117)? Above all, they ask what we should *do* with the literary work. Should we accept its invitations, or hold it at arm's length? Become immersed in the author's world, or rationally dissect it? Consult the literary work as a source of wisdom, or interrogate its assumptions? Excavate the text as an historical artifact, or surrender to its aesthetic qualities?

In this book, I want to explain how these types of questions may be brought fruitfully to bear on the efforts of any person who wants to read well and appreciatively, and to unite the knowledge wrought by a small selection of the best literary critics, from the past and from today, with any reader's ambitions toward a richer experience of literary art. For with practice, people do learn to become more mature, discriminating, noticing readers. Is there a special quality or disposition that makes some people casual readers—people who read mostly to kill time or only read what's popular—and others critical readers, people who choose what they read with care, who guard their reading lives from the invasion of social obligations and distracting technologies, who carry around in their heads a private library of meaningful books? Many people read books, and many people read a lot. But there are some people who, quite simply, seem to get more out of reading. They're *really reading*. Is it what they choose to read that matters, or is it how they go about it?

Literary readers do not belong to a special caste, and this book is not intended as an initiation into the secret practices of the highly literate. It can be dangerous and irresponsible to judge a person's intelligence, politics, or moral feeling by the books she reads (or doesn't read). Categorical thinking of that sort may become a tool of elitism and censorship. So I like the judicious way C. S. Lewis writes about two kinds of readers in the first chapters of *An Experiment in Criticism* (1961). He wants to reverse the usual assumption that criticism is about judging the merits of different books, and suggests that instead we turn our attention to the reader: what we would call a "good book" is read in one way, and a "bad book" is read in another way. Lewis characterizes the majority of readers as people who never read a book twice, who read as a last resort when there's nothing else going on, who finish a book without noticing its effects on them, and who seldom talk about their reading. Other people, the reading minority, go about it differently. They enjoy rereading the same books, they feel lost when they're deprived of time to read, they know that reading is a momentous experience that alters their consciousness, and they long to talk about books. It seems clear that for some people, reading is a pursuit, more than just a pastime. Yet Lewis warns against prejudices or oversimplifications about these types or categories of readers. We probably all have friends or family members who have never read a novel from start to finish, and they are none the worse for it—they do their jobs conscientiously, love their families, and ably perform the duties of citizenship. After all, as the Marxist critic Terry Eagleton has argued, people who don't sit down at night to read Henry James or Toni Morrison constitute the social majority and they could hardly be labeled as imaginatively bankrupt or morally obtuse. C. S. Lewis reminds us that the majority of readers include people "who are equal or superior to some of the [minority] in psychological health, in moral virtue, practical prudence, good manners, and general adaptability" (1961: 5). He even objects to the use of the word *serious* as applied to reading (as in, "Marcus is a serious reader") since that equivocal adjective often wrongly suggests solemnity, studiousness, and a kind of literary puritanism that equates literary difficulty with moral discipline.

Rather, writes Lewis, the "true reader reads every work seriously in the sense that he reads it whole-heartedly, makes himself as receptive as he can" (1961: 11). He is able to read "in the same spirit as the author writ": he can analyze British imperialism in *Mansfield Park* and still enjoy Austen's moral insight, or discuss *The Great Gatsby*'s presentation of masculinity and still be moved by Fitzgerald's lyricism. Reading wholeheartedly includes our natural responses, from pleasure in rhyme and meter to the pull of narrative suspense. Importantly, these true readers do not necessarily read the way trained academics, professors, professional reviewers, and scholars read—and they shouldn't. The poet W. H. Auden has a fine observation about the distinction between the reading practices of professors and those of the common reader. In answer to the question, "What is the function of a critic?" Auden replies:

1 Introduce me to authors or works of which I was hitherto unaware.
2 Convince me that I have undervalued an author or a work because I had not read them carefully enough.
3 Show me relations between works of different ages and cultures which I could never have seen for myself because I do not know enough and never shall.
4 Give a "reading" of a work which increases my understanding of it.
5 Throw light upon the process of artistic "Making".

6   Throw light upon the relation of art to life, to science, to economics, ethics, religion, etc.

(1962: 8–9)

Auden claims that the first three items on the list demand scholarship—extensive and valuable knowledge that may be imparted to other people. It goes without saying that we should be hugely grateful to scholars and professors for their help in offering context and information about a work of literature; it's rather important to know about the American south in William Faulkner's fiction, John Milton's position during the English Civil Wars, the impact of colonial rule on Derek Walcott's poetry. Literary study would be crippled and impoverished without this kind of knowledge.

But Auden suggests that the aim of close, critical reading is not *only* that kind of knowledge. We may with equal dignity be headed for something harder to measure, and perhaps harder to attain: for the last three items on the list require "not superior knowledge, but superior insight" (1962: 9). Auden doesn't mean a flash of recognition or some kind of momentary illumination, though these things do happen. He means discernment—a habit of noticing what an author's doing, and a way of making connections with other books and with a world of ideas. Item number 4 on Auden's list might constitute the product of this process. To "give a reading," a critic zeroes in on certain features of the text he has noticed and responded to and makes an argument based on his ideas about what he's noticed. A good close reading extends our appreciation of the aesthetic features of a work, shows us something about what it may mean, and opens it up for critical debate.

Close reading, like all modes of literary interpretation, is based on a theory about how to read and criticize literature. But in a way, close reading also supersedes theory because it's the end or goal of theorizing—it's what we *do* with literature, and as such it's a practice we can learn by studying good models. Witnessing the labor, invention, and care that go into close critical reading should get us to appreciate our investment in English studies, and help us when we try our own hand at writing a literary critique. So throughout this book I offer many examples by formalist, subjective, and ethical critics to show the different ways close reading may be done, and to set before us the pros and cons of each. To see how these approaches can be welded together creatively, in fruitful and interesting ways, in Chapter 5 below a group of distinguished contemporary critics do close readings of a selected poem or story. Throughout this book, I hope to display the richness of the literary encounter when the focus is on the work itself rather than theoretical or social contexts, and thereby testify to the value and pleasure of close literary reading when the job is undertaken with creativity, precision, and delight.

What is needed for literary satisfaction is not, "this is beautiful because of such and such a theory," but "this is all right; I am feeling correctly about this; I know the kind of way in which it is meant to be affecting me."

(Empson 1953: 254)

Poetry, drama, and fiction have a peculiar relation to knowledge because literary works demand the exercise of cognition and emotion, intellect and intuition. Literature asks us to occupy two kinds of mental space at once: we are invited to accept the functionality of words that have the ability to point to things we already know or recognize in the real world—courtship rituals or nightingales or war—yet at the same time to observe the instability of the same words to signal oblique or unfamiliar things that we may only sense. As the philosopher Gordon Graham has suggested, literature has the peculiar ability "to reveal to us 'how it feels' as well as 'how it is.' "[4]

In 1930, William Empson, a student at Cambridge University, published an astonishingly original book called *Seven Types of Ambiguity*, in which he tackled the problem of how poets manage to get language to be effective in several ways at once. He argued that although no critical explanation will adequately account for the greatness of a poem, a reasonable analysis of its language may be applied in a way that helps us appreciate how the poem succeeds.

Most people are probably familiar with Shakespeare's sonnet 73, which begins:

> That time of year thou mayst in me behold
> When yellow leaves, or none, or few, do hang
> Upon those boughs which shake against the cold,
> Bare ruined choirs, where late the sweet birds sang.

Here is what Empson has to say about the fourth line:

> [T]he comparison holds for many reasons; because ruined monastery choirs are places in which to sing, because they involve sitting in a row, because they are made of wood, are carved in knots and so forth, because they used to be surrounded by a sheltering of buildings crystallized out of the likeness of a forest, and coloured with stained glass and painting like flowers and leaves, because they are now abandoned by all but the grey walls coloured like the skies of winter, because the cold and Narcissistic charm suggested by choir-boys suits well with Shakespeare's feeling for the object of the Sonnets, and for various social and historical reasons (the protestant destruction of the monasteries; fear of puritanism), which it would be hard now to trace out in their proportions; these reasons and many more relating the simile to

its place in the Sonnet, must all combine to give the line its beauty, and there is a sort of ambiguity in not knowing which of them to hold most clearly in mind. Clearly this is involved in all such richness and heightening of effect, and the machinations of ambiguity are among the very roots of poetry.

(1953: 2–3)

By minutely studying the resonance of just this one line, Empson demonstrates how *ambiguity* is the engine that drives poetic meaning. If we pause to examine a word or a metaphor in a poem, its vibrant possibilities stand out like a brilliantly colored thread in a tightly woven tapestry. It's true that Empson's close readings were undertaken with a kind of amiable ferocity, and he was aware that some of his contemporaries might feel his ruthless verbal analysis destroyed the atmosphere of the poem and sterilized the reader's emotional response. But Empson retorts that reading this closely may actually make the reader feel more confident in her response, stronger in her appreciation, and better able to distinguish between an accidental reaction and one that can be repeated because it can be explained in reference to the poet's choices (1953: 254). "[T]he more one understands one's own reactions," Empson declares, "the less one is at their mercy" (1953: 15).

To begin, of course, we have to just read—read all the words, read to the end. But Empson assumed that when we set out to analyze a work of literature we are progressing from just reading to a different stage of comprehension and appreciation—from what he called intuitive knowledge to intellectual knowledge. We may understand the poem alone, in our minds, but when we try to criticize it we place it in a field with other objects and we talk about it to other people (1953: 251–252). The great Canadian literary critic Northrop Frye wrote that, "the end of reading or listening is the beginning of critical understanding, and nothing that we call criticism can begin until the whole of what it is striving to comprehend has been presented to it" (1963: 8). Frye means that it is only when we have finished reading and have absorbed the work of literature as a whole that we can take the next step in a cognitive process that may inaugurate a series of recognitions, whether these are of meaningful patterns in the work's design, a larger encounter with the mind of the author, a better sense of the big picture of literary history, or even a personal epiphany. Everyone who enjoys reading, whether epics or detective stories, will have what Frye calls a "pre-critical" or "participating" response to what is being read: going along with the text, hearing the author out, being sped along by the words and worlds she's created. There's a second kind of response, though, which Frye characterizes as "thematic, detached, fully conscious," a sense-making effort toward a better understanding of the work, or toward a value judgment about it, or maybe both (1963: 8–9). In her essay "How

Should One Read a Book?" Virginia Woolf expresses the idea with typical elegance:

> The first process, to receive impressions with the utmost understanding, is only half the process of reading; it must be completed, if we are to get the whole pleasure from a book, by another. We must pass judgment upon these multitudinous impressions; we must make of these fleeting shapes one that is hard and lasting.
>
> (1989: 266)

What I am calling *close reading* is essentially this second type of response: the cultivation of self-consciousness about the reading experience, a desire for more awareness of what's going on—the kind of reading that opens the door to a deeper, more critical understanding of the *particular* work being read, and of the *experience* of reading as a whole.

When we read with full attention, it may be because we are drawn to a poem's or novel's aesthetic features; we are attracted and pleased by its *form* and want to examine in detail the way it is designed. At other times, we may want to know and understand what's behind the artistry, to grasp the work's *content*, the concepts or worldview that is being shown to us, and to meet the mind that devised it. Then again we may read for solace, or to feel less alone during a difficult time in our lives. Close reading is a technique we use to shrink the distance between ourselves and a writer or a text. We can still disagree with the author's ideas or find her style flavorless—close doesn't mean merging with the author's worldview, and we'll see that judging the literary work is unavoidable. But close reading—critical reading—gets us to think rationally about an experience that is fundamentally estranging, because ordinary language is being used in unfamiliar, incongruous, or bizarre ways (such as "Bare ruined choirs, where late the sweet birds sang"). Close reading also gets us to think analytically about what we've read without losing hold of the emotional part of the whole experience (and in this sense close reading may be applied to films and other non-reading events). Finally, close reading requires that we temporarily put away our own habits of thinking, our opinions and certainties, and make space for another's ideas, look through another's eyes. My definition of close reading, then, is this: a deliberately undertaken activity that asks for attention to the real-time experience of reading a literary work united with an effort to step back from the experience in order to better understand (1) the work's *form*, its craftsmanship and artistry, (2) the work's *feeling*, or its personal and psychological resonance, and (3) the work's *ethos*, its implied commentary on human values.

This back-and-forth of objective and subjective is, I believe, at the root of all good close reading, no matter what theoretical position a critic or a reader may assume. So what I am calling close reading is something many poets and critics have written about: it is the interplay of the *active* and *reflective* aspects of reading. In a comment on William Blake in the essay already cited, Northrop Frye sees in Blake's poetry the uncompromising belief that an artist "demonstrates a certain way of life: his aim is not to be appreciated or admired, but to *transfer to others* the imaginative habit and energy of his mind" (1963: 4, my italics). Samuel Taylor Coleridge, the Romantic poet, wrote that what makes Shakespeare a great poet is that "he has made *you* one—an active creative being" (Scott 2009: 193). Similarly, the twentieth-century French theorist Maurice Blanchot says, "The reading of a poem is the poem itself" (1983: 198). Or as Marcel Proust puts it, in a sort of looking-glass version of Blanchot, "Every reader, as he reads, is actually the reader of himself" (quoted in Kundera 2006: 96). What each of these writers suggests is that even if someone applies the most rigorous theoretical tools to decipher the operation of language or the production of meaning in a literary work, literary reading is still fundamentally relational, or *intersubjective*: a self-to-other, self-to-world, and even self-to-self experience. Even the strictest objective critic understands that a literary creation is vitally recreated in the minds of readers. And so close literary reading requires imagination, focus, receptivity, intellectual endurance, the expectation of pleasure, a willingness to be surprised, curiosity, and a bracing capacity for risk. These are the intangibles that belong to the practice that I am calling close reading, critical reading, or engaged reading, and I will return to them often in this book. But I also want to bring into focus some of the more learnable skills that belong to close reading, a practice I think almost everyone would agree is foundational for any serious study of English.

Although some works require and reward critical scrutiny more than others, close reading in the sense I am using it does not apply only to works of fiction, poetry, or drama, or only to "high art," canonical texts. We can do a close reading of Charles Darwin's *Origin of Species*, Plato's *Republic*, Virginia Woolf's diaries, John Green's *The Fault in Our Stars*, or the screenplay for *Fight Club*. Close reading is essentially about understanding different levels of coherence in written communication, and this is a skill very much worth learning. In a great essay called "Reading in Slow Motion," published in 1962, Reuben Brower argued that a

> course in interpretation is a course in definition by contexts, in seeing how words are given rich and precise meaning through their interrelations with other words. The student who acquires this habit of definition will be a better reader of philosophy or law or any other type of specialized discourse, and he may learn something about the art of writing, or how to control context in order to express oneself.
>
> (1962: 11)

I hope the personal and practical value of forming this intellectual habit and acquiring the skills and competencies close reading fosters will become apparent in the chapters to follow, as we work through some sophisticated critical positions, and explore an array of literary works.

As the contemporary scholar Jane Gallop has recently argued, close reading is by no means a new idea in literary criticism; it was the very practice that turned English into a discipline, and it is still the most valuable thing English has to offer (2007: 183). Yet some scholars are beginning to feel that, in the last half decade or so, close reading skills have been crowded out of the field by a set of other practices that have tended to move away from the relational aspect of reading that I want to emphasize. Although a simplification, I think it's fair to say that these orientations to the literary work have tended to look at determinants of the way language can be used in society (sometimes referred to as cultural discourse) and at the abstract social and political machinery that generates patterns of behavior. In this view, literature is seen as part of a socio-linguistic system. So some critics attack the job of reading a novel or a poem by interrogating certain categories supposed to be in any product of culture, such as economics or gender, looking for political and ideological assumptions that the text may have smoothed out or hidden from its original audience. The author himself is pretty irrelevant, in this view, because systems of language and technologies of writing have already determined his attitude of expression, his metaphors, his symbols, his assumptions about genre. If a view of the world is being expressed in *Hamlet*, it is not Shakespeare who expresses that view, but the text of the play *Hamlet*, an arrangement of language inextricable from other texts that came before and will come after. A similar strand in critical theory insists on the instability of language, implying that words don't refer to anything "out there" in what we call "reality," but only to more words; to talk about the "meaning" of a poem is irrational, since all we really have are grammatical patterns generating more grammatical patterns. A single work of literature, then, may be seen to dissolve into *intertextuality*, its position beside other works of literature or other discourses, or else it is understood as a matrix of cultural codes, which it is the theorist's job to unlock.

In another critical orientation, labeled New Historicism, the way into the text is through particular historical and cultural contexts surrounding the literary work. Like all writing, poems and plays are historical documents, artifacts of a whole, complex culture. New Historicists might not even want to see a text as the unique creation of a single author, so the author's biography or her purported intentions are not given much weight in the work of interpretation. Instead, New Historicists seek the traces and leftovers of the author's culture, excavating the literary work for fragments of everyday life, and so placing it on a continuum with other evidence from the culture—paintings, pamphlets, buildings, photographs, maps, etc. Rather than piously studying a play by Shakespeare as a timeless work of art that transcends its historical moment, this kind of critic might explore an embedded discourse of Roman Catholic ritual in *Hamlet*, teasing out all the references to bread or confession or Purgatory, and place the play against Elizabethan documents on the Protestant Reformation. Similar to the methods of anthropologists, these critics take a small bit of cultural evidence from a text and tug on it like a piece of loose thread in order to unravel a network of evocative symbols awaiting their cultural analysis. This critical position encourages readers to approach literature with suspicion, wary of its designs upon us. So although New Historicists *do* pay attention to literature's formal qualities (language, rhetoric, genre, allusion) and they are often very exacting close readers, that enterprise is undertaken not in a spirit of poetic appreciation, but rather to expose apparently aesthetic qualities as complicit in historical facts or in ideologies of power. Indeed, two of the originators of New Historicism, Catherine Gallagher and Stephen Greenblatt, claim straightforwardly that this model of criticism comes with an attitude: it is "skeptical, wary, demystifying, critical, and even adversarial" (2000: 9).

Alongside the historicist approach is cultural studies, a model of inquiry that tends to situate literature in relation to the social sciences. Cultural studies critics are especially interested in the economics of literary production and in power relations. To find out about the race, class, and gender dynamics of the American literary marketplace, for instance, these critics might look at how Jack London's stories were solicited and sold, where they appeared and how they were advertised, how they were received by consumers and reviewers, and the cultural forces that gave rise to London's status as a celebrity author. They might be interested in how a society defined or policed certain identities, studying, say, the figure of the physician in a bunch of nineteenth-century novels (some well known, some all but forgotten), in order to speculate on the power structure of the Victorian medical establishment, its policing of the female body, and its latent representation in bourgeois novels. Because in their view, culture is not identical with "high culture"—with texts that are endowed with a degree of importance in society, and therefore preserved in archives, anthologies, and libraries—these critics eagerly take up popular and non-literary material, both unpublished and published pieces of writing (comic books, diaries, etiquette manuals, court documents) and other media products, from vampire films to sit-coms, gospel music to sporting events. A cultural studies critic would be curious about *Hamlet* and *Star Trek*, or *Hamlet's* cultural mobility and Chinese films, or how interpretations of the role of Ophelia expose assumptions about women and madness in different historical periods. Related fields of specialization, such as textual studies, media studies, geospatial studies, the history of the book, and studies in material culture and visual culture, embrace as their subject all forms of human communication.

In both cultural studies and New Historicist approaches, the essential questions revolve around the capitalist, patriarchal, or imperialist contexts of the work's production, its packaging, and its consumption by readers or viewers. The point is to get beneath the entertaining surface and make bare or *demystify* the power structures that are always implicated in literature—and, indeed, to dismantle the idea that some works have a special status or aura because they are high art products, capital-L literature. Using a psychoanalytic paradigm, what has been called *symptomatic reading* assumes there is repressed, often violent, cultural information just below the pleasant veneer of the novel or the poem. As the critics Stephen Best and Sharon Marcus explain,

> When symptomatic readers focus on elements present in the text they construe them as symbolic of something latent or concealed; for example, a queer symptomatic reading might interpret the closet, or ghosts, as surface signs of the deep truth of a homosexuality that cannot be overtly depicted. Symptomatic readings also often locate outright absences, gaps, and ellipses in texts, and then ask what those absences mean, what forces create them, and how they signify the questions that motivate the text, but that the text itself cannot articulate.
>
> (2009: 3)

This critical position mistrusts what a novel seems to say, and instead theorizes what the text doesn't know or can't say. When we read *against* the text, we look not for what the author may have wanted to communicate, but for cultural tensions and truths that make their way into the work regardless of the author's apparent aims. The moral trajectory of *Jane Eyre* is ostensibly toward the heroine's achievement of autonomy, but as many readers have observed, Charlotte Brontë's novel also communicates Victorian culture's anxiety about female aggression. Bram Stoker's *Dracula* is supposed to make our flesh creep, but underneath the campy vampirism lie profound fears of racial difference, foreign invasion, and sexual anarchy. Indeed, cultural studies critics have been industrious when it comes to vampires, especially regarding Stephanie Meyers's popular saga—in just the last five years almost a dozen books have been published, with clever titles such as *Images of the Modern Vampire: The Hip and the Atavistic*; *Theorizing Twilight: Critical Essays on What's at Stake in a Post-Vampire World*; *The Vampire Goes to College: Essays on Teaching with the Undead*; and *Bitten by Twilight: Youth Culture, Media, and the Vampire Franchise*.

Historical contexts and theoretical tools should not be abandoned in our reading and critical practice—indeed, I don't think it's possible to abandon them. Professional literary critics and well-informed readers should know something about an author's life and historical situation, a text's publication history, and the cultural forces that were at work when it was published. We can be deeply moved by Walt Whitman's great poem "When Lilacs Last in the Dooryard Bloom'd" without knowing about the assassination of Abraham Lincoln, but we will probably get more out of the poem if we have some details about the event that inspired it.

Also, I don't think there is anything wrong with approaching a text through a calculated critical position. In the last thirty years hundreds of extraordinary literary works have been added to the American and British canons because of the committed scholarly labor of feminist, queer, Marxist, and postcolonial scholars—now canonical works by women, such as Charlotte Perkins Gilman's "The Yellow Wallpaper," Kate Chopin's *The Awakening*, and Zora Neale Hurston's *Their Eyes Were Watching God*, the writings of postcolonial authors such as Chinua Achebe, and long-suppressed works by Native Americans and gay and lesbian authors. And many so-called masterpieces have been cracked wide open by a generation of critics who studied them for the first time with an eye toward the representation of women, sexuality, social class, and race and ethnicity. So a feminist reading of *Hamlet* that zeroes in on Gertrude as way to understand women and power in the reign of Elizabeth I is not necessarily a distorted interpretation of the play. Reading Charlotte Brontë's *Jane Eyre* with an eye out for racist and imperialist assumptions and tropes makes sense given the expansion of British imperial power in the nineteenth century, just as it might cast a light on the Victorian class struggle if we look up statistics about a governess's wages in 1847 and compare them to those of a factory worker. Looking at the articles and advertisements published alongside Oscar Wilde's *The Picture of Dorian Gray* in *Lippincott's Magazine* for July 1890 might give readers a glimpse into some odd, late-Victorian hobbies relevant to the world of the novel. Similarly, we can excavate Emily Dickinson's poetry through women's fashions of the time, finding new meaning in the tippets, capes, calicoes, and gaiters that appear in many of her poems. It can be argued that these kinds of approaches attempt to demonstrate the many ways literature takes part in the real world, and how literary works are woven into the texture of history and politics, place and identity, popular culture and everyday life.

In recent years, though, established and influential scholars have asked why contemporary criticism must be an investigation of grammatical systems and power grids, why it is always dependent on historical contexts and hidden truths, or on situating literature in relation to media studies and the social sciences. Some have begun to express surprise at the state of affairs in humanities departments, and even a bit of consternation at what passes for literary criticism today.[5] They wonder if valuable aesthetic and moral features have been forgotten when we look at literature merely as an appendage of history. Some of these scholars are also asking if including all kinds of textual objects and media, from nineteenth-century fashion magazines to cult movies, shopping malls, and Google Maps under the umbrella term "English" is the right way to promote the kind of work that once belonged to a distinguished tradition of literary criticism, whose task (to cite T. S. Eliot one last time) had been to help readers "to *understand*

and *enjoy*" poetry, fiction, and plays (1957: 130, original italics). It has been argued that the ascendancy of cultural studies, and another area of critique called textual studies, a burgeoning field now often assimilated into English programs, has pushed the study of literature into a rather small and irrelevant corner. In opening the door for scholars to freely explore everything out there (what *isn't* a text?), have English departments lost their justification, and made the close reading of literature irrelevant? If students over in the English department are not actually reading literature and learning how to write about it, what *are* they doing? Maybe historicism and cultural studies have tilted English departments too much toward theoretical abstractions or specialized categories of inquiry, so that the literature we study is presented not as a source of ideas about how to live, but as a reflection of an ideology. As David Mikics (2013a) puts it, in many of today's college English classrooms "books, whether theory or not, have become tools for making predictable references to big concepts (capitalism, gender, modernity) rather than what they should be, guides to life."

Whether or not we agree with Mikics's idealism about literature's potential, it is probably true that, in some situations, theoretical paradigms, cultural analyses, and abstract ideas have almost taken the place of reading literature for its intrinsic value. To cite Reuben Brower once again, because literary texts "are often presented in some broad historical framework," a work of imaginative literature is deployed principally as an illustration of an historical fact. The "rich and special experience" of reading fiction or poetry is "too readily reduced to crude examples of a historic idea" (1962: 18). Today, more than fifty years after Brower's essay, the internet has made so many kinds of information easily available that there's probably more data about Elizabethan theater, modernist little magazines, or Victorian serials than non-academic, non-specialist readers can meaningfully apply to the study of literary texts—to say nothing of products and websites that make the actual reading experience either irrelevant or an extension of the entertainment industry.[6]

To be clear, I am not talking about scholarship in the digital humanities, which can be extremely helpful for students and scholars who might want to know different sorts of things about a work they're studying. Digitization has made hundreds of literary works available to researchers who are adding new knowledge to many areas of study. The digital humanities is changing our research methodologies and the way we think about studying literature, and there will be concrete and probably irreversible repercussions in the future study of English. There may be no going back to what Stephen Ramsay has wryly called the "old-school, analogue humanities," iconically represented by a person in an armchair holding a leather-bound book.[7] Perhaps in the future, literature students will learn not how to do close reading, but how to do code!

In fact, English instructors have for decades augmented the traditional five-page essay with assignments that deploy new instructional tools, often in order to give students more hands-on involvement with the culture that's being studied. What's wrong with that? It may be fun and creative to use a software program to construct a nifty magazine on eighteenth-century London coffee-houses, or good research practice to design an elegant Powerpoint presentation on the Bloomsbury group, or efficient and convenient to buy an app about *The Waste Land* when you read the poem on your device. Students learn from these assignments and activities. But my suspicion is that when we embark on specialized historical research or use the amazing technological aids to reading that are all around us, it feels as if we are working on something, doing something—or in Stephen Ramsay's articulation, building something—whereas reading Eliot out loud in your room, puzzling out the parodies in *A Tale of a Tub*, or letting *Mrs Dalloway* wash over your mind can look a bit like idleness.

Literary critics cannot simply and straightforwardly adapt the methods of anthropologists and social scientists, the research and training of historians, or the rubrics of computer programmers—and literary readers should not try to take on those roles or positions either. For as everyone knows, at least intuitively, what happens when we read literature, listen to music, or experience works of art cannot be tabulated and put on a graph, their effects assessed in terms of measurable, long-term outcomes.[8] The three critical practices I have chosen to isolate in this book beat against the currents of contextualist and media studies trends. As we'll see, their emphases and methodologies are very different, but what they share is an orientation toward the relational paradigm I mentioned earlier: the understanding that reading literature is a special kind of encounter that calls for the engagement of the whole person—a balance of thought and feeling—and a sense of responsibility to the work being read. Reading a poem or a story involves careful attention to both the details of a text and the lived experience of processing imaginative language, whether by turning actual pages, scrolling, clicking, listening, or whatever new technologies of reading the future brings. These three approaches, formalism, reader-oriented criticism, and ethical criticism, postulate that literature can offer an experience of resonant and beautiful language; of psychological insight and self-knowledge; and of different people's minds, situations, and choices that we can refer to in our interactions within a complex moral world. But these things can only be understood if we take the time to really read the words on the page—to attend to the author's artistic decisions, to tune in to the cadences of language, to seek social and other forms of knowledge through the questions and responses the work provokes, and to reflect on the reading experience, whether alone or in conversation with other readers.

Each of the three critical strands I discuss is represented by examples from critics and theorists, for we should remember that critics are also fine writers, and some of their essays are models of clarity, insight, and wit that deserve to be read, rather than summarized. I have selected these particular critics and literary texts because I find their style and the presentation of their ideas accessible and enjoyable or because their angle on the questions attached to close reading and critical reading seem to get to the heart of the matter. If I frequently reach back to the mid-twentieth century and earlier, it is because the critics I value take for granted the centrality of literary culture in a democracy and so seem to speak to a broader constituency of readers.[9] But there are a great many voices in this discussion besides those I have put in the spotlight. In the process of thinking about close reading, we may discover other critics who help us learn how to get the most out of reading literature—our own "perfect critic" or role model.

Chapter 2 addresses formalism, beginning with what came to be called New Criticism in the years before and after World War II, and continuing up to very current debates about what is at stake in returning to close-grained or aesthetic reading that might focus on matters of literary form: style, genre, voice, and those qualities that make a work of literary art unique, with its own internal rules and energies. The New Critics have a reputation for promoting a stance of objectivity, placing the literary work under glass, disallowing historical or biographical information to affect the interpretive act. They definitely fall on the "thought" side of the divide— though they are suspicious of reading for a text's articulation of ideas alone. New Criticism sees the relationship between the reader and the text as stable and knowable: there is a meaning in the work of literature that an astute and careful reader can comprehend and explain. The text is a "verbal icon" and the center of our intellectual inquiry should be the poem alone—not the reader or history or the needs of society. Literature *does* communicate values and it certainly can be seen as a "form of knowledge" (Wimsatt 1954: xii), but that information is best explained by analyzing certain dimensions of the text. According to New Critics Cleanth Brooks and Robert Penn Warren,

> The mere presence in a piece of fiction of an idea which is held to be important in itself on ethical, religious, philosophical, sociological or other grounds does not necessarily indicate anything about the importance of the piece of fiction.... The idea is important in a story in so far as it is incorporated into the total structure.
>
> (1947: xv–xvi)

A novel may stimulate the reader to consider the workings of history or what happens when we die, but unless the ideas presented are really and truly profound, its formal qualities—its "grammar"—will have an equal claim on our critical attention.

This approach seems to make the reader a kind of coldblooded literary sleuth, objectively on the lookout for internal facts and evidence of meaning. But when we actually read some of the New Critics—Cleanth Brooks, John Crowe Ransom, Robert Penn Warren, William Empson,

Allen Tate, W. K. Wimsatt—it becomes clear that these men (they were all men) did respect the role of the reader in bringing the literary work to life, and they were not afraid of exploring the emotions a poet sought to convey in his work. They were also deeply concerned about the declining role of the humanities in mid-twentieth century American society and they took their profession as literary critics and teachers very seriously (many of the New Critics were also accomplished poets). They turned to more objective or "scientific" criteria partly because they wanted to give weight and validity to the study of literature in post-war American society, which was being rapidly transformed by scientific innovation and the rise of a prosperous, consumption-driven middle class. The New Critics sometimes declined to release a literary text from a quasi-scientific method of critical analysis, insisting on "general criteria against which a poem could be measured" (Brooks 1947: 217), locating touchstones in a poem (such as paradox, ambiguity, and irony) and defining critical argumentation (such as the affective and the intentional fallacies). Much of the New Criticism was not interested in the social background of a literary work, or in moral and psychological applications of its meaning. "I insist," wrote Cleanth Brooks in 1947,

> that to treat the poems discussed primarily as poems is a proper emphasis, and very much worth doing. For we have gone to school to the anthropologists and the cultural historians assiduously, and we have learned their lesson almost too well

—so well, in fact, that there's a danger we won't be able to recognize what makes a poem a poem (1947: 217). Some of the New Critics sounded an elitist, patriarchal, Ivy League note that annoyed (and still annoys) some readers. But against their opponents, they repeatedly and wearily apologized for simply doing a critic's job: distinguishing good poems from bad poems and making normative judgments. With all their fussiness, superiority, and yardsticks, the New Critics, taken together, were important in establishing the English literary canon and formalizing literary study at the high school and college levels. The descriptive term *close reading* originated with the New Critics, whose demand that disinterested attention be given to the words on the page as the author wrote them was delivered not only to professional critics, but also to the students in their classrooms, a great many of them young men who took advantage of the G.I. Bill after the end of World War II. Their methodology trained a generation of the most prestigious literary critics of the second half of the twentieth century, including Marjorie Garber, Stanley Fish, J. Hillis Miller, and Helen Vendler.

As we will see in Chapter 2, contemporary scholars are beginning to appreciate anew what very fine close readers and interpreters the New Critics could be, and there has been a revival of interest in their methods and ideas.[10] For formal close reading can illuminate even a familiar literary work with stunning clarity; it can be quite exciting to be shown, in brilliant detail, how a poem such as "Ode on a Grecian Urn" turns on its deployment of paradox (as Brooks famously did in *The Well Wrought Urn*). Some contemporary critics also want to liberate the literary work from the constraints of ideological interpretation. One scholar has even called the reassessment of New Criticism, the return to close reading, and the study of formal matters nothing less than "the defense of the literary" (Rooney 2000: 25). Yet other practitioners of the New Formalism (more a convenient label than a coherent school of thought) wonder if these critics are too enamored with "the literary" as a space for intellectual pleasure and emotional play. Is there a way to combine a wish to delve into the aesthetic complexity of a literary work with a concern for its life in politics and history? Can we make a case that the literariness of literature, an author's style and originality of expression, is the very feature that plunges readers into a critique of the standardizations and ideologies of modern life? So-called "activist formalists" seek a compromise between the New Critical bent toward non-historical and aesthetic reading and the important work of historicists, Marxists, and feminists from the 1980s and after.

New Criticism's emphasis on objective measures and its air of authority, polished appraisal, and erudition was bound to trigger a backlash. Instead of training the focus on the text's rhetorical structure and isolating its formal and aesthetic effects, another group of scholars decided it was time to pay serious attention to the *reader*'s experience. These critics present an entirely different set of critical questions than those of the formalists, for they want to tunnel into the mind and heart of the reading subject—they're definitely on the "feeling" end of the critical spectrum. Subjectivist critics want to probe what happens when we read—cognitively, emotionally, even unconsciously—and how we use literary texts in our lives.

A lot of early reader-response theory tended to look at "the reader" as a kind of abstract entity. As Vincent B. Leitch explains in his overview of the reader-response movement, there developed "a rich panoply of types of readers—informed readers, implied readers, actual readers, virtual readers, super-readers" (Leitch 1995: 34). My focus will be less on these reader taxonomies than on an earlier experiential or relational approach to literary reading, modestly introduced under the looming shadow of New Critical objectivity by the American scholar Louise Rosenblatt in *Literature as Exploration*, first published in 1938 (it is now in its fifth edition). Rosenblatt promotes what she calls a "transactional" theory of reading, one that looks at the reading situation as reciprocal: meaning is not "in" the text, nor is it "in" the reader, but rather involves a range of unique factors that contribute to create a full, responsible, sensitive encounter. In all of her books and essays, Rosenblatt is consistently concerned with teaching and with the importance of literate citizens in a democratic society. She is especially committed to restoring agency to students' responses to literary works, and in this regard challenges the authoritative stance of some of the New Critics as both critics and teachers of literature. What Rosenblatt and the formalist critics she cites in her book share, though, is a solid faith in the method of close reading, in the self-and-other encounter or interface of author and reader, without the excessive mediation of historians or theorists.

Rosenblatt's work should be put in conversation with some contemporary critics who have written eloquently about the place of close reading in the study and teaching of English, such as Rita Felski, Cristina Vischer Bruns, and Eve Kosofsky Sedgwick. These critics, and those working in the related field of affect studies, want to get critics talking about the transformative power of literary reading and return to concepts that have been long out of fashion with the rise of historicism and textual studies, such as identifying with characters, allowing personal reactions to be voiced in literature classes, going to literature for consolation or enchantment, using novels and poems as sources of knowledge or of truth. To some critics, this kind of reading may seem naïve, but as J. Hillis Miller argues, "Unless one has performed that innocent first reading, nothing much exists to resist or criticize" (2002: 159).

In philosophy, *phenomenology* inquires into the relation of the perceiver to myriad objects encountered in the world—to phenomena. The writings of phenomenologists of reading, such as Wolfgang Iser and Georges Poulet in the late 1960s and 1970s, tend to focus on a dialectical model of the way a supposedly generic reader (but actually a highly educated and sensitive one) might experience the picture-making, illusion-generating, suspenseful, real-and-not-real experience of being absorbed in reading. Phenomenological reading theories can help us to become more in tune with the heartbeat of our reading experience, to focus in on "consciousness, perception, and judgment" (Felski 2008: 17), and even to identify what psychoanalysts have called transitional objects—those images, places, things, sounds, words, and especially works of art that trigger understanding or let certain kinds of knowledge about the world emerge into consciousness. We can also read with a heightened awareness of the mysterious process of artistic creation and examine how reading brings us into contact with another person's inner world and imagination, perhaps assisting our own excavations into the self, a dense landscape of dreams and memories. How do we respond to the proliferation of keys, windows, and doors in Emily Brontë's *Wuthering Heights*, the recurrence of cuts, blood, and moons in Sylvia Plath's poetry, the repetition of names and sounds in Samuel Beckett's novels and plays? "A writer's working out of *a relationship to objects*, through the handling of the line of prose and other textual features," writes the philosopher Frank Farrell, "can generate a space of heightened significance for whatever enters into it" (Farrell 2004: 13, my italics). Readers, like writers, need this intermediate space for psychic rest from the demands of the world, and to potentially revive an exhausted or lost experience of the self.

The critics I discuss in Chapter 4 on ethical criticism share a concern for the real-world effects of literary reading. Daniel R. Schwarz writes, "The representation of the relationship between author and reader is the representation of an ethical relationship" (2001: 3). Schwarz means that reading, and especially close reading of sophisticated literary works, is an experience of *alterity*—engagement with another point of view, another person, another world—and so always involves an ethical component. The story of the rise of ethical criticism in the 1990s is sometimes referred to as an *ethical turn* in literary studies and as the *narrative turn* in philosophy: a shift in both disciplines away from postmodern theories of language, what was called the *linguistic turn*, and toward an exploration of the ways literature, and especially stories and novels, are embedded with news about our moral lives. Although in many ways this approach to reading literature seems natural and even inevitable, ethical criticism was for many years considered inadequate as a model of intellectual inquiry.

There are a number of reasons for this. The wave of poststructuralist theory that washed over departments of English in the 1970s, with its strong emphasis on linguistic codes and systems, was quickly followed by the tsunami of ideology-driven criticism focused on race, class, and gender, a model of critique that emphasized literature's complicity with all kinds of power structures. Instead of reading with an attitude of receptivity to the author's voice and perspective, and even with a sense of humility or reverence toward the work's authority, critics scrutinized the many ways political conditions are revealed in a text's language and an author's representations. These theorists taught students to read vigilantly for evidence of a text's hidden agendas—its falsifications or its naturalization of power relations—and to identify frameworks of oppression, binary thinking, and the privileging of certain points of view (middle-class, male, white, Western, heterosexual). Their aim was to detect and make visible the operation of social and economic forces, the policing of identity, and the ubiquity of politics in all works of literature, and so they deliberately read against the grain of a more traditional, humanist approach in which works of literature are viewed as articulating and dramatizing a moral sensibility. In making an activist claim for literary theory and criticism, these critics invited readers to see themselves as empowered players in movements of political resistance or social change. For some ideological critics, too, the problem with an ethical approach to reading is that it seems reductive or merely descriptive. What else is there to say once you "get" the moral point of *Huckleberry Finn* or *Gulliver's Travels*? Isn't it a kind of trivial exercise to talk about Twain's or Swift's moral sensibility or satiric intentions, as if they weren't implicated in the ideological assumptions and values of their particular historical time and place?

The reply to these critics from the advocates of ethical criticism is that whether or not we choose to embrace a form of ethical critique, when we read literature seriously, as Schwarz has claimed, we have already entered into an ethical situation. Ethical critics have also pointed out that the laudable political urgency that motivates feminist, queer, postcolonial, or Marxist critics is inextricable from *ethical* questions concerning justice, equality, and respect for difference (and that even poststructuralists, who insist that texts be accepted as indeterminate, or that the subject position is an unstable linguistic construct, are operating on the ethical assumption that there's a right way and a wrong way to read literary works). Furthermore, there are so many dimensions to ethical criticism that it's a vast oversimplification to equate this practice with just making moral judgments about literature. Some ethical critics are concerned principally with *narratology*, or theories about how the structure of stories communicates moral content and affects the way we perceive the world; others are interested in a variety of genres, such as poetry and life-writing, which pose questions about voice and self-representation; still others focus on the responsibility of readers toward texts, and the complex intersecting relationship between private reading and public ethos—character, values, actions, and judgments. A simple way to put it is that ethical criticism believes that literature offers readers "arenas of ethical reflection" (Buell 1999: 13). As so many artists and writers have claimed, unlike other types of writing or discourse in modern society, including works of moral philosophy, works of the imagination offer invitations to remake ourselves, and can shape our future responses to the world we encounter.

Chapter 4 tries to untangle the kinds of questions ethical criticism likes to ask, borrowed chiefly from works by Wayne Booth, James Phelan, and Marshall Gregory. What does it mean to be responsible to the text? Why is it important to talk about our reading with others? What is at stake in the ways in which we interpret metaphors or understand fictional characters? Is all criticism of literature necessarily ethical? Should certain works be commended as strengthening our ethical sensibilities? Does ethical inquiry produce knowledge or merely enforce personal prejudices? Throughout this chapter I try to link ethical criticism with the story I am telling about close reading, returning to both denunciations and defenses of formalist and New Critics, as well as to the problem of empathy and identificatory reading in some subjective or reader-response approaches.

At this point, questions about the role of the humanities and reading literature in public life will have to be addressed. Philosophers from Sophocles to John Dewey have said that the central project of free individuals is to discover and enlarge the self. I hope this book about three different approaches to reading literature validates our personal involvement in reading as something that helps us "become who we are" (in Nietzsche's words) as well as an activity that, over time, can reinforce a *social* imagination that helps us see other people non-instrumentally, as complexly motivated ethical agents. In 2007, a report published by the U.S. National Endowment for the Arts, *To Read or Not to Read*, concluded, "Good readers, and not only literary ones, enjoy [the] privilege of understanding and appreciating the outlook of others while enlarging their own identity. Perhaps because of this active empathy, they contribute in measurable ways to civic and social improvements." So although this book is designed to trace a line of critique within English studies, questions about the role of reading in civic life also have a place in this discussion.

In a small introductory English class I once observed, students who had just read Ernest Hemingway's *The Sun Also Rises* were asked which of the critical theories they had studied opened their eyes the most. The answers were eager and candid: "I related to the feminism one," "Queer theory was cool," "I *think* I liked structuralism," "The Marxist one was depressing," and (my favorite) "I liked New Criticism because, you know, a lot of times writing is *hard*." After almost everyone in the circle had volunteered a reply, one student raised her hand: "I kind of wanted to know, though— what did Hemingway mean, like, what did he want to say? Is there a school of criticism for that?"

What did Hemingway want to say? What was his take on things? This question is fundamental to literary reading. For an essential part of close reading involves making sense of the author's version of life for oneself, deciding if the novel, play, essay, or poem has something in it to learn from or deeply enjoy, or even live by. Critics and teachers who view literature defensively, or who are afraid of being labeled old-fashioned or apolitical, may have forgotten that one reason people read literature is for help in deciding how they want to live their lives and what kind of person they want to become. Mark Edmundson (2004a) has written eloquently about the value of literary study as a way to achieve what he calls "secular rebirth":

> To me, the best way to think about reading is as life's grand second chance. All of us grow up once: we pass through a process of socialization. We learn about right and wrong and good and bad from our parents, then from our teachers or religious guides.... Yet for many people, the process of socialization doesn't quite work. The values they acquire from all the well-meaning authorities don't fit them. And it is these people who often become obsessed readers. They don't read for information, and they don't read for beautiful escape. No, they read to remake themselves. They read to be socialized again, not into the ways of their city or village this time but into another world with different values. Such people want to revise, or even to displace, the influence their parents have had on them. They want to adopt values they perceive to be higher or perhaps just better suited to their natures.

Edmundson uses the example of a thirty-five-year-old carpenter who went to his job in Brooklyn every day, carrying with him the sandwich his mother made for him and something to read during his lunch hour—the essays, perhaps, of Ralph Waldo Emerson. He would sit on his pile of boards at the noon hour reading, and then go back to his job of building houses, his father's trade before him. But Emerson's writing changed this young man's orientation to the modern world of nineteenth-century America, and more importantly it initiated a creative awakening. "I was simmering, simmering, simmering," he later confessed. "Emerson brought me to a boil."

Not everyone is going to become Walt Whitman. But perhaps a lot of people are simmering, not quite aware that they're ready to tap into their potential—people from all social classes, and with or without the kinds of material advantages that are needed to remake themselves—until a poet or a novelist provides the words, ideas, images, or characters that allow them to admit the possibility of resocialization and change.

Possibly the strong presence of critical theory, entirely salutary in some circumstances, has intimidated less experienced readers. So someone who responds to Frances Hodgson Burnett's *The Secret Garden* as a positive story about overcoming psychic trauma or discovering self-acceptance is dismissed as naïve by the theorist who sees the novel in unquestionably negative terms—as a work that endorses submissive feminine behavior, or British imperial power, or environmental exploitation.[11] All readings are fair readings, so it goes, if they can be defended by evidence in the text. But as Edmundson has observed, critical argument that is merely a set of adroit intellectual moves without ethical investment is not what the study of literature should be about (2004b: 43–44). By itself, theory, ideology, or history may be a small tunnel by which to enter the broad universe of a novel or a poem.

Understandably, students who have been taught to read only through theoretical models might wonder what reading and criticism will look like if we downplay theory, as well as a text's social and cultural contexts. In the early 1920s, I. A. Richards gave his undergraduates at Cambridge University thirteen poems to read without revealing the author's name or any other extraneous or explanatory matter. He was interested in exploring "the difficulty of judging verse without a hint as to its provenance" (1929: 5). Richards had several aims in mind. First, he was curious to see if his students' personal responses and interpretive efforts would shape themselves into a kind of readable survey of contemporary thought. As he put it, between subjects that can be discussed in terms of verifiable facts (physics, mathematics) and subjects that can be handled by rules and conventions (commerce, law) there is an enormous "middle field" that includes "everything about which civilized man cares most … ethics, metaphysics, morals, religion, aesthetics, and the discussions surrounding liberty, nationality, justice, love, truth, faith, and knowledge" (1929: 5). Because poetry, Richards argued, is a central form of communication in that middle field, we might gather data on "human opinions and feelings" (and on what constitutes useful literary training) by studying people's uncensored responses to verse. He was conducting an unofficial ethno-graphic experiment.

But Richards had another end in view as well: he wanted to insert psychology into the strictly objective practice of reading and of literary criticism. He scrutinized his students' motives, both reasoned and intu-itive, for their interpretations of the poetry he gave them—their dif-ficulties, frustrations, moral qualms, insights, misapprehensions, emotional reactions, and rationalizations. What he found was that his students felt baffled and defeated by what they read and they were ter-rible at discerning literary quality. Again and again, the students fell back on rough guesses, personal feeling, or conventional opinions about the meaning of a poem. After documenting and analyzing hundreds of responses, published in *Practical Criticism: A Study of Literary Judgment* (1929), Richards concluded that the basic difficulty in all reading is "the problem of *making out the meaning.*" What is a meaning and what are we doing when we try to get at it? This, says Richards, is the funda-mental question underlying literary reading and the master-key to all the problems of criticism (1929: 174, original italics).

Richards put his finger on the challenges we face when we decide to read *Beloved* or *Macbeth*, the poems of Seamus Heaney or the essays of Ralph Waldo Emerson. For we want to take away something real from the time we spend reading, and we want to stand our ground with a great writer as best we can. We want to get it! Richards is credited with identifying a method to help students, and all interested readers, to "make out the meaning," and so get the most satisfaction from their intellectual efforts: *close reading*, the work of mindfulness applied to our language, to our feelings, and to our situation as moral agents in the world.

Richards is a figure whose ideas have influenced the three critical methods addressed in this chapter and those to come. First, he was a ded-icated formalist. Richards wanted to stick to the poem to figure out how it manages to generate several kinds of meaning. In his experiment, the stu-dents were required to read and reread only the text they had before them—English words set on a page in a certain order by someone at some time in the history of humane letters. His emphasis on reading closely for how meanings can be extracted from a careful analysis of tone, symbol, metaphor, and sound definitely influenced the New Critics—indeed, William Empson, one of Richards's students at Cambridge, wrote *Seven Types of Ambiguity* based on Richards's ideas about multiple meanings. It has become a landmark text of New Criticism. Second, Richards had a huge influence on subjective approaches to reading and criticism (in fact, his emphasis on psychology alienated some of the New Critics). Louise Rosenblatt learned much from Richards about students' reluctance to take risks and offer fresh interpretations of poetry because they were dominated by "stereotyped ideas and conventional feelings" (Rosenblatt 1995: 96), exactly the things literature and a literary education rejects. Reuben Brower was also Richards's student at Cambridge, and he pays full tribute to Richards's method of close reading in the first chapter of his book *Fields of Light*. Finally, Richards's faith in the importance of literature in contemporary society resonates with ethical criticism. He believed fervently in the power of poetry and the arts to open our small, individual worlds to the minds of others. If reading literature is like traveling to new places, responsible literary criticism is an instrument of navigation: "the art of knowing where we are wherever, as mental travellers, we may go" (Richards 1929: 10).

I wonder how Richards's experiment would work today. How does a student write an English paper without getting on the internet to read a biographical snapshot or research the author's time and place, or without finding a useful theory to apply to the text, or even without skimming some prior criticism about the work? Does close reading mean we cannot accept any help from the authorities in trying to understand a poem or a play? Should we honestly spend time talking about an author's decisions, getting tied up in boring matters of craft, style, rhetoric, and prosody? Does close reading throw us into the ring with a difficult work—John Donne's "The Canonization" or George Eliot's *Middlemarch*—without any equipment to help us to read it? If we're put face to face, alone and unprotected, with the work of literature, are we just supposed to respond personally? Should we ignore questions about identity and social power, and forget about the political dimension of reading literature? And what about the canon? Is that elitist and exclusionary? Or are there really a relatively small number of literary works that can help us toward living a satisfying, meaningful, and fulfilling life? Is it even valid to go to literature for news about the world we live in, or for moral advice and a model of how to live?

Close reading doesn't banish context from the literary experience, or insist that we ignore data that could enrich our understanding and our pleasure; facts and speculations about the author's life, the values of her society, and economic imperatives that may have affected the work we are reading are needed background that should still be brought to the table. A commitment to close reading does not mean placing a work of literature under a microscope in order to analyze it to death; it does not mean there are deep, hidden meanings in every breath the poet takes. And certainly close reading does not assume a desire to preserve a text from the contaminations of theory, or guard it as a precious aesthetic object, valued above all for its timeless truths and supposedly universal qualities. But because close reading asks for a direct encounter with a work of literature, it has the potential to restore agency to both the reader and the text, as well as reveal details of the world and of our own consciousness that we could not see without the help of the literary work. Like a camera obscura, the pinhole of literary attention lets in the transforming light that makes the world larger. It makes it seem different. It makes it seem endless with possibilities.

Notes

1 Some recent reappraisals of close reading in the literary academy include Lentricchia and DuBois (2002); Culler (2010); Gallop (2000, 2007, 2010); Armstrong (2011); Best and Marcus (2009); Bialotosky (2006); and Guillory (2010). The *ADE Bulletin* 149 (2010) includes a cluster on close reading, and the essays in *Representations* 108.1 (Fall 2009) focus on reading practices. Some of this discussion, no doubt, has been generated by our technology-dominated lives, as both professors and general readers think about the fate of reading in the digital age. See for example Hurley (2012); Hayles (2010); and Birkets (2010). Jessica Pressman's Introduction in *Digital Modernism: Making It New in New Media* (2014) defends close reading as a vital practice in the digital humanities. There's a lot of healthy flexibility in the "return to reading" lexicon—there's immersive reading, microreading, deep reading, surface reading, wakeful reading, attentive reading, and slow reading. There are also books directed at general readers who want to slow down: Jacobs (2011); Ulin (2010); and Mikics (2013b).
2 For one example, see Chace (2009).
3 It's difficult to track down the very first use of the term "close reading." Most scholars attribute it to I. A. Richards: "All respectable poetry invites close reading" (1929: 195). The *OED* credits the first usage (not "close reading" but "close analysis") to F. R. Leavis in 1932, followed by John Crowe Ransom's "close criticism" in 1937, and then by Virginia Woolf in 1938: "I think to fill in the time quietly by forcing myself to do a Horace Walpole sketch for America. Why not? It means close reading."
4 Quoted in Fessenbecker (2013: 117).
5 Three recent books have influenced my own thinking on these issues: Rita Felski, *Uses of Literature* (2008); Frank Farrell, *Why Does Literature Matter?* (2004); and Cristina Vischer Bruns, *Why Literature?* (2011).
6 Such as booktrack.com, where reading a book may be accompanied by an appropriate soundtrack.
7 http://stephenramsay.us/text/2011/01/08/whos-in-and-whos-out/.
8 If you need verifiable proof that reading literature is good for you, you may want to look into the science of literary study, or neuroaesthetics. See Patricia Cohen, "The Next Big Thing in English: Knowing That They Know That You Know," *The New York Times*, March 31, 2010; Annie Murphy Paul, "Reading Literature Makes Us Smarter and Nicer," *Time*, June 3, 2013; Laura Miller, "Your Brain Loves Jane Austen," *Salon*, September 19, 2012; Pam Belluck, "For Better Social Skills, Scientists Recommend a Little Chekhov," *New York Times*, October 3, 2013; and Jennifer Schuessler, "Wired: Putting a Writer and Readers to a Test," *The New York Times*, November 30, 2013. Schuessler reports an experiment designed by the Dutch novelist Arnon Grunberg. He wears electrodes to scan his brain while writing a novella, and when it is published his readers will also be scanned to determine the similarity of their responses. A Google search of "neuroaesthetics" or "neuroaesthetics and reading" will come up with many online magazines and blogs. See also Armstrong (2013).
9 John Guillory has described the gap between reading practiced by academics and by ordinary readers. What he calls "professional reading" is characterized by four features. Reading is *work*; it is governed by conventions within the *discipline*; it is *vigilant* (aimed at sustained reflection, rather than immediate delight); and it is *communal*, conscious of a potential audience of scholars or students. Nonprofessional or "lay" readers, on the other hand, practice at the site of *leisure*; the *conventions* of reading are nondisciplinary; they are usually motivated by a desire for relaxation or *pleasure*; and reading is largely a *solitary*

activity. Guillory argues that the difference between these reading practices is relatively incommensurable. No wonder misunderstandings persist about what goes on in English departments. Lay readers, for example, might think English professors have betrayed their traditional responsibility to offer guidance about how best to read, while academics keep justifying their existence in terms of political effects. Yet I believe an intermediate position is possible, that the gap can be breached with the assistance of articulate, interesting, and committed literary criticism. See Guillory (2000: 29–46).

10 For a good anthology of New Critical writing see Davis. Hickman and McIntyre's (2012) edition offers contemporary scholars' engagements with the New Critics. Two important edited collections that engage current debates about formalism and historicism are Rasmussen (2002), and Wolfson and Brown (2006), as well as Theile and Tredennick (2013).

11 The example is from one of my English classes, in which an extremely bright feminist and sharp critical reader unfortunately made her case with a high-handed air that deflated the class and shut down the discussion. Students who liked *The Secret Garden* were afraid of appearing stupidly sympathetic to the author's retrograde political views.

References

Armstrong, Paul B. (2011) "In Defense of Reading." *New Literary History* 42.1 (Winter): 87–113.

Armstrong, Paul B. (2013) *How Literature Plays with the Brain: The Neuroscience of Reading and Art*. Baltimore, MD: Johns Hopkins University Press.

Arnold, Matthew [1865] (1970a) "The Function of Criticism at the Present Time," in *Selected Prose*, ed. P. J. Keating. Harmondsworth: Penguin, 130–156.

Arnold, Matthew [1880] (1970b) "The Study of Poetry," in *Selected Prose*, ed. P. J. Keating. Harmondsworth: Penguin, 340–366.

Auden, W. H. [1948] (1962) *The Dyer's Hand and Other Essays*. New York: Random House.

Best, Stephen and Sharon Marcus (2009) "Surface Reading: An Introduction." *Representations* 108.1 (Fall): 1–21.

Bialotosky, Don (2006) "Should College English Be Close Reading?" *College English* 69.2 (November): 111–116.

Birkets, Sven (2010) "Reading in a Digital Age." *The American Scholar*. March 1.

Blanchot, Maurice (1983) *The Space of Literature*. Trans. Anna Smock. Lincoln: University of Nebraska Press.

Brooks, Cleanth (1947) *The Well Wrought Urn: Studies in the Structure of Poetry*. New York: Harcourt Brace.

Brooks, Cleanth and Robert Penn Warren [1943] (1947) *Understanding Fiction*. New York: F. S. Crofts.

Brower, Reuben (1962) "Reading in Slow Motion," in *In Defense of Reading: A Reader's Approach to Literary Criticism*, ed. Reuben Brower and Richard Poirier. New York: Dutton, 3–21.

Brower, Reuben [1951] (2013) *Fields of Light: An Experiment in Critical Reading*. Philadelphia: Paul Dry Books.

Bruns, Cristina Vischer (2011) *Why Literature? The Value of Literary Reading and What it Means for Teaching*. London: Continuum.

Buell, Lawrence (1999) "In Pursuit of Ethics." *PMLA* 114.1 (January): 7–19.

Chace, William M. (2009) "The Decline of the English Department." *The American Scholar*. September 1.

Culler, Jonathan (2010) "The Closeness of Close Reading." *ADE Bulletin* 149: 20–25.

Davis, Garrick, ed. (2008) *Praising It New: The Best of the New Criticism*. Athens, OH: Ohio University Press.

De Bolla, Peter (2001) *Art Matters*. Cambridge, MA: Harvard University Press.

Edmundson, Mark (2004a) "The Risk of Reading." *The New York Times*, August 1.

Edmundson, Mark (2004b) *Why Read?* New York: Bloomsbury.

Eliot, T. S. [1943] (1957) "Frontiers of Criticism." *On Poetry and Poets*. New York: Farrar, Straus, and Giroux, 113–131.

Eliot, T. S. (2011) "The Perfect Critic." *The Sacred Wood: Essays on Poetry and Criticism*. West Valley City, UT: Waking Lion Press, 1–11.

Empson, William [1930] (1953) *Seven Types of Ambiguity*. London: New Directions.

Farrell, Frank B. (2004) *Why Does Literature Matter?* Ithaca, NY: Cornell University Press.

Felski, Rita (2008) *Uses of Literature*. Malden, MA: Blackwell, 2008.

Felski, Rita (2009) "Everyday Aesthetics." *Minnesota Review* 71/72 (Winter/Spring): 171–179.

Fessenbecker, Patrick (2013) "In Defense of Paraphrase." *New Literary History* 44.1 (Winter): 117–139.

Frye, Northrop (1963) "The Road of Excess," in *Myth and Symbol: Critical Approaches and Applications*, ed. Bernice Slote. Lincoln: University of Nebraska Press, 3–20.

Gallagher, Catherine and Stephen Greenblatt (2000) *Practicing New Historicism*. Chicago: University of Chicago Press.

Gallop, Jane (2000) "The Ethics of Reading: Close Encounters." *Journal of Curriculum Theorizing* (Fall): 7–17.

Gallop, Jane (2007) "The Historicization of Literary Study and the Fate of Close Reading." *Profession*: 181–186.

Gallop, Jane (2010) "Close Reading in 2009." *ADE Bulletin* 149: 15–19.

Guillory, John (2000) "The Ethical Practice of Modernity: The Example of Reading," in *The Turn to Ethics*, ed. Marjorie Garber. London: Routledge, 29–46.

Guillory, John (2010) "Close Reading: Prologue and Epilogue." *ADE Bulletin* 149: 8–14.

Hayles, N. Katherine (2010) "How We Read: Close, Hyper, Machine." *ADE Bulletin* 150: 62–79.

Hickman, Miranda B. and John D. McIntyre, eds. (2012) *Rereading the New Criticism*. Columbus: The Ohio State University Press.

Hurley, Thomas G. (2012) "New Media and the Teaching of Reading: Our Janus Moment." *ADE Bulletin* 15: 54–64.

Jacobs, Alan (2010) *The Pleasures of Reading in an Age of Distraction*. Oxford: Oxford University Press.

Kundera, Milan (2006) *The Curtain: An Essay in Seven Parts*. Trans. Linda Asher. New York: HarperCollins.

Lawrence, D. H. [1928] (1973) "John Galsworthy," in *Selected Literary Criticism*, ed. Anthony Beal. New York: Viking, 118–137.

Leitch, Vincent B. (1995) "Reader-Response Criticism," in *Readers and Reading*, ed. Andrew Bennett. London: Longman, 32–65.

Lentricchia, Frank and Andrew DuBois, eds. (2002) *Close Reading: The Reader*. Durham, NC: Duke University Press.

Lewis, C. S. (1961) *An Experiment in Criticism*. Cambridge, U.K.: Cambridge University Press.

Mikics, David (2013a) "Cultural Studies: Bane of the Humanities." *Chronicle of Higher Education*, Oct 7.

Mikics, David (2013b) *Slow Reading in a Hurried Age*. Cambridge, MA: Belknap Press.

Miller, J. Hillis (2002) *On Literature*. London: Routledge.

Pressman, Jessica (2014) *Digital Modernism: Making It New in New Media*. Oxford: Oxford University Press.

Rasmussen, Mark David, ed. (2002) *Renaissance Literature and Its Formal Engagements*. London: Palgrave Macmillan.

Richards, I. A. (1925) *Principles of Literary Criticism*. New York: Harcourt Brace.

Richards, I. A. (1929) *Practical Criticism: A Study of Literary Judgment*. New York: Harcourt Brace.

Rooney, Ellen (2000) "Form and Contentment." *Modern Language Quarterly* 61.1 (March): 17–40.

Rosenblatt, Louise M. [1938] (1995) *Literature as Exploration*. New York: Modern Language Association.

Schwarz, Daniel R. (2001) "A Humanistic Ethics of Reading," in *Mapping the Ethical Turn: A Reader in Ethics, Culture, and Literary Theory*, ed. Todd F. Davis and Kenneth Womack. Charlottesville: University Press of Virginia, 3–15.

Scott, Matthew (2009) "Coleridge's *Lectures 1809–1819: On Literature*," in *The Oxford Handbook of Samuel Taylor Coleridge*, ed. Frederick Burwick. New York: Oxford University Press, 185–203.

Tate, Allen [1951] (2008) "Is Literary Criticism Possible?," in *Praising It New: The Best of the New Criticism*, ed. Garrick Davis. Athens: Swallow Press/Ohio University Press, 61–71.

Theile, Verena and Linda Tredennick, eds. (2013) *New Formalisms and Literary Theory*. London: Palgrave Macmillan.

Ulin, David (2010) *The Lost Art of Reading: Why Books Matter in a Distracted Time*. Seattle: Sasquatch Books.

U.S. National Endowment for the Arts (2007) *To Read or Not to Read: A Question of National Consequence*. Washington, D.C.: National Endowment for the Arts.

Wimsatt, W. K. (1954) *The Verbal Icon: Studies in the Meaning of Poetry*. Lexington: University of Kentucky Press.

Wolfson, Susan and Marshall Brown, eds. (2006) *Reading for Form*. Seattle: University of Washington Press.

Woolf, Virginia [1932] (1989) "How Should One Read a Book?," in *The Second Common Reader*, ed. Andrew McNeillie. New York: Harcourt, 258–270.

2 The verbal icon

To see the object as in itself it really is.

(Arnold 1970a: 130)

The first law to be prescribed to criticism ... is that it shall be objective, shall cite the nature of the object rather than its effect upon the subject.

(Ransom 1938: 342)

In this chapter, we will dive into a time-honored approach to literary reading and criticism: the thought-over-feeling model, or the objective approach to writing and talking about poems, plays, and works of fiction. Although objective criticism has sometimes been dismissed as a misapplication of scientific principles to works of art, as apolitical and myopic, or as too narrowly concerned with technical matters—the "lemon-squeezer school of criticism," as T. S. Eliot (1957: 125) wrote in a pestered humor—there is much to admire, value, and imitate in this approach to reading literature. For one thing, objective or formalist criticism invites us to think about some of the fundamental questions about how literature works—about the ambiguity of words, the uses of figurative language, the verbal and aural techniques employed by poets and novelists, and important matters such as structure, meter, rhyme, symbol, metaphor, variation, and tone. So the questions often asked by objective critics begin with the *how* of literature: how does the poem work, how does its meaning get communicated through the arrangement of these particular words and sounds in this order on the page or screen? This kind of careful attention to the details of the literary work and to the operations of language are what most people understand by the term *close reading*: to read slowly and attentively in order to explain, analyze, explicate, and argue for your reading from the evidence of the text itself. As the scholar Barbara Johnson puts it, this traditional use of close reading teaches students "how to notice things in a text that a speed-reading culture is trained to disregard, overcome, edit out, or explain away; how to read what the language is doing, not guess what the author was thinking" (quoted in Culler 2010: 23). But this method of objective, evidence-based close reading—a mainstay of literature classes in the U.S. and U.K., and the indispensable skill for any self-respecting English major or doctoral student—was not always the way literature was read, taught, or analyzed.

The New Critics mentioned in Chapter 1—René Wellek, John Crowe Ransom, Robert Penn Warren, Allen Tate, W. K. Wimsatt, Cleanth Brooks, and Austin Warren, among others—are largely responsible for the emphasis on close textual analysis in today's English classrooms. These critics, who wrote about and taught literature in the years before and after World War II, waved the banner for objective criticism when other orthodoxies such as historical study, literary biography, and philology (the study of language) prevailed. They were determined to achieve two things.

First, the New Critics wanted to validate and organize the study of literature as a discipline in American colleges and universities. In their landmark book, *Theory of Literature*, published in 1948, René Wellek and Austin Warren go to great lengths to explain the difference between "the art of reading," or "appreciation"—an ideal for personal cultivation and enjoyment—and "literary scholarship," a more systematic undertaking, and one they strongly advocate. Like history, philosophy, the sciences, or other academic disciplines, the study of literature should be structured, coordinated, and legitimized as a form of knowledge.

Second, the New Critics wanted to establish fresh criteria for literary criticism and so redefine the role of the literary critic, her methodology, subject matter, and audience. These dogged promoters of a more professionalized, objective attitude to literary reading should also get credit for placing front and center very difficult aesthetic problems that would impact the study and practice of literature for decades to come. They persisted in asking hard questions: how should one analyze a poem, what separates literature from the other arts, how do we get to the meaning of a text, how do poems and stories communicate knowledge and ideas, and how may we distinguish between critical concepts, such as form and content, structure and texture, sound and sense? They also asked important questions about how we go about deciding what is and what is not literature, and how to define the public and pedagogic role of the literary critic in a modern society.

When Victorian poet and critic Matthew Arnold wrote in the mid-nineteenth century that the critical practice of modern European letters should be the effort to "see the object as in itself it really is," he articulated a basic assumption of criticism that still holds up today: that the literary work is an independent thing with an objective existence, like a table or a chestnut tree. Its nature remains the same, its essence or meaning is consistent and knowable. Following Arnold's lead, the New Critics advocated well-reasoned judgments, a flexible and patient method of inquiry, and the unbiased critique of the poem as an integrated aesthetic structure. Also like Arnold, these critics repeatedly asked and argued about the function of literature in modern society and the purpose of literary study, always urging its fundamental importance to human lives and human interests. Many of these critics despised what they called the relativism of most critical readings and sloppy judgments about poetic merit, and a few of them were seriously worried that popular forms of art—sappy verse, bestsellers, cinema—would erode the public's taste and dilute the appetite for great literature. Literature and poetry are important, it was argued, because unlike ordinary people who are satisfied with stock responses to whatever their culture offers them, novelists and poets are more alive to stimuli and see the complex connections among actions, thoughts, symbols, and images. Instead of suppressing or toning down her emotional and intellectual responses to the world, the writer organizes and expresses them. The professional critic should recognize this quality of awakeness as a characteristic of the creative mind and cultivate a matching vigilance—not in the sense of wariness about the text's ideological underpinnings, but rather a focused attention on what the author has set out to achieve and which demands a discriminating and ordered response.

For objective criticism, judgment cannot rest on simply liking or not liking a poem.[1] One should be able to explain why a poem by Ella Wheeler Wilcox is inferior to a poem by Christina Rossetti, why Edgar Allan Poe's "The Raven" works but his "Ulalume" doesn't. Debates about the varying quality of poetic achievement sharpen the critical instinct. Similarly, objective critics are opposed to the *interestedness* of readers whose judgment of a literary work is colored by the degree to which the author appeals to their own religious, political, or personal beliefs. The ideal attitude is *disinterestedness*, Matthew Arnold's insistent word for the kind of clear-eyed, unbiased inquiry into the total effect of the creative arrangement of words that truly objective criticism should aspire to.

The context of Arnold's energetic claims for disinterestedness is worth mentioning here, for he saw beyond the ancient libraries of nineteenth-century Oxford. With the rise of the Victorian middle class, the spread of liberalism and democratic ideals among all classes, and the distressing and widening gap between wealthy capitalists and the working poor and unemployed, people seemed to recklessly and automatically take the side of their own group or political party without bothering to examine the question at issue, and many of them were easily swayed by the persuasions and beguilements of advertising and popular entertainment. Disinterestedness—the critical spirit, or objective reasoning—was for Arnold a beacon of hope in the wilderness of a newly industrialized society; he wished to see critical thinking cultivated not among the educated classes only, but among all citizens. For Arnold, critical objectivity was a social principle opposed to the spread of conformity and the kind of lax thinking he worried would crush originality and deaden intellectual culture. Fifty years later, I. A. Richards described the value of disinterestedness as well—not only for modern society as a whole, but also for the individual person. Aesthetic responses, he wrote, open many facets of the mind which may be amplified and focused if we develop an objective perspective:

> To respond, not through one narrow channel of interest, but simultan-eously and coherently through many, is to be *disinterested* in the only sense of the word which concerns us here. A state of mind which is not disinterested is one which sees things only from one standpoint or under one aspect. At the same time since more of our personality is engaged the independence and individuality of other things become greater. We seem to see "all round" them, to see them as they really are; we see them apart from any one particular interest which they may have for us. Of course, without some interest we should not see them at all, but the less any one particular interest is indispensable, the more *detached* our attitude becomes. And to say that we are *imper-sonal* is merely a curious way of saying that our personality is more *completely* involved.
>
> (1925: 251–252, original italics)

What I think Richards is saying in this complex passage is that if we view a work of art or read a poem with genuine receptivity, as an involved observer, we release the work from a base utilitarianism (what's in it for me) and so remain open to unexpected pleasures and insights. We simply can see the text more clearly if we're not trying to make it match our own values, loyalties, or point of view. The *detachment* Richards men-tions does not imply cold indifference or lack of interest, but rather an "unselfing" before the work of art which allows us to experience it more vividly and completely—a more transcendental kind of disinterestedness, perhaps.

The New Critics believed that literature has the power to communicate universally. Yet they realized that questions of value are always difficult, fraught with psychological, social, and moral problems, to say nothing of the precariousness of language itself. These weighty matters have generated a range of passionate and complex discussions among intellectuals about the role of literature and the humanities in our public and private lives, including by some of the scholars exploring the movement that has been called New Formalism, as we will see at the end of this chapter. In order to understand just what objective critics are opposed to and what kinds of reading practices they want to promote, we'll begin by looking at a few of the main tenets put forth by some of the New Critics and test out their ideas by reading samples of objective criticism.

> Honest criticism and sensitive appreciation is directed not upon the poet but upon the poetry.
>
> (Eliot 2011: 37)

In 1938, two American literary critics, Cleanth Brooks and Robert Penn Warren, young colleagues in the English Department at Louisiana State University, published an important and widely adopted textbook, *Understanding Poetry* (a second edition was published in 1950). *Understanding Poetry* was based on a series of pamphlets Brooks and Warren created to help their students grasp and analyze different types of poetry, and to explain plainly the nature of poetic language and the purpose of poetry in everyday life. Brooks and Warren laid out their formalist agenda in the first sentence of a preliminary section called "Letter to the Teacher": "This book has been conceived on the assumption that if poetry is worth teaching at all it is worth teaching as poetry" (1950: xi). They then went on to argue that the way students have been taught to read and write about poetry has been seriously misguided. For decades, students have been encouraged to apprehend poetry as a stand-in for something else, either as a vehicle for ideas or morals that can be dug out from under the poem, or as something belonging more to historians than to literary critics. No, they insisted: poetry is not history or morality, its language is not the language of science, commerce, or religion. Poetry—literature—uses language differently, operates according to different laws, and has different aims, and these distinctions can and should be formally studied, taught, and understood. Brooks and Warren wanted especially to overturn three debilitating critical and educational trends.

First, they wanted to do away with teaching students to paraphrase a literary work—to prove that they get the gist of the poem, and then be done with it (a practice still alive and well, and assisted by numerous internet sites). Although paraphrase and summary are good places to start in terms of basic comprehension, there's probably more to say about John Keats's "Ode to a Nightingale" than "The song of the nightingale brings sadness and exhilaration to the poet and makes him long to be lifted up and away from the limitations of life. The seventh stanza is particularly beautiful."[2] This kind of blah paraphrase leads to a disastrous vagueness that takes students no closer to a reading of the poem than when they set out. They argued that summary statements about a poem take the reader away from the center of the work itself. In the church of objective criticism, Brooks reviled "the heresy of paraphrase."[3] A poem is not an idea wrapped up in emotional language, a novel is not prose decorated with sensuous imagery and difficult metaphors. Condensation of a text into a sound bite is a violation of its very essence as a work of art, which is meant to be experienced in its entirety. Poetry relies essentially on its structure *as a poem* to communicate meaning, and not only on its summarizable content.

But for Brooks and Warren it was equally malfeasant for professors to require students to approach a poem like statisticians, making them count and classify the kinds of figures of speech in it, for instance, or memorize rules for identifying meter and rhyme. It's great if a student can locate one caesura and identify six different degrees of light and heavy stresses in

"Ode to a Nightingale," but unless she places those features in relation to the whole poem, her apprehension of Keats's ode—the ideas engaged, the mood, the poet's state of mind—will be pretty limited. As I. A. Richards writes, "We pay attention to externals when we do not know what else to do with a poem"—counting stresses is sort of the last-ditch effort when the meaning of the poem eludes us (1925: 24). Much as Brooks and Warren care about attention to the details of the poem, any approach that leaves behind what they called the *organic* nature of poetry—how its many factors contribute to the overall effect and to the poem's meaning—is sadly mechanical and legalistic. Brooks and Warren (1950) insist that the kind of analytical, objective critique they champion is *not* about taking a poem apart, turning over its components, and putting it back together, like an auto mechanic reassembling an engine. They argue that the all-important thing is the relationship among the elements in a poem, which are intimate and fundamental to the way its meaning is communicated. The many kinds of poems offered to the reader in *Understanding Poetry*, combined with the authors' close analyses, prove that the purpose of placing sharp focus on the different elements that make a poem—metaphor, meter, rhyme, speaker, tone, etc.—is to develop a richer experience of the *whole* poem.

Their second objection to then-current methods of teaching literature was the emphasis on historical material or on the author's biography. They concede that historical background can help to clarify an interpretation, but it should be a means to an end, not the goal of literary study itself. (In the second edition of *Understanding Poetry* they included a section on context that is well worth reading today.) Similarly, it's fine to supplement the reading of a work of literature with information about the author's biography and his participation in the events of his day—after all, we are naturally curious about other people, and who wouldn't want to look up details about the person who created *The Metamorphosis* or *Frankenstein*? But to an objective critic, a reader gets into trouble if she makes too many assumptions about historical influences or an author's supposed intentions. A historian may read William Wordsworth to learn more about the effects of the Enclosure Acts on the rural poor in England, just as a psychologist would be interested in studying this poet to explore the mental process of artistic creation. But the historian and the psychologist would then be interested in reading Wordsworth's bad poems as well as his good poems, and a mass of other documents as well. The student of literature, on the other hand, has a different interest: the nature of the poem itself, its success as a poem. Brooks and Warren worried that, especially for inexperienced readers, focusing on the poet's life or historical situation may distort the reading experience and lead students (and critics) into a labyrinth of suppositions.

W. K. Wimsatt and Monroe Beardsley, writing in the 1940s, called this critical pothole the *intentional fallacy*. They give an interesting example of an interpretation that in their opinion weighs too heavily on the side of historical context and leaps to conclusions about authorial intent. These lines are from John Donne's great poem, "A Valediction: Forbidding Mourning":

> Moving of th' earth brings harmes and feares,
> Men reckon what it did and meant,
> But trepidation of the spheares,
> Though greater farre, is innocent.

Wimsatt and Beardsley cite an eminent scholar who interprets these lines in the context of the new astronomy of the sixteenth and seventeenth centuries, very plausibly arguing that Donne, as is well known, was familiar with the works of Copernicus, Kepler, and Galileo and thought deeply about the implications of this new science for theology (Donne was an Anglican priest). Wimsatt and Beardsley point out, however, that before jumping to historical conclusions, the critic should have analyzed the text more closely. Wouldn't the celestial motion described by Copernicus be smooth and regular rather than violent and fearsome? Could "Moving of th' earth" refer to an earthquake, and might "trepidation" echo the shaking implied in that image? In any case, "trepidation of the spheres" is "greater far" than an earthquake, but not much greater than the earth's movement around the sun. Then there's a problem of tense: reckoning "what it did and meant" suggests that the event is over, like an earthquake's tremors, but not like the motion of the planets, which is perpetual. John Donne was interested in scientific developments, and that fact may add another shade of meaning to the poem. But these critics conclude that to make the new and old astronomy the core of Donne's metaphor "is to disregard the English language, to prefer private evidence to public, external to internal" (1954: 12–14). Psychoanalyzing an author, inserting historical facts that are not explicit in the poem, or digging around for evidence of the author's motives by uncovering what she was reading when she wrote the poem—all of these methods are off-limits for objective critical inquiry, mere hypotheses that stray too far beyond the margins of the text, the words on the page, the English language as it is used by a particular author in a particular poem.

The intentional fallacy exerted quite an influence on literary studies in the twentieth century, and it's an idea that is still debated among some critics. If we could travel back in time and ask Oscar Wilde what he meant to imply in his allusions to Dorian Gray's sins, or examine T. S. Eliot on certain passages in *The Waste Land* (as determined readers actually did), would our experience with the novel or poem be significantly different? Would their comments even be reliable? If I read a novel by Cormac McCarthy or J. D. Salinger, two American novelists famously reticent about their work, and then come across a rare interview or a stash of letters, what should I do with that information when I reread *Blood*

Meridian or *Catcher in the Rye*? Should an author's commentary on what was meant in a novel or his articulation of a philosophy direct or influence a reader's encounter with the text, or not? It's a difficult question. For Wimsatt and Beardsley, literary critics should assume that the work's meaning is discernible without recourse to inside information from the author, whether in interviews, award speeches, letters, memoirs, or sketches on cocktail napkins. T. S. Eliot, who was of two minds about the question, makes a good point about authorial intention in "The Frontiers of Criticism," asserting that each reader has to decide in each particular case how important it is to have information about the author's intentions. One critic may argue that Wordsworth's affair with Annette Vallon in France had a determining influence on his subject matter and the development of his style; another critic asserts the clue lies not in the affair with Annette but in Wordsworth's affection for his sister Dorothy. Who knows? These speculations might be very important if we want to understand the man, Wordsworth, but "the real question," says Eliot,

> which every reader of Wordsworth must answer for himself is: does it matter? Does this account help me to understand the Lucy poems any better than I did before? For myself I can only say that a knowledge of the springs which released the poem is not necessarily a help towards understanding the poem: too much information about the origins of a poem may even break my contact with it.
>
> (1957: 124)

The point in objective criticism is that the critic should try not to let biographical information, psychological speculation, or iffy facts about the author's marital record, writing habits, alcohol consumption, or literary tastes and temperament get in the way of his experience with the object the author has created and brought into the world—the language before him, the poem, play, or novel itself.

The third tendency rejected by Brooks and Warren goes along with this distaste for private speculation and personal preference. Students should not be encouraged to read literature only for inspiration or moral instruction, and they should not confuse critical reading with didactic interpretations—reading to discover a life lesson, a kernel of wisdom, a confirmation of one's instincts or beliefs. They call this common type of misreading "message-hunting," a practice that drastically oversimplifies most poems by treating a work of literature as a source of practical information or a pearl of wisdom. But, we might protest, why shouldn't ordinary readers look for precepts to apply to their lives? For thousands of years, the arts have been a destination for people who want to make sense of the turbulence of human experiences. The most constant and pressing thoughts we have about life are the subjects of literature: the awareness and anticipation of death, the inchoate longing for beauty or God, the confusing blaze of love and sexual desire. But if we think we've actually *read* a poem because we found a quotable message or an uplifting thought, we are giving up on a deeper experience of the text. Such readers are more interested in finding a mirror to reflect their own lives than they are in the author's vision and her art. To be clear, Brooks and Warren aren't out to deflate a reader's enjoyment of a poem, or to remove the consolations and encouragements that literature can offer. In fact, they point out that most readers who approve of what a poem says also seem to enjoy something intangible about it: its "message" is inextricably bound to its texture and its poetic features, maybe to what they perceive as its beauty—sound, meter, rhyme, figurative language, ambiguity, and voice.

Here is the last stanza of a well-known poem by Robert Frost (1998: 49):

> I shall be telling this with a sigh
> Somewhere ages and ages hence:
> Two roads diverged in a wood, and I—
> I took the one less traveled by,
> And that has made all the difference.

To many readers (especially American readers), these lines offer a satisfying philosophy, something like, "Trust yourself and follow your own path in life" or "To be self-reliant and to take risks has both its challenges and its rewards." The pace and formal structure of Frost's poem (rhyming iambic tetrameter), the precise way the speaker's mood is conveyed by a sighing pause after "I" in the middle of the stanza, the absence of an emphatic stress pattern in the slow, nearly monosyllabic final line communicate a feeling of restraint, a mood of wistfulness combined with resolution and acceptance—the perspective of some people in the middle of their lives as they look back at the choices they have made.

But quite a few literary critics have argued that to read these lines without irony, as morally uplifting or as an expression of American individualism, is totally misguided. Even if we leave aside the story of the poem's composition and publication in 1916–1917, and Frost's own commentary on it, there is enough equivocation in the text itself to read the "message" very differently.[4] In an influential critique from 1995, the critic Frank Lentricchia argued that the last stanza's "strongly sententious" tone is actually an ironic prediction of the "happy American construction" the poem has been understood to endorse; the poem is a comment on naïve readers who prefer consolatory platitudes to the challenges of modernist poetry. For Lentricchia, what the lines say, in fact, is the *opposite* of Emersonian self-reliance, nonconformity, and self-determination:

> Frost's speaker does not choose out of some rational capacity; he prefers, in fact, not to choose at all.... The good American ending, the last three lines of the poem, is prefaced by two lines of storytelling

self-consciousness in which the speaker ... in effect tells his auditor
that in some unspecified *future* he will tell it otherwise, to some gullible audience, tell it the way they want to hear it.

He concludes that Frost's meaning in the last stanza is that "our life-
shaping choices are irrational, that we are fundamentally out of control"
(1975: 75). Not everyone will agree with Lentricchia's interpretation,
but he makes a good case; indeed, this ironic reading of the poem is
widely accepted among critics of Frost's poetry. Yet the upbeat message
prevails with many readers who are not trained critics, and understandably so. A very famous poem by an iconic American author is always
liable to be reassembled by some readers into inspirational bumper-
stickers, self-help books, patriotic websites, and email signature tags—
doubly ironic, in the case of "The Road Not Taken," if those readers
feel the point of the poem is nonconformity! Because the presumed
message resonates with readers or strikes them as true, the poem is not
read carefully, thoroughly, or questioningly, nor is it studied for problems of voice and consistency. Frost himself called "The Road Not
Taken" a tricky poem.

Finally, the New Critics argued that just as readers should try to avoid
the pitfalls of message-hunting—finding a moral in the poem to live
by—they should avoid the trap of assuming that literature should have
nothing to do with the real world or with morality, and that art is about
only itself. On this point the New Critics have often been misunderstood,
and opponents who assume that their focus on the autonomous work of
art represented a throwback to "art for art's sake" couldn't be more
wrong. The New Critics argued forcefully that it is because literature has
important use and relevance to the world that the critic has a public role to
play in setting standards and aiding readers' appreciation and understanding. As John Crowe Ransom wrote, a novel or play is "an artistic object,
with a heroic human labor behind it, and on these terms it calls for public
discussion," not a glass case in a museum (1938: 342). What objective criticism rejects is mushy aestheticizing: the theory that a work of literature
should be defined as the distillation of a pure feeling or of a basic human
truth. This implies that the proper reader is someone who experiences the
meaning of the work on some kind of spiritual or emotional level. These
readers incorrectly think of the work of art as ineffable and transcendent,
as "pure realization," a "beautiful statement of some higher truth," only
accessible through a pleasing combination of sounds and images (Brooks
and Warren 1950: xlvi–xlix). The New Critics said over and over that
poetry and literature are *not* religion. Critics who dwell on metaphysics
dilute the purpose of literary criticism and befuddle the reader with
abstractions about the truth of literature, the enchantment of literature,
and dreams of an escape from the sordid real world into a realm of art and
beauty. This amounts to saying that good poems create intense feelings in

the reader, and bad poems leave the reader cold or indifferent—and any judgment based only on feelings is bound to be wobbly and unreliable.

Wimsatt and Beardsley called this the *affective fallacy*. Their argument is that Romantic assumptions about art in the nineteenth century have held far too much sway in the world of letters, breeding generations of "introspective amateurs and soul-cultivators" masquerading as authorities on literary quality (1954: 29). Indeed, Matthew Arnold warned against what he called "the personal fallacy" in 1880, in his great essay, "The Study of Poetry":

> Our personal affinities, likings and circumstances, have great power to sway our estimate of this or that poet's work, and to make us attach more importance to it as poetry than in itself it really possesses, because to us it is, or has been, of high importance. Here also we overrate the object of our interest, and apply to it a language of praise which is quite exaggerated.
>
> (1970b: 342)

Arnold wanted to wave away the mist before the reader's eyes when she leans too far toward either an historical estimate of a work (over-rating poems because they've been around a long time) or a private estimate (over-rating poems because we relate to them). Wimsatt and Beardsley, though, went much further than Arnold in delineating the snares and deceptions of affective criticism, which may take devious shapes. There's the emotive theory, for instance, which assumes that language by its very nature carries emotional resonance. If we read the word "sultry," whether in a rap song, a cosmetics ad, or a poem by Anna Laetitia Barbauld, we're going to have feelings associated with sultriness. There's also the imaginative or empathic theory, in which the reader can lose the self through immersion in the reading experience or through intense identification with a character, object, or image. Perhaps most offensive to objective critics is the so-called physiological branch of affective criticism, where a poem's success is judged by the reader's somatic response—the bristling-skin, tingling-spine, pit-of-the-stomach theory of reading. (In the 1940s, these reactions were measured in laboratories with a galvanometer; today they're tallied up with magnetic resonance imaging in the emerging field of neuroaesthetics.) We are all certainly entitled to our emotional reactions to works of art—poems are not information systems, and we do not aspire to be computers or robots. The problem with affective criticism, though, is that it removes the focus from the work of literature to the reader's subjective responses—indeed, as Wimsatt and Beardsley argue, the competence and sincerity of the critic become an issue, since we can never know the subjective basis for her likes and dislikes. Are her positive feelings aroused by the bright vernacular language and clever rhymes in the poem "Still I Rise," or by a strong identification with Maya Angelou as a black woman?

If she dislikes Hemingway's novels is it because she finds his style uncongenial, or is there some personal distaste for the way he portrays women characters? If the critic's job is to explain certain concepts about how literature works and to analyze how meaning is made and communicated in specific texts, merely personal reactions are irrelevant. They are extraneous to the work itself. This doesn't mean that objective critics are not allowed to have emotions about Ophelia's madness or Tess Durbeyfield's fate— assuming a posture of aloofness or coldbloodedness isn't really *reading*, since we must surrender something of ourselves when we take up a work of fiction or poetry. But the responsibility of the critic is to examine how emotions are structured by and created within the text itself.

Wimsatt and Beardsley are very clear about the implications of this split between objective and subjective criticism: "The critic whose formulations lean to the emotive and the critic whose formulations lean to the cognitive will in the long run produce a vastly different sort of criticism." And their essays on the two fallacies are still defended by critics who advocate what they call cognitive critique. The critic cannot ignore the emotional effects of literature, but her role is to offer a specific account of the *reasons* for the emotion so that sufficiently informed readers will be led back to the work itself. The literary critic, as a more experienced reader, is both a teacher and a role model, and as such she has a duty to other readers, as well as to the literature, to justify her interpretations based on the data of the text. So really useful criticism "will not talk of tears, prickles, or other physiological symptoms, of feeling angry, joyful, hot, cold, or intense, or of vaguer states of emotional disturbance," write Wimsatt and Beardsley.

> The critic is not a contributor to statistically countable reports about the poem, but a teacher or explicator of meanings. His readers, if they are alert, will not be content to take what he says as testimony, but will scrutinize it as teaching.
>
> (1954: 34)

The critic-as-teacher, then, in the objectivist model, has a delicate and demanding task, one that involves judiciousness, reason, and great self-awareness. Emotion is not banished from criticism, of course, but it is analyzed as an inextricable aspect of the poem's artistic status. One of the New Critics described the critic's job as balancing the *evaluation of literature* with the *communication of insights*—adding (discouragingly) that neither of these can actually be taught in the classroom. For if the instructor offers her own evaluation of a work—telling her class that Sylvia Plath's *Ariel* is really overrated, or that Henry James's *The Turn of the Screw* is the pinnacle of his work—she disseminates a hierarchy that may stultify the student's personal response. On the other hand, insights can't be taught, only exhibited, and they're difficult to explain to readers who haven't read as much as the professor has (Tate 2008: 65–68). After all, insights may be both professional and personal, intellectual and emotive: one reader sees, for example, a line of thought in Jane Austen's descriptions of people's emotions that can be traced to David Hume, while another realizes rather painfully why she understands Emma Woodhouse. So we're back to some of the original problems faced by formalist critics: can a work of literature adequately be studied as a self-contained art object, without reference to the social conditions that brought it into existence? Can a reader—even a highly trained one—make rational, evaluative, and true statements about the quality of a novel or poem? Can he test the validity of a poem's ideas? Can she deliver a reasonable assessment about the feelings and ideas the work communicates? And then there is the thorny matter of evaluation, or justifying one's judgments about literary worth.

Formalists believe judgments should be based on something qualitative in the work, whether creative imagery, organic structure, concentration of expression, or thematic coherence. This is where some people part ways with the New Critics, whose judgments about literary quality seemed deliberately blind to the sociopolitical and historical conditions under which literature is written and published—factors such as education, wealth, breadth of experience, opportunity, and literary connections that are crucial to an understanding of women's poetry in the seventeenth century, for instance, or the writings of Native Americans in the 1800s. The New Critics tended to work with a very small group of Western canonical works, most by men and mostly poetry.

This comparative narrowness has turned many people off. If we should not rely on our religious or political beliefs to criticize literature, then we should not fall back on elitist assumptions about the superiority of works from the past to works from the present (Arnold's "historical fallacy"), or the presumed value of "highbrow" art over popular works. A great many people find artistic worth and enjoyment in successful authors such as Dan Brown, Stephen King, and J. K. Rowling. Even I. A. Richards, in 1929, recognized that literary critics had better pay some attention to popular culture. "Best-sellers in all the arts," he wrote, "are worthy of very close study. No theory of criticism is satisfactory which is not able to explain their wide appeal and give clear reasons why those who disdain them are not necessarily snobs" (1929: 203). Or why those who like them are not necessarily gullible or unsophisticated. A New Critic would say that it is the job of the literary critic to explain why these authors are or are not excellent, why they are or are not worth reading for their complexity and insight, whether what they do technically, stylistically, and thematically with narrative art is fine and original, or careless and predictable.[5] Given the prominence of courses on popular genres in today's college classrooms—Westerns, detective fiction, mysteries, hip hop, children's literature, graphic novels, sci-fi—shouldn't the methods of objective criticism also be applied to non-canonical or even non-literary texts? Would those texts fail to stand up to objective scrutiny? Does it matter? And so there has grown a chasm between literary studies and cultural studies. If some people in literary studies feel that the traditional focus on fiction, poetry, and drama has been unfortunately displaced by film, popular culture, and digital media there are people in cultural studies who wonder if their activist concern with the operations of class or gender ideology has been hijacked by English departments that keep harping on formal or aesthetic matters. Yet both sides could pursue their interests using close reading strategies. As Jane Gallop observes, a scholar of cultural studies who has literary training will likely notice different sorts of things than someone trained as a sociologist or an historian and so have something original to contribute to the reading of a text (2010: 15). Close textual analysis, even if objectivity is not desired, is a valuable skill that can be applied to any cultural product.

But there remains the problem of artistic value and of excellence, which the New Critics took very seriously indeed. Although the dust has settled from the literary "culture wars" of the 1980s and most English departments are comfortable with a canon that is multicultural and fairly inclusive, a few outspoken scholars today echo the New Critical demand for quality above *all* considerations. In 2011, for example, the esteemed Harvard scholar Helen Vendler reviewed a new anthology of twentieth-century American poetry by the equally esteemed poet Rita Dove (a United States poet laureate) in which she criticized Dove's selection of 175 poets as far too welcoming and indiscriminate. She asked, "Which of Dove's 175 poets will have staying power, and which will seep back into the archives of sociology?" Vendler argued that Dove's judgment was colored by her concern for "multicultural inclusivity," rather than literary worth.[6] Her standards were too low, or else were skewed by non-literary interests. Like the New Critics who were her teachers, Helen Vendler insists that some poets are better than others—some much better—and that the job of the critic or anthologist is to guide and educate readers on the merits of poetry *as poetry*.

No doubt some people think this point of view calculating, elitist, or just hard to justify. How does one prove that one poem is quantifiably better than another? The New Critics laid down a method for writing and talking about literature that was based on the legalistic or scientific language of evidence, truth, and facts. The reader must demonstrate that he has read the text closely, consulted relevant works of criticism about it, and then go on to prove that his judgment is correct or his interpretation solid and convincing based on the criteria he has established and the evidence of the text itself. This is a very difficult task, and it takes practice. In *Understanding Fiction*, Brooks and Warren argued that evaluation should come later in the critical process—that the first problem is to teach readers to understand "the nature of the fictional structure," to get them to move beyond "stock responses and threshold interests" (1947: xiv). To ask inexperienced readers to pit two differently successful stories against one another can lead to "critical vindictiveness and literary priggishness." Even if we feel confident enough to make broad evaluative judgments, we must remain open-minded and generous toward other readers' opinions. There is no place for "a literary dictator," wrote Brooks and Warren, in the democratic "republic of letters" (1947: xiv). In fact, T. S. Eliot wrote that one of the dangers of objective criticism "is that of assuming that there must be just one interpretation of the poem as a whole, that must be right" (1957: 126). Critics are allowed to disagree, and it's often through their disagreements that we're able to get a clearer reading of the text. But they still have to make their case for why a story or poem is interesting, half-decent, brilliant, or forgettable. Let us wade carefully into the swamp of literary judgment and address some of the difficulties that ensue when formalist critics disagree about formal matters—about the sense and meaning of a word or a line, the value of an expression, the success of an image, or the seriousness of the author's purpose.

> [W]e must also set our standard for poetry high, since poetry, to be capable of fulfilling such high destinies, must be poetry of a high order of excellence. We must accustom ourselves to a high standard and to a strict judgment.
>
> (Arnold 1970b: 341)

> Is it possible to say that Poem A (one of Donne's *Holy Sonnets*, or one of the poems of Jonson or of Shakespeare) is better than Poem B (Collins' *Ode to Evening*), or vice versa?
>
> If not, is it possible to say that either of these is better than Poem C (*The Cremation of Sam Magee* or something comparable)?
>
> (Winters 2008: 75)

Matthew Arnold wanted to establish clear-cut measures—he called them "touchstones"—to help educated readers sift through the best and worst of English poetry, and so learn to distinguish a true classic (Homer, Shakespeare, Dante) from a "dubious" or "false" classic (Chaucer). He was serious about the value of rating and ranking and sifting through literary worth because he saw that a very, very large commercial market was opening for people to make a lot of money hawking trashy novels and sentimental verse. There had to be a set of standards for great literature and, as Oxford University's Professor of Poetry, Arnold felt he was qualified to supply them: truth, high seriousness, superior diction, a strong manner, a fitting style. A group of mid-twentieth-century critics, including Eliot and F. R. Leavis in Britain and the New Critics in America, inherited Arnold's belief that literary critics have to hold certain standards in order to make objective judgments. You could even say, as Allen Tate did emphatically in an essay from 1940, that as teachers or experts, they have a *moral obligation* to make judgments, to develop a method of understanding how the formal features of a poem work in unity, and to apply these methods to their reading of both contemporary and past works (1940: 455).[7] Do ordinary readers also have an obligation to judge? Not in the same way as paid professionals, of course, yet if we care about reading and want to read well, there is no escaping judgment. When we talk about a novel or a film in class, or even casually with a friend, we're bound to fall into language that involves evaluative criteria. As the contemporary scholar Rita Felski says, "evaluation is not optional: we are condemned to choose, required to rank, endlessly engaged in practices of selecting, sorting, distinguishing, privileging, whether in academia or in everyday life" (2008: 20).

This famous poem was published in 1875, by the Victorian poet William Ernest Henley:

Invictus

Out of the night that covers me,
    Black as the pit from pole to pole,
I thank whatever gods may be
    For my unconquerable soul.

In the fell clutch of circumstance
    I have not winced nor cried aloud.
Under the bludgeonings of chance
    My head is bloody, but unbow'd.

Beyond this place of wrath and tears
    Looms but the Horror of the shade,
And yet the menace of the years
    Finds and shall find me unafraid.

It matters not how strait the gate,
    How charged with punishments the scroll,
I am the master of my fate:
    I am the captain of my soul.

Let's first approach the poem using the methods *contra* Brooks and Warren: paraphrase, history and biography, and message-hunting.

After we learn the title is Latin for "unconquered" or "unvanquished,"[8] we might paraphrase the poem by saying that it is about a person's determination to overcome all the accidents and terrors of his life, with or without the existence of God or belief in an afterlife. It is striking, for example, that the poem mixes Christian imagery about the day of judgment—"strait the gate," "the scroll," and the word "soul" twice—with some ambiguous classical or pagan references—"gods," "circumstance," "chance," and "fate" (we'll leave aside for now the question of whether this suggests muddled thinking from the poet or something quite profound about the human condition). Next, we may want to place the poem in the context of the Victorian age and the crisis of faith. When we learn in addition that Henley was a staunch supporter of late-Victorian imperialism and the cult of masculine adventure, and later became the well-connected editor of a successful literary magazine, the poem takes shape as a reflection of a cluster of ideas and beliefs belonging to the political, social, and literary cultures of the poet's time. The fact that Henley suffered the grievous misfortune of having his leg amputated and wrote the poem while hospitalized might be relevant to an interpretation of its message: a declaration of courage and defiance in the face of life's cruelty and injustice, or as inspiration to continue to fight a hard personal battle such as illness, personal loss, or political oppression. I'm probably safe to say that many readers enjoy "Invictus" because they embrace its message. Some people in the public eye have even used it to communicate something important about their beliefs—people as differently situated as Nelson Mandela, Gordon Brown, and Timothy McVeigh.[9]

Although the historical and biographical material take us deeper into the world of the poem and add an important dimension to it, an objective critic might ask if that information helps us to experience the poem as a poem. To reduce the poem to a moral message likewise seems irrelevant to interpretation. And does the fact that so many people have publicly claimed that this poem has personally inspired them to endure hardship mean that it is a good poem? Does the fact that its title and some of its lines have entered popular discourse, from *Mass Effect 3* to the name of a rock band, from an episode of *Star Trek* to a popular tattoo, mean it is worth preserving as a poem?

An objective critic wants to know one thing above all: is this a good poem or a bad poem, according to certain criteria of poetic worth? Let us consider the views of two literary critics writing at the height of the New Criticism. First, Marshall McLuhan's negative verdict, published in 1944:

> Henley provides himself with a Satanic backdrop as he comes forward to announce his own virtues. (The image is vaguely nautical, evoking the common notion of man's wayfaring. But the main suggestion of "Pit" is that of a hell-trap. This is reinforced by "Clutch.") He is appealing oratorically for the sympathetic admiration of an audience which he well understands. Almost every line contains a hard-bitten cliché which propels the "thought" along to the shrill double emphasis on "I" in the last two lines.
>
>   Verse of this sort has no internal organization. It doesn't hang together by a poetic action, which always manifests itself in the interaction of the language and the metaphors, but simply by an external

appeal to audience assumptions. (Contrast it in this respect with a genuinely successful poem such as [Thomas] Hardy's "Neutral Tone" [*sic*] or consider how the superficially rhetorical credo of Tennyson's "Ulysses" succeeds as poetry by reason of the original pressures in the rhythms of its language and the adequacy of the dramatic situation from which it grows.) The lines

Beyond this place of wrath and tears
Looms but the horror of the shade,

are the least foolish of the whole series of hyperboles. There is a crude sort of surprise intended in calling this life hell and the next a relief. The only example of restraint or tension in the entire poem is in the "but" of that second line.

For their full effect, one has to imagine these verses being recited by an actor employing extreme gestures and the utmost emphasis of delivery. The setting for the drama is Hell and Judgement, the posture is defiance, the imagery banal, the effect that of a terrified man screwing his courage to the sticking point.

From this brief exegesis, I could conclude that our critic's implicit standards for excellent poetry are: (1) it should avoid clichés; (2) it should have crisp images; (3) it should not rely on a "shrill" or exaggerated tone to achieve its effects; (4) it should not appear self-indulgent; (5) it should be organized by the relation of its parts, such as language, metaphor, rhythm, or dramatic action; (6) it should avoid hyperbole and exhibit restraint or understatement; (7) it should treat a serious idea without resorting to either cheap theatrics or banality. Against these standards, "Invictus" is a very bad poem indeed.

Here is another critic, in a direct response to McLuhan's analysis:

It is possible to be too harsh on this lyric, and I think that Mr. McLuhan in his total condemnation has been a little unkind to a poem which has found its way into so many anthologies and which has given courage to so many readers. The objection that the poem has no "internal structure" is equally true of Shakespeare's "Under the greenwood tree," "When icicles hang on the wall," and many another fine lyric as well. The lyric is the expression of a mood, an emotion, or an idea without development. If it develops it becomes didactic or philosophical just because of this development.

Let us break "Invictus" into its parts. Certainly it is full of triteness: "black as a pit," "from pole to pole," "fell clutch," "head … unbowed," "the place of wrath and tears." What about the metaphors? Altogether there are eight—in a poem of sixteen lines evidence enough that the poet's memory or imagination is working. Are they hyperbolic? That is a matter of opinion. When Shakespeare calls Sylvia "Holy, fair, and wise" he has exaggerated too. When he says the "tooth" of the wind is keen, he is using hyperbole; but he is hardly more rash than Henley, who speaks of the "bludgeonings of chance" and the "menace of the years."

What about [the poem's] theology? To any one believing in the doctrine of free-will Henley's conclusion will appear largely orthodox.... It is a truism, I think, that the truth or falsity of a poem's ideas does not determine whether or not it is a poem. A work of art must be judged by its art.

"Invictus" is to be contrasted, not with Hardy's "Neutral Tone" [*sic*] but with [George] Herbert's "The Collar." ... Both poets are trying to produce a resonant effect in language, intended, of course, to fit the ideas each has in mind. Much of the effectiveness of both poems lies in their sound. Both poets lean heavily on alliteration and the use of open vowels "o," "ou," the liquid "l," and the rolled "r." The effect is thunderous, as intended by both poets, in one to affirm the power of God, in the other to assert the courage of man.

Whatever the psychological factors in Henley's nature or the characteristics of late Victorianism, the poem has to be judged as a work. "Invictus" has its faults—even serious ones, of which triteness is certainly the worst—but the skillful use of vowel and consonant, the careful adaptation of sound to meaning, has kept this poem alive when most of Henley's effusions are being forgotten.

This critic, J. M. Purcell (1945), shares some opinions with his colleague— he concedes the poem's language is often trite or clichéd, for instance—but he defends the poem on other grounds: (1) it is a particular type of poem, a lyric, and lyrics are characterized by the expression of a mood; (2) it shows imagination in the proliferation of metaphors; (3) hyperbolic or exaggerated language may have a purpose in poetry; (4) a poem should be judged as a work of art, not as a statement of theology; (5) the poet uses alliteration and vowel sounds effectively to convey his thoughts; (6) the poet's historical milieu or his personal quirks have proved irrelevant to the poem's popularity and endurance. So although it may not be the greatest composition of all time, in Purcell's reading Henley's poem earns a measure of success and is deserving of its fame.

As objective critics, McLuhan and Purcell make an effort to read the poem without too many references to Henley's life or to the context of Victorian belief (though both see that this context cannot be erased entirely). Both eschew message-hunting; as Purcell says, "Invictus" should be studied as a work of art, not as a piece of philosophical doctrine. It is appropriate for both critics to allow glancing comparisons with similar works by other poets (Hardy, Tennyson, Shakespeare, Herbert) in order to clarify their own judgments. And other than a certain testiness in McLuhan and a tone of mild dissent in Purcell, each critic strives to communicate his opinion of the poem unclouded by any emotional involvement in its truth or untruth for him, personally. "Invictus," then, presents a useful test case for objective criticism.

Well—maybe, and maybe not. Despite this poem's continuing appeal to a great many ordinary readers and its reliable place in poetry anthologies, there has been comparatively little expert commentary on "Invictus." Largely this is because most minor Victorian poets went out of critical fashion in the twentieth century. But it may also be because, to a perspicacious critic, poems such as "Invictus" are too obvious, too easy to dispatch. The New Critics were drawn to complexity. They especially championed the knotty metaphysical poetry of John Donne and the modernist experiments of Eliot, Wallace Stevens, Ezra Pound, and William Carlos Williams. These critics liked to work on poems where there was a level of difficulty in getting at the meaning, where the poet's symbolism, persona, wit, irony, and allusiveness invited a scrupulous attention to formal details. One of the most telling features of formalist criticism, then and now, is a fascination with the multiplicity of meanings generated by language. Poetry, as one of the richest uses of language possible, offers a goldmine of potential meanings, a wealth of connotative ambiguity. Even "Invictus" contains words that can be read in different senses—when used as an adjective, the word *fell* can have three meanings: harsh and cruel; sinister, as in with an evil purpose; or destructive and deadly. Depending on the interpretation, "the fell clutch of circumstance" may mean either that Fate is indifferently brutal or really malevolent and out to get you.

To some readers, it doesn't make much difference—either meaning will do. They find the elusiveness of literary language and the profusion of possible meanings frustrating, as if poets are in the business of obscuring what they mean rather than revealing it, and many readers give up when a work seems to persist in teasing their comprehension. For close formalist readers, though, *paradox, irony*, and *ambiguity* are the bread and butter of literary reading. Words can't always be stared at directly for their meaning, like headlights on a dark road. They carry nuances, lights and shadows that are illuminated by the words surrounding them, the speaker's tone, the narrative line. It is when we study the way words bend and chase each other, shift and glitter—when we open up to *how* several senses of a word's import can illuminate or complicate the poem's meaning—that the excitement and challenge of objective close reading takes off.

> Poets who can compel slow reading have thus an initial advantage. The effort, the heightened attention, may brace the reader, and that particular intellectual thrill which celebrates the step-by-step conquest of understanding may irradiate and awaken other mental activities more essential to poetry. It is a good thing to make the light-footed reader work for what he gets.
>
> (Richards 1926: 195)

The English poet Gerard Manley Hopkins (1844–1889) was almost an exact contemporary of W. E. Henley, but most of his poems were not published until 1918, almost thirty years after his death. He became a sort of honorary modernist when I. A. Richards and his student, William Empson, offered two readings of Hopkins's poem, "The Windhover," in the 1920s, opening the door to a landslide of competing interpretations that continued for more than forty years. Critics remain fascinated by Hopkins's metrical invention, his use of tension and surprise, and his original and puzzling metaphors. His poems celebrate the lavishness of the English language and the sheer abundance of its possibilities, but they also exhibit great control and formal ingenuity.

Hopkins called "The Windhover" the best thing he ever wrote, and readers have examined this poem from an astounding range of perspectives. In this section, we're going to narrow it down to a few confident objective critics who, dictionaries in hand, have determined to stick to the words on the page—especially to one word, which has generated piles of critical commentary in scholarly journals, and a volley of feisty letters to the editor of a prestigious literary review. Before we engage these critiques, there are some basic data about Hopkins and "The Windhover" that we should know.

First, the poem is a sonnet, traditionally a form made up of fourteen lines in rhyming iambic pentameter, with an octet and a sestet that communicate the progress of the poet's meditations on a subject: the last six lines of the poem comment on or develop the thoughts or images set up in the first eight lines. The subject of "The Windhover" is a kestrel, a small falcon or hawk, balancing on the early morning wind (octet) and then diving after its prey (sestet). (Most of the critical arguments about "The Windhover" are about the sestet.) Second, Hopkins developed an idiosyncratic meter which he called "sprung rhythm," designed to convey the uniqueness and naturalness of every subject he addresses in his poetry—its "thisness," or what he called its *inscape*, the essence of its existence, the energy of its being. In Hopkins's metrical system, every poem might have a unique number of stressed and unstressed syllables, braided together in a tapestry of assonance and alliteration, repetition, internal rhyme, and near rhyme. Hopkins even stretched the rules of grammar when he felt the poem demanded a certain sound or sense. So although "The Windhover" is a sonnet of fourteen lines, and it does have a rhyme scheme, its stress pattern is there to communicate the freedom of "windhoverness," not the strictness of "Petrarchan sonnet." Also, Hopkins strongly believed that effective poetry relies on the sounds of words arranged together. In his letters he often urged his friends to read his poetry aloud, to "take breath and read it with the ears as I always wish to be read." He inserted accents over words to insure that when read aloud they would convey the push or force of the syllable or the gliding sound in a given line. Finally, one biographical detail: in 1867, Hopkins entered a Jesuit novitiate. He destroyed all the poetry he had written until then, and did not write again until 1875. Many critics have argued that because Hopkins wrote "The Wind-hover" four months before he was ordained as a Jesuit priest, the sonnet requires a Christian interpretation—indeed, six years later Hopkins inserted the dedication "To Christ Our Lord," which is always printed with the poem. Others, though, argue that the language of the poem may imply a spiritual or psychological conflict, pointing to the tension between desire and repression, freedom and obedience, and that a strictly religious reading closes off the poem to further interpretations (other readers just want to see it as a nature poem). These ideas inevitably come into play in a poem that expresses great excitement and emotion, but our task is to test the mettle of objective critics who stick emphatically to the evidence of the text, and for whom the maze of Hopkins's language is the important thing. They insist that a reader cannot get at the general *meaning* of the poem, which is the whole point of interpretation, if she does not pay minute attention to the words the poet has chosen and what his language is trying to achieve.

The Windhover:
To Christ our Lord

I caught this morning morning's minion, king-
    dom of daylight's dauphin, dapple-dawn-drawn Falcon, in his riding
    Of the rolling level underneath him steady air, and striding
High there, how he rung upon the rein of a wimpling wing
In his ecstasy! then off, off forth on swing,
    As a skate's heel sweeps smooth on a bow-bend: the hurl and gliding
    Rebuffed the big wind. My heart in hiding
Stirred for a bird,—the achieve of, the mastery of the thing!

Brute beauty and valour and act, oh, air, pride, plume, here
    Buckle! AND the fire that breaks from thee then, a billion
Times told lovelier, more dangerous, O my chevalier!

    No wonder of it: shéer plód makes plough down sillion
Shine, and blue-bleak embers, ah my dear,
    Fall, gall themselves, and gash gold-vermilion.

Critics more or less agree that the words *minion, kingdom, dauphin, mastery, valour,* and *chevalier* (pronounced *chev-al-year,* to rhyme with "here") convey a crusading knight motif, evoking the elegance and grandeur of the age of chivalry—although one contemporary critic points out that many of these words are derived from the French, and may convey decadence and waste, while another points out that *minion* (a favored servant) and *dauphin* (a princeling) bear connotations of subordination, not mastery (Cosgrove 450–451). I. A. Richards took the lines *Rung upon the rein* as a term from a riding academy, when a trainer causes his horse to circle around on a long rein, or perhaps the falcon rides upon the air like a knight upon his steed. That reading has been contradicted by bird-watchers, who observe that to "ring" is a technical term in falconry meaning to rise spirally in flight. Walter Ong (1974) has read the images as composite, so that falcon-horse-rider combine symbolically to convey lightness and strength, energy and grace, heroism and tragedy. But does a kestrel spiral up, or does it *stride* and then hover, using its wing to *rein* in the wind, to keep its place? Or perhaps *rung* means "to linger in the ear or the memory, to sound, like a bell, perhaps rung in triumph, perhaps a summons to prayer." It can even suggest a "coin thrown on a counter, to test it, and so suggests the testing of a man's soul" (Deutsch 1969: 63). *Wimpling wing*, it has been suggested, could gesture toward a medieval nun's headcovering (a wimpling, or wimple, looks a little like wings), or it could be used as an adjective indicating "to curve or twist," or both. The falcon's sweeping movements are then compared to how *a skate's heel sweeps smooth on a bow-bend*: it is like a figure skater sweeping powerfully along the ice—although one critic said the image could be of an English crossbow. Ong manages to see the image as referring to the falcon-rider symbol combined: "the skate's heel carries a strong suggestion of the horse's hoof: skates cannot only clip and clop beneath one … but provide a kinesthetic sensation of contact with the earth" (Ong 1974: 6).

There's been a little more discussion about *My heart in hiding/Stirred for a bird*—in fact, this is the point where critics start to disagree, and have to prove that their interpretation is correct based on the text of the poem. "Why in hiding? Hiding from what?" asked I. A. Richards. "I should say the poet's heart is in hiding from Life, has chosen a safer way, and that the greater danger is the greater exposure to temptation and error than a more adventurous, less sheltered course," but then he adds that an "equally plausible reading is this: Renouncing the glamour of the outer life of adventure, the poet transfers its qualities of audacity to the inner life" (1926: 198–199). So something is going on between safety and danger, the outer life and the inner spirit. William Empson took this interpretation even further by suggesting the lines must point to an expression of deep self-division:

> Confronted suddenly with the active physical beauty of the bird, he conceives it as the opposite of his patient spiritual renunciation; the statements of the poem appear to insist that his own life is superior but he cannot decisively judge between them, and holds both with agony in his mind.
>
> (1953: 225)

These critics make us think about the elasticity of Hopkins's language: is the heart in hiding from something it wants or from something it fears? Yet another critic, N. S. Lees, strongly objects to the heart-in-conflict theme; it is something that has been added to the poem "by the psychologist seeking involuntary self-revelation." Lees says Richards and Empson have been too influenced by knowledge of Hopkins's life (it was known that Hopkins worried that writing poetry was incompatible with his religious calling). Furthermore, their secularity makes them unable to sympathize in any way with Hopkins's voluntary "submission to the Jesuit discipline" (Lees 1950: 32). Richards is entitled to offer a *comment* on the poem, but that, says Lees, is not the same as an exposition of it.

Further readings argue that the poet's heart hides from "the bitter implications of life and from Christ's insistent challenge to a more heroic plane of activity" (Schoder 1969: 36). Does the Jesuit priest fear the burden of his calling? Denis Donoghue thinks that is a bit labored, and that the lines simply express "inadequacy and weakness in the poet, aroused by the sight of the bird's positive strength and activity" (Donoghue 1969: 93). But it *is* possible to see a more terrifying aspect in the line's sense: "What stirs the heart," according to one commentator, is "the hidden dread of the powers against which the bird contends ... a sense of this brutish world's threat to the understanding, and the thought that spiritual triumph may come with pain and loss" (Deutsch 1969: 63). Are all of these readings plausible? They certainly exemplify nuanced interpretations (and we should reread the octet to see if they hold up), but there is at least some consensus on the general import of the lines: *My heart in hiding/ Stirred for a bird* suggests basically that the poet sees his own weakness or timidity because he is awestruck at the mastery of the falcon balancing on the wind. So far, so good.

Serious disagreement, though, begins with the sestet. As Carl Woodring wrote, "At the words *here/Buckle*, interpretations scatter like the legs of an inksplotch"—and they spread to the contested imagery of the plough and the embers in the second tercet as well (Woodring 1950: 62). Why do so many literary critics pause at the word *Buckle*? It has seemed to many readers the structural center, the pivot on which the sonnet turns. I'd like to present a few close textual readings of the last six lines of "The Windhover" as examples of the studiousness, integrity, and rigor of objective criticism. Yes, the high-stakes tone and superior attitude in which some authors register their dissent may sound a little outdated, and there are limits to this kind of literary dissection—as one critic put it, that first tercet might be "atomized into a kind of radioactive dust destructive of all life in the poem" (Lisca 1969: 110). Even the New Critics knew that too intent a reading may come down like a pulverizer on a work of literature. On the other hand, careful analysis on a literal level should be the starting point for all responsible literary criticism if the intent is to introduce fresh meanings through pertinent explication. Let's have the first tercet before us again:

> Brute beauty and valour and act, oh, air, pride, plume, here
>   Buckle! AND the fire that breaks from thee then, a billion
> Times told lovelier, more dangerous, O my chevalier!

William Empson threw down the gauntlet, in a section of *Seven Types of Ambiguity*, on the double meanings in Hopkins's word choice:

> *Buckle* admits of two tenses and two meanings: "they do buckle here," or "come, and buckle yourself here"; *buckle* like a military belt, for the discipline of heroic action, and *buckle* like a bicycle wheel, "make useless, distorted and incapable of its natural motion." *Here* may mean "in the case of the bird" or "in the case of the Jesuit"; *then* "when you have become like the bird" or "when you have become like the Jesuit"; *Chevalier* personifies either physical or spiritual activity; Christ riding to Jerusalem, or the cavalry-man ready for the charge; Pegasus or the Windhover.
>
> (1953: 225)

Empson sees these possible meanings as profoundly significant, not only for a reading of Hopkins, but for anyone who cares about the operations of language and the human mind:

> [W]e seem to have a clear case of the Freudian use of opposites, where two things thought of as incompatible, but desired intensely by different systems of judgment, are spoken of simultaneously by words applying to both: both desires are thus given a transient and exhausting satisfaction, and the two systems of judgment are brought into open conflict before the reader. Such a process, one might imagine, could pierce to regions that underlie the whole structure of our thought; could tap the energy of the very depths of the mind.
>
> (1953: 225–226)

Today we might call this phenomenon cognitive dissonance. In any case, it looked like a far stretch from Hopkins's poem for some readers. First of all, does Empson's stress on multiple meanings smudge the poem's imagery? It's hard to see what the poet wants us to picture if the words are gesticulating in so many directions, from belts to bicycle wheels. Then to imply that the poet didn't know what he was doing when he chose his language, or that something in the recesses of his mind produced a "half-conscious pun" (in the words of one dismissive opponent), is a ridiculous and irresponsible speculation, and takes us no closer to the meaning of Hopkins's sonnet. (Is it relevant, for instance, that there is a pub called The Hawk and Buckle near the college where Hopkins was studying theology at Cambridge?) And why must we read into the lines an agonized spiritual struggle? The expression of the poem is joyful and positive! "The conflict between artist and ascetic," writes one dissenter, "is simply not there. The bird's 'achieve' and mastery are admired as those of a creature of God and as a great symbol of Christ. And 'buckling' ... is not self-destruction, but self-dedication" (Ritz 1955: 84–85). In fact, to say that *Buckle* could be read in several ways is no help at all. "We must decide *which* it means," insists Lees, "and I suggest that it has *not* like a bicycle wheel meaning." Lees strongly disagrees that "Buckle!" has a negative sense in the poem:

> "to come together, meet, join, engage," as with a belt ("This belt buckles neatly"), with an overtone of "engage" as in action ("He buckles to the task"), even, indeed, a military action ("I will buckle thee with blows") is surely the meaning and not the contradictory development of the same word to "bending" or "crumpling." ... And the word has emerged in the poet's mind with tones from words like spar*kle*, twin*kle*, crac*kle*, swash*buckle*, which increase and point its vivacity.
>
> (Lees 1969: 74–75)

Lees's interpretation was published in a letter to the editor of London's illustrious *Times Literary Supplement* in 1954, and it was followed by ten more letters in the following months, including two from Empson. Buckling on armor, collapsing, buckling down to work: how many meanings should we allow this word to have? And if we do allow for different meanings, should we read them as *symbolic* or *descriptive*? One symbolic reading offers, "the example of Christ's life linked together three relevant and complementary meanings of 'Buckle!'—buckle within (discipline), buckle to (labour), buckle under (sacrifice)" (Gardner 1969: 17). But another insists that we have to rule out the "submit now" interpretation of *here/Buckle!* if it suggests that the falcon is defeated by the wind (by falling below it) for "then the poet's emotion exceeds its stimulus"—in other words, there must be more to Hopkins's language than the excitement of your average birdwatcher (Woodring 1950: 64). Yet another reader argues that the falcon "does no diving in this poem, and those who see it swoop down have been reading ornithological dictionaries or fanciful definitions of the word 'Buckle' rather than the poem Hopkins wrote" (Litzinger 1969: 140). The bird has rather stopped in flight; it characteristically and skillfully *hovers* and the poet's heart utters a cry of admiration. While one commentator argues confidently that to read *buckle* chiefly as "collapsing" "cannot fit a context which asks for a quick decisive snapping together" (Grigson 1969: 88–89), another more tentatively says, "We cannot be positive that we understand the imagery. The key word 'buckle' is unruly. It can mean 'to break' or 'to join'—with variations. It can be a statement or a command" (Grady 1969: 28). So from the definition of buckle, we come again to the grammatical mood as expressed in the poem. For the following critic, "buckle" is definitely *not* an imperative (a command), and its meaning can only be comprehended if we pay attention to the words that come after it:

> Something buckles and something breaks through. Readers who buckle belts neglect the second half of this statement, though Hopkins capitalized AND between the parts. It will not do to take buckle as an imperative either, as many writers do, for that leaves AND hanging loose and destroys the sentence. It is neither armor nor belt, nor Mr. Empson's bicycle wheel, that buckles or breaks; the pivotal image is of a higher order of magnitude. Decks or bulkheads of a ship buckle before fire breaks through; walls of a building buckle before they crash or burn. In "The Windhover" the whole material world buckles, "AND the fire" of the spiritual world—or Christ—"breaks" through.
>
> (Schneider 1969: 113)

This is quite ingenious! But what if it *is* a command or a wish? How would that change the sense of the lines? There are also questions about who is being addressed in these lines as "thee" and "my chevalier." Is it the falcon, the poet's heart, or, as more than one reader has suggested, Christ, to whom the poem is dedicated?

We'll lay that problem aside for now, and look briefly at the imagery of the second tercet:

> No wonder of it: shéer plód makes plough down sillion
> Shine, and blue-bleak embers, ah my dear,
> Fall, gall themselves, and gash gold-vermilion.

There are two images here: a plough making furrows in the soil (*sillion* means "a furrow turned over by the plough")[10] and the glow of ash or embers. But does the blade of the plough shine, or the newly turned clods of earth? Empson insists that the furrows shine: "at least they do in the heavy wheat land that I came from—they look greasy. The idea is that the plough-man makes a beautiful shape though he is simply trying to plough as well as he can" (Empson 1969: 77). But it is certainly possible to picture the plough being polished to a bright shine by the soil—the ploughman's plodding labor makes a homely farm tool brighter and lovelier. Both readings do seem to work. We also have to decide how to read the embers (do they spark? glow? flash?), and if the line *Fall, gall themselves, and gash gold-vermilion* evokes Christ's crucifixion, martyr's blood, the gold that painters have used for the haloes of saints, a cup of wine mixed with gall, the self-consuming fire of the spirit, the sudden flaring up of coals, or the flame-red glory of the dawn with which the poem began. All of these meanings have been read into them. The reader also must work to link the image of the falcon with that of the plough and the embers. And then there is the whole matter of the aural pattern in the sonnet and its rhymes, which are inextricable from the total effect.

The debates about Hopkins's "The Windhover" attest to the merits and limitations, revelations and frustrations, of these super-close readings, the pros and cons of objective critique. One thing is certain: reading a well-executed close reading requires patience and attention to both the text *and* the critic's argument about it. We can learn a few things about close reading from this sampling of objective criticism. One is that rather than assume that our confusion over the meaning of a word, its sense or purpose in the context of the poem, is the poet's fault for not being more clear, we should accept the radical ambiguity of the literary uses of language. Ambiguity complicates and enriches meaning, and good writers know how to exploit this. Hopkins wanted to represent a startling natural phenomenon by wringing multiple meanings out of English words, stretching language almost to its breaking point—perhaps the poem itself *buckles* at the crux of its ambition to communicate?

Another consideration basic to the critical enterprise centers on the author's successful realization of his or her efforts. Does Hopkins's sonnet have the internal stamina and artistic integrity to bear so many close readings? Is it good enough (as Henley's poem, perhaps, was not) to generate the critical history we've seen? Or are these critics just making clever moves in an elaborate chess game? This latter view was taken by the critic Stanley Fish in the 1980s. In his provocative book *Is There a Text in This Class?* (1980), Fish pointed out that if an objective critical judgment relies on evidence in the text, on "seeing the object as *in itself it really is*," there cannot be more than one "true" reading of a text. If words have determinate meanings and literary texts can be interpreted through close critical analysis of the words on the page, disagreements can only be resolved by referring to the so-called evidence of the text. But, argues Fish, interpretations do supplant one another, and they do so by referring to "a new set of obvious and indisputable facts," or new evidence. Where does this "evidence" come from if it is not embedded in the text? Fish argues that it is constructed by what he calls *interpretive communities*—a cluster of readers who share the same assumptions about how a text should be approached critically. "Of course each new reading is elaborated in the name of the poem itself," he says, "but the poem itself is always a function of the interpretive perspective from which the critic 'discovers it'" (Fish 1980: 341). In other words, there's no authorial "meaning" in the poem other than what the critic finds there (or, as Fish would say, puts there). Fish's concept that critics' interpretive strategies determine the text's meaning might sound cynical. What about the reader's capacity to really be shaped by what he reads, and what about the author's role in the meaning-making process? A more comforting view would be that the game of interpretation is "a testimony to the capacity of a great work of art to generate multiple readings" (Fish 1980: 342). Or as Oscar Wilde wrote, "Diversity of opinion about a work of art shows that the work is new, complex, and vital" (1989: 48). Nevertheless, in their determination to supply a correct reading based on objective analysis, some readers may look more like magicians or conquistadors than literary critics. They lose sight of the goal of criticism, which should be to elucidate the poem for other readers and awaken fresh appreciation.

"The Windhover" raises a third question about the aims and usefulness of objective criticism. The critics who didn't agree with Richards's initial psychological reading or Empson's ambiguity-driven one complained that in their determination to find tension in the poem, they lost sight of the image Hopkins was trying to draw—they didn't keep their eye on the bird and its movements. This is a valid critique. Close objective reading often should begin with a literal-minded reading of a text, taking the images at face value. One critical essay on "The Windhover," for example, suggests that the uncertainties in the poem are quite comprehensible if we just read them literally:

> Gerard Manley Hopkins once saw a kestrel in the wind, first hovering, then ringing, and then gliding, and it seemed wonderful. But when the hawk dived, the poet saw an even superior achievement, and he did his best to give us an image of this intangible beauty. His best was not perfect, but it is enormously good when we first see exactly what he saw: namely (in the octave), a hawk on the wind, and (in the sestet), a hawk, a plough and some embers flaming in their descent.
>
> (Gwynn 1969: 60)

In my view, one of the merits of New Criticism is that by making us account for the aesthetic effects of a good poem—by working through what it's saying and how it manages to give structure and shape to a private experience—we may come to appreciate the skill and vision behind a fine work of literature. As this critic acknowledges, Hopkins did his best to show the reader what he saw. A poem such as "The Windhover" is the product of a mind interested in its own associations and meanderings, of a person awake to the things of the world, and as such it is an undertaking of great faith in the power of mere language to communicate, almost miraculously, a resonant and beautiful moment. Although it is a challenging poem, executed with exceptional skill, imagination, and word-consciousness, it is not as formidable as it might have seemed at the first reading. If we start with the literal or concrete situation, learn to think of the work as a deliberate, formal structure, pay attention to details that stand out—strange words and groups of words, rhymes and near-rhymes, pacing, patterns of imagery and repetition—if we keep a good dictionary handy, stay away from mere paraphrase and message-hunting, and if we are willing to return to the work and reread it (probably the first and most important rule), we'll develop the skills of a good, objective close reader.

The New Critics demonstrated that a reader who wants a hard-and-fast paraphrase, and wants it in a hurry, does not understand the more subtle operations of imaginative writing. They argued that the purpose of literary analysis is not to get the reading over with, and it is not to deliver a final statement or a proposition, whether about history, the author's intentions, or our tingling spines. Nor do we have to force the text to fit an interpretation or take apart every possible intonation. Yes, the critics I've cited here are a little nit-picky and they do try to make convincing arguments for their take on the poem's meaning. But isn't it part of our responsibility as students of English to defend how we have arrived at our literary judgments, our interpretations? Stanley Fish might say that proving we're clever readers and making a good argument is our stake in the game. Indeed, close reading and literary criticism have always been touted as valuable exercises in critical thinking skills such as reasoning and analysis—the skills that are supposedly being tested in standard placement examinations on literature and reading comprehension.

Yet developing a skill set is not the only purpose of literary study (at least not to me). Of course, critical arguments must be made. But at some point we have to recognize that they're provisional, that they're only arguments, not eternal verities, and they will likely be supplanted by new readings and new intellectual trends. Empson warned that at some point we have to "protect our sensibility against critical dogma," lest we become paralyzed by doubts about the rightness or wrongness of an interpretation (1953: 255–256). Then we'll wonder why we are bothering to read poetry at all. Even a doctrinaire formalist or card-carrying New Critic may be brought to admit that there are features of the literary work that can't be pinned down and completely understood. When a work of literature is fully realized by its author, sensitive readers often feel that they have experienced something that cannot be explained in the usual terms of practical criticism. The complete meaning of "The Windhover" hovers just outside our intellectual grasp. This doesn't mean that we should abandon objective analysis—just the opposite, in fact. For among the many rewards of close, formalist reading may be a deeper appreciation of the mystery and wonder of form itself.

Despite their occasional crankiness, The New Critics were once the free-thinkers of the English academy. It's instructive to remember that this generation of scholars emerged in revolt against historical, bibliographical, and content- or theme-oriented criticism. When they emerged on the scene in the 1930s and 1940s they had vigorous opponents in the academy, and because some of them took a sharp or pungent tone in their manifestos for criticism, their aims were often misunderstood. They were labeled as either strict art-for-art's-sake formalists, codifiers who wanted to turn criticism into a science, or blinkered anti-historicists. Yet all they insisted upon was that literary critics focus their attention on the elementary units of literary art, what René Wellek and Austin Warren defined carefully in *Theory of Literature* as the intertwining of "structure, sign, and value," on euphony, rhythm, meter, image, metaphor, and symbol in poetry, on narrative structure, voice, point of view, characterization, dynamic development, setting, conventions, and genre in fiction (1949: 158). Wellek recalls "the acrimony of the conflict" between teachers who wanted to pursue *criticism* and those who supported the prevailing doctrines of philology and history. "Most of the New Critics were college teachers, and had to make their way in an environment hostile to any and all criticism ... it was an uphill fight" (1978: 614).

It seems ironic that only a few years later the New Critics, once trailblazers in U.S. colleges and universities, came to be seen as abominably retrograde and reactionary. Their critical values suffered a backlash on several fronts, representing the first part of a major shift in the way literature was going to be read and taught in the next half century. Why did formalism and objective close reading become the *bête noire* for the next generation of English scholars? The answer is complicated. For one thing, progressive intellectual currents and sweeping cultural and social changes challenged the New Critical assumption that literature and politics were two separate spheres of human action. Younger professors and theorists wanted to incorporate activism into their intellectual pursuits, and so began to analyze literary works as logical extensions of political and social systems and historical events. (The fact that some of the most eminent New Critics were white southern men or politically conservative Christians also fired the backlash.) Marxist critics viewed the idea that art has a special "aura" as a manipulative fiction, one already rendered obsolete by film, mass media, and Leftist politics.[11] They expressed suspicion of a Kantian notion of beauty that, in Heather Dubrow's words, "privileges privilege"—celebrates the work of art at the expense of the worker, or as she puts it, "the poet who spends hours polishing the rhyme scheme of his sestina ... is dependent on a society where some in turn have the obligation to polish well-wrought urns for minimal wages and others the leisure to admire them" (2000: 61). But there were also more deliberate *literary* rationales for the rejection of objective or formalist critique based on radical new ideas about how literature should be taught and studied. These objections took several directions.

First, the New Critics were accused of having no sense of the importance of history in the creation and afterlife of a literary work. Younger literary critics strongly objected to the New Critical tendency to isolate literature from its historical contexts, a move that struck them as socially and politically disengaged at best, or as in collusion with sexist, racist, bourgeois society at worst. When the New Critics talked about literary value and artistic excellence, the response from some New Historicists was puncturing. For them, literature was just another product of ingrained political interests. It is well to study literature, but not because the arts "enlighten" the population or assist social progress, as humanists like to advertise; instead we should study literature in light of its function in society. They thought it irresponsible to read literature for mere "appreciation" of its formal features, urging instead a more resistant model of engagement.

Other scholars expressed serious misgivings about the New Critics' influence on the formation of the literary canon, which, it was pointed out, largely excluded women and gave no place to entire groups of people who had not the educational, economic, or social advantages of the Ivy League elite. Conscientious critics demanded a re-examination of the entire category of "Literature," something invented, owned, and packaged by a privileged white male class of self-anointed experts. There were also allegations that the New Critics' formalism went no further than dreary explications of poems that ended up trapping them in a barren intellectual framework without considering the operations of an individual's reception of the work or the function of pleasure, beauty, or even transcendence in the literary experience. In *Against Interpretation*, the American intellectual Susan Sontag (1966: 7) wrote that modern methods of interpretation were "stifling. Like the fumes of the automobile and of heavy industry which befoul the urban atmosphere, the effusion of interpretations of art today poisons our sensibilities." The recondite analyses practiced by formalist critics were seen as a symptom of a moribund culture—dry academicians denying the living quality of the work of art, sealing up poems in libraries rather than carrying their vivid and potentially revolutionary messages into the streets. As we will see in Chapter 2 below, attention was also moving away from the self-contained text to the reader and his responses, from the rigidity of the verbal icon toward a more intuitive, fluid, and subjective approach to the way literature works. A return to biographical and psychological approaches and to the uses of myth and archetypes was also in the air.

The influence of French theorists, usually lumped together under post-structuralism and, later, deconstruction, should also be mentioned here. The motivating philosophy behind some of these theorists was to formulate a science of semiotics, and so their approach to texts was largely anthropological and materialist, rather than properly critical. They were not at all concerned with making literary judgments, for instance, a mainstay of the New Critics. Then there was the enormous influence, in Britain and America, of the writings of Michel Foucault. Whereas you could argue that some postmodern theorists who downplay context and perform granular readings of texts might be on a continuum with the formalism of the New Critics, that's not quite the case for Foucault. Foucault argued that literary texts are part of a system of social and political discourses and as such are subject to the hidden laws of knowledge production. Nothing escapes the discipline of discursive regimes; texts don't have discoverable "meanings," but are contained in social and cultural systems. Graduate students and professors who studied Foucault would be disinclined to discuss a novel as the labor of an individual author with ideas and feeling; instead, they would frame it as one sociohistorical practice in a web of discursive practices, almost wholly determined by the ideological system it participates in.[12] What one scholar has called the "deconstructive model of the self-undermining text" turned the agency and integrity of the literary work and its formal features on its head (Farrell 2004: 133).

As early as 1994, the critic George Levine wondered why the "formalism of the New Critics is, for many of my students and colleagues, merely a mistake, and has nothing to teach them" (1994: 1). In *Aesthetics and Ideology*, Levine and a group of eminent literary critics set out to examine the pros and cons of what he called the "radical transformation of literary study" that had taken place in the previous two decades—the turn toward New Historicism and the operations of cultural forces (1994: 3). He and his colleagues wondered if the New Critics had been unfairly maligned—if maybe there were some valuable ideas behind their interest in formal analysis and close reading. Perhaps instead of minimizing the author's craft and analyzing how texts bring to light significant aspects of culture, it might be important to affirm the value of individual writers who offer ways of thinking that may be necessary for that culture's continuation. This concern was readdressed at the turn of this century by well-respected scholars from different disciplines who wanted to incorporate cultural and political questions into their close formal readings of Romantic poetry, Shakespeare, or Austen.[13] Today, the growing number of teachers and scholars who want to re-examine, and perhaps learn from, the New Critical practice of placing attention on words, definitions, details, sense, sound, image, and metaphor—on *form*, rather than only on sociological contexts—have been given the name New Formalists.[14] But as Marjorie Levinson points out in an overview of important new scholarship in this area, the tag identifies not a methodology, but more a tendency or movement that has slowly gathered momentum.

She identifies two strains of the new turn to formalism. The first, what she calls "activist formalism," does not want to reject the contributions of more ideologically oriented critics and historicists who have crucially opened up the canon and brought matters of grave social consequence— the effects of economic class, of gender and sexuality, and of race—back onto the literary table (others have used the terms "engaged formalism," "strategic formalism," and "indexical formalism"). These scholars want to continue to see literature as a product of history and culture, while at the same time treating the poem or novel as a somewhat autonomous object, worthy of aesthetic attention. This strategy was the basis of New Historicist methodology in its early years, but over time literary reading was diverted into tracking down any possibly relevant historical reference. It seemed that the mere mention of, say, an Indian shawl or the price of sugar in a nineteenth-century novel would "get the machinery of 'archeology' and archive-churning going" (Levinson 2007: 560), and instead of reading *Mansfield Park*, the scholar would unearth documents on abolition that Austen might have encountered or newspaper reports about the East India Company, and give prime place to those texts in their analysis. There is no doubt that this critical strategy has yielded brilliant, subversive, and substantive readings of Jane Austen's novels, pulling back a curtain on the political realities of her world. But there is now a perceived need to maximize attention to the text itself rather than the surrounding archival materials, however relevant or fascinating those may be. This strand of New Formalism purports to study form while still pointing to the culture that produced the text; in other words, form is one dimension of ideology and so deserves careful scrutiny. As Douglas Bruster writes, New Formalism is "a critical genre dedicated to examining the social, cultural, and historical aspects of literary form, and the function of form for those who produce and consume literary texts" (2002: 44). The object of study may not even be a work of literature, but some other product of culture read closely for or through its formal features.

The second New Formalist strand Levinson identifies prefers to emphasize what sets a work of art apart from other cultural or historical texts—to point up the difference between "discourse" and "literature." These practitioners, whom she calls "normative formalists," view form as the *condition* of art, the very feature that differentiates literature from other types of communication. In this respect, some New Formalists have much in common with the New Critics: *form* is what makes a poem or a story different from an editorial or a history book, and it is why we value literature above other kinds of texts. Also called "aesthetic formalism," this concept of literature and art can be traced back to Immanuel Kant's definition of the aesthetic as a distinct and separate realm of human knowledge, one that helps us understand ourselves and binds people together. New Formalism in this vein stresses the reader's "susceptibility to pleasure, our somatic self-awareness, our sense of shared humanness, our sense of wonder"—all of which have been "under siege by the collective forces of modernity" and the ascendency of postmodern theory, historicism, and cultural studies (Levinson 2007: 560). Levinson uses the term *normative* formalism not because these critics want to lay down the law or regulate the future of literary criticism. Rather, like some of the New Critics, they seek to balance a concern for the formal qualities of poems, novels, and plays that are integral to their status as literature with a model of human agency that has been challenged by many contemporary philosophers. In other words, the "normative" or "aesthetic" formalists tentatively want to restore to literature its power to actually change people—their thoughts about the world, their psyches, their actions. They look to form as one important way to comprehend *how* literary art gets its work done in that special self-making, knowledge-producing, life-assisting sense.

These two strands of New Formalism don't run on separate rails, but spiral into a helix—and happily so, for both are interested in ways of rethinking the predominance of sociopolitical and media studies in English teaching and scholarship. I should stress *rethinking*. For as Heather Dubrow has suggested, an adversarial model that pits historicists against formalists, or generational clashes in which the old New Critics are surpassed by the young New

Formalists, is unhealthy for English departments in the business of promoting the free play of the mind on all matters (as Matthew Arnold would say). Dubrow writes, "New Formalism can best establish its relationship to other movements by sifting and winnowing rather than uncritical emulation and … rivalry" (2013: xv). In fact, Dubrow, Levinson, Ellen Rooney, Susan Wolfson, and other scholars share a hope that a return to close formal reading will unite scholars and teachers and reshape the study of literature. For the rise of New Formalism may be traced partly to pragmatic demands about the future of literary study and partly to sincere concern for our literary inheritance and our democratic institutions, which seem to have been left out of the picture when English turned away from literature toward semiotics, theory, historicism, ideology, and popular culture. If New Formalism has anything in common with the New Critics, it's the desire to restore value and importance to both works of literature *and* literary criticism; it signals a "rededication," as Levinson says, to the study of the text itself, the words on the page, to literature as literature—and to close reading (2007: 561). In a way, the urge toward a new formalism boils down to what Ellen Rooney calls "a *reading* matter," the belief that actual, attentive reading is at the center of the critical pursuit (2000: 24).

It's probably true that a New Formalist approach is not easy to differentiate from any really good close reading of a work of literature, especially if historical contexts, postmodern theory, and cultural studies are not exactly banished from the critical field. In fact, it's been claimed that what New Formalism lacks is a theory to hold it together, what Verena Theile calls "a driving force and an intentionality" that will give it clout and staying power as a methodology (2013: 16). So many recent essays specifically identified as formalist criticism seem to be about the effort to reconcile formalism with political commitment—to theorize it—and in this the modern turn to formalism shows a reluctance to declare firmly that our subject is literature, not politics or culture. There's a disinclination among some formalists (but not all) to declare too loudly or absolutely that it's time to put aside the cultural-historical model of criticism, roll up our shirtsleeves, and do an old-fashioned, New Critical reading of a poem ("The Windhover," anyone?). That kind of critique still strikes some people as merely descriptive—talking about the features of the art object isn't doing the hard work of interpreting its content or meaning, or of situating it among other texts. As the editors of *Shakespeare Up Close* explain, "An approach to analysis that privileges the textual object may feel limited because this act of reading does not make assertions about anything beyond the way language is working" (MacDonald et al. 2012: xxvii).

But attention to the way language works does not necessarily mean context is irrelevant—indeed, for most literary critics, history, context, and theory are part of the job of analyzing literature. To return to my example of Jane Austen: both the normative and the activist New Formalists could acknowledge the context of British imperialism, the Napoleonic Wars, or the abolition of the slave trade, and each might do a fine-tuned analysis of any and all references to the British Navy or the West Indies. But the focus would stay on how the backdrop of current affairs is made relevant through literary performance. Theoretical and historical contexts could frame the discussion, but a formalist analysis would make the centerpiece a reading of Austen's linguistic choices and her moves as a novelist. Indeed, because her novels subordinate the historical and political realities of the Regency period to other matters—personal and family relationships, social mores, or marriage—Jane Austen might be a good author on whom to practice close, formal reading. Students who almost automatically approach literature from the perspective of history would have to contend with Austen's staging of her world before they dig into cultural contexts.[15]

In 1978, René Wellek published an essay in which he addressed an array of disparaging opinions about New Criticism just as English studies was tilting towards the hermeneutics of suspicion, deconstruction, and Marxist and feminist theory, and when it was at the threshold of Foucault and the swerve toward interdisciplinarity and cultural studies. In his conclusion, he wrote this:

> I will not conceal my own conviction that the New Criticism stated or reaffirmed many basic truths to which future ages will have to return: the specific nature of the aesthetic transaction, the normative presence of a work of art which forms a structure, a unity, a coherence, a whole, which cannot be simply battered about and is comparatively independent of its origins and effects. The New Critics have also persuasively described the function of literature in not yielding abstract knowledge or information, message or stated ideology, and they devised a technique of interpretation which often succeeded in illuminating not so much the form of a poem as the implied attitudes of the author, the resolved or unresolved tensions and contradictions: a technique that yields a standard of judgment that cannot be easily dismissed in favor of the currently popular, sentimental, and simple. The charge of "elitism" cannot get around the New Critics' assertion of quality and value. A decision between good and bad art remains an unavoidable duty of criticism. The humanities would abdicate their function in society if they surrendered to a neutral scientism and indifferent relativism or if they succumbed to the imposition of alien norms required by political indoctrination. Particularly on these two fronts the New Critics have waged a valiant fight which, I am afraid, must be fought over again in the future.
>
> (1978: 622)

Wellek's defense of New Criticism here has four main principles: (1) the work of literature is autonomous and independent; (2) literature is not information, and the study of literature is not equivalent to the study of politics, sociology, or history; (3) the function of criticism is to apprehend as best one can the author's implied attitude and to form a judgment about it; (4) judgment is unavoidable, for there will always be some works that are superior to others in literary execution, in their aims and values, and in their contributions to humanity.

It remains to be seen whether or not English departments in the twenty-first century will pay attention to Wellek's challenge and return to the "duty of criticism" and the "basic truths" about the place of literary study in modern society. Is objective criticism the right way to go about the difficult task of protecting literary studies from the complexities of the modern world—from the reach of global politics, capitalism, social injustice, and dangers to our environment? Is it possible, or even desirable, to go back to Arnoldian disinterestedness or to the erection of artistic standards? Will English scholarship in the next few decades differ significantly from the cultural studies model? These are all open questions. Perhaps we can conclude that objective criticism teaches us that *form*—the author's selection of language, the work's structure and unity—does matter. What is close reading without it? Scholars, students, readers, and teachers of English should welcome its return.

Notes

1 And how do we know what we like? I. A. Richards points out that many people's reactions are manufactured by their unthinking consumption of popular culture: "Even the decision as to what constitutes a pretty girl or a handsome young man," he wrote in 1928, "an affair apparently natural and personal enough, is largely determined by magazine covers and movie stars" (1925: 203). One valuable social aspect of objective criticism is that it helps train people how to think independently, rather than follow the pack.

2 This is the negative example Brooks and Warren (1950: xi) use, taken from a literature textbook of the time.

3 See *The Well Wrought Urn*, Chapter 2, "The Heresy of Paraphrase."

4 See Pritchard (1993: 125–128).

5 In 2003, when the National Book Foundation gave a lifetime award to horror writer Stephen King, the eminent literary critic Harold Bloom was outraged. He wrote that King is "an immensely inadequate writer on a sentence-by-sentence, paragraph-by-paragraph, book-by-book basis." He also thinks J. K. Rowling is "terrible." "Rowling's mind is so governed by clichés and dead metaphors that she has no other style of writing." See Bloom (2003).

6 For a passionate defense of her selections, see Dove (2011).

7 But note, "the moral obligation to judge does not necessarily obligate us to make a moral judgment" (Tate 1940: 455).

8 The title was added in 1902, not by the poet but by the editor of the *Oxford Book of English Verse*. Subsequent readers' judgments would be colored by this grand title (and it's in Latin, which conveys inescapable authority).

9 On April 19, 1995, Timothy McVeigh set off a bomb at the Alfred P. Murrah Federal Building in Oklahoma City, killing 168 people and injuring over 600. He presented "Invictus" as his last statement before his execution in 2001. Gordon Brown was British Prime Minister from 2007 to 2010. Nelson Mandela, who died in 2014, was the first black President of South Africa.

10 The *OED* uses "The Windhover" in its definition of *sillion*. Even this has been debated. Frederick L. Gwynn insists that "sillion" does *not* mean "furrow" but "a narrow strip lying between two furrows" or "a strip of land under cultivation." Hence he says,

> the troublesome analogy of the plough should be paraphrased thus: the (utter, steep, bright, sharp) progress of a ploughshare through the earth makes it shine—even as the dive of a bird (which looks and acts something like a ploughshare) through the air produces fire.
>
> (Gwynn 59–60)

11 A famous essay on this topic is Walter Benjamin's "The Work of Art in the Age of Mechanical Reproduction" (1939).
12 This isn't to say that some Foucauldians don't go in for close reading. D. A. Miller's *The Novel and the Police*, one of the most influential books of the 1980s, comes to mind immediately as an ideology-driven work of criticism that is minutely attentive to language, repetition, and imagery.
13 *Modern Language Quarterly* 61.1 (March 2000) is devoted to the New Formalism. See also Rasmussen's *Renaissance Literature and its Formal Engagements* (2002) and Susan Wolfson's *Formal Charges: The Shaping of Poetry in British Romanticism* (1997).
14 The term seems to have been first used in 1989 by the early modern scholar Heather Dubrow. See Bruster (2002: 44–45).
15 D. A. Miller, for example, in *Jane Austen, or the Secret of Style* (2003), brilliantly anatomizes the social and sexual meaning of Robert Ferrars's toothpick-case in *Sense and Sensibility* without departing from the novel for a moment (or hauling in eighteenth-century advertisements for toothpick-cases). Miller, a queer theorist, offers granular readings of Austen's novels that epitomize (or satirize) close reading. He suggests that another way to understand close reading is as "an almost infantile desire to be *close*, period, as close as one can get, without literal plagiarism, to merging with the mother-text" (2003: 58).

References

Arnold, Matthew [1865] (1970a) "The Function of Criticism at the Present Time," in *Selected Prose*, ed. P. J. Keating. Harmondsworth: Penguin, 130–156.

Arnold, Matthew [1880] (1970b) "The Study of Poetry," in *Selected Prose*, ed. P. J. Keating. Harmondsworth: Penguin, 340–366.

Benjamin, Walter (1969) "The Work of Art in the Age of Mechanical Reproduction," in *Illuminations*. Trans Harry Zohn. New York: Schocken Books, 217–251.

Best, Stephen and Sharon Marcus (2009) "Surface Reading: An Introduction." *Representations* 108.1 (Fall): 1–21.

Bloom, Harold (2003) "Dumbing Down American Readers." *The Boston Globe*. September 24.

Brooks, Cleanth and Robert Penn Warren (1947) *Understanding Fiction*. New York: F. S. Crofts.

Brooks, Cleanth and Robert Penn Warren (1950) *Understanding Poetry*. New York: Henry Holt.

Bruster, David (2002) "Shakespeare and the Composite Text," in *Renaissance Literature and Its Formal Engagements*, ed. Mark David Rasmussen. London: Palgrave, 43–66.

Cosgrove, Peter (2004) "Hopkins's 'The Windhover': Not Ideas About the Thing But the Thing Itself." *Poetics Today* 25.3 (Fall): 437–464.

Culler, Jonathan (2010) "The Closeness of Close Reading." *ADE Bulletin* 149: 20–25.

Deutsch, Babette [1952] (1969) *Poetry in Our Time*. New York: Holt, Rinehart and Winston. Reprinted in *Gerard Manley Hopkins: 'The Windhover,'* ed. John Pick. Columbus, OH: Charles E. Merrill, 61–65.

Donoghue, Denis [1955] (1969) "The Bird as Symbol: Hopkins's Windhover." *Irish Studies* XLIV (Autumn). Reprinted in *Gerard Manley Hopkins: 'The Windhover,'* ed. John Pick. Columbus, OH: Charles E. Merrill, 91–99.

Dove, Rita (2011) "Reply to Helen Vendler." *The New York Review of Books.* December 22.

Dubrow, Heather (2000) "Guess Who's Coming to Dinner? Reinterpreting Formalism and the Country House Poem." *Modern Language Quarterly* 61.1 (March): 59–77.

Dubrow, Heather (2013) "Foreword," in *New Formalisms and Literary Theory,* ed. Verena Theile and Linda Tredennick. London: Palgrave Macmillan, vii–xvii.

Eliot, T. S. [1943] (1957) "Frontiers of Criticism." *On Poetry and Poets.* New York: Farrar, Straus, and Giroux, 113–131.

Eliot, T. S. (2011) "Tradition and the Individual Talent." *The Sacred Wood.* West Valley City, UT: Waking Lion Press, 33–42.

Empson, William [1930] (1953) *Seven Types of Ambiguity*. London: New Directions.

Empson, William [1954] (1969) Letter. *Times Literary Supplement.* October 1. *Gerard Manley Hopkins: 'The Windhover,'* ed. John Pick. Columbus, OH: Charles E. Merrill, 76–78.

Farrell, Frank B. (2004) *Why Does Literature Matter?* Ithaca, NY: Cornell University Press.

Felski, Rita (2008) *Uses of Literature*. Malden, MA: Blackwell.

Fish, Stanley (1980) *Is There a Text in This Class? The Authority of Interpretive Communities.* Cambridge, MA: Harvard University Press.

Frost, Robert (1998) "The Road Not Taken." *101 Great American Poems.* New York: Dover Thrift Editions, 49.

Gallop, Jane (2010) "Close Reading in 2009." *ADE Bulletin* 149: 15–19.

Gardner, W. H. [1948] (1969) *Gerard Manley Hopkins: A Study of Poetic Idiosyncrasy.* Oxford: Oxford University Press. Reprinted in *Gerard Manley Hopkins: 'The Windhover,'* ed. John Pick. Columbus, OH: Charles E. Merrill, 15–18.

Grady, Thomas J. [1944] (1969) "Windhover's Meaning." *America* LXX (January 29). Reprinted in *Gerard Manley Hopkins: 'The Windhover,'* ed. John Pick. Columbus, OH: Charles E. Merrill, 25–29.

Grigson, Geoffrey [1955] (1969) *Gerard Manley Hopkins*. London: The British Council. Reprinted in *Gerard Manley Hopkins: 'The Windhover,'* ed. John Pick. Columbus, OH: Charles E. Merrill, 87–90.

Gwynn, Frederick L. [1957] (1969) "Hopkins' 'The Windhover': A New Simplification." *Modern Language Notes* LXVI (June). Reprinted in *Gerard Manley Hopkins: 'The Windhover,'* ed. John Pick. Columbus, OH: Charles E. Merrill, 57–60.

Henley, William Ernest [1939] (1957) "Invictus." *The Oxford Book of English Verse 1250–1918*, ed. Arthur Quiller-Couch. Oxford: Oxford University Press, 1027–1028.

Hopkins, Gerard Manley (1970) "The Windhover." *The Poems of Gerard Manley Hopkins*, ed. W. H. Gardner and N. H. MacKenzie. Oxford: Oxford University Press, 69.

Lees, F. N. (1950) "The Windhover." *Scrutiny* 17.1 (Spring): 32–37.

Lees, F. N. [1954] (1969) Letter. *Times Literary Supplement*, September 3. Reprinted in *Gerard Manley Hopkins: 'The Windhover,'* ed. John Pick. Columbus, OH: Charles E. Merrill, 13–75.

Lentricchia, Frank (1995) *Modernist Quartet*. Cambridge, U.K.: Cambridge University Press.

Levine, George, ed. (1994) *Aesthetics and Ideology*. New Brunswick: Rutgers University Press.

Levinson, Marjorie (2007) "What Is New Formalism?" *PMLA* 122.2: 558–569.

Lisca, Peter [1957] (1969) "The Return of 'The Windhover.'" *College English* xix (December). Reprinted in *Gerard Manley Hopkins: 'The Windhover,'* ed. John Pick. Columbus, OH: Charles E. Merrill, 109–112.

Litzinger, Boyd [1967] (1969) "Once More, 'The Windhover.'" *Victorian Poetry* V (Autumn). Reprinted in *Gerard Manley Hopkins: 'The Windhover,'* ed. John Pick. Columbus, OH: Charles E. Merrill, 139–141.

MacDonald, Russ, Nicholas D. Nace, and Travis D. Williams, eds. (2012) *Shakespeare Up Close: Reading Early Modern Texts*. London: Bloomsbury.

McLuhan, Marshall (1944) "Invictus." *The Explicator* 3.3 (December): Item 22.

Miller, D. A. (1988) *The Novel and the Police*. Berkeley: University of California Press.

Miller, D. A. (2003) *Jane Austen, Or the Secret of Style*. Princeton, NJ: Princeton University Press.

Ong, Walter (1974) "Bird, Horse, and Chevalier in Hopkins's 'Windhover.'" *Hopkins Quarterly* 1.2 (July): 61–75.

Pritchard, William H. (1973) *Frost: A Literary Life Reconsidered*. Amherst: University of Massachusetts Press.

Purcell, J. M. (1945) "Invictus." *The Explicator* 4.13 (January): Item 13.

Ransom, John Crowe (1938) *The World's Body*. New York: Scribner's.

Rasmussen, Mark David, ed. (2002) *Renaissance Literature and Its Formal Engagements*. London: Palgrave Macmillan.

Richards, I. A. (1925) *Principles of Literary Criticism*. New York: Harcourt Brace.

Richards, I. A. (1926) "Gerard Hopkins." *The Dial* 81.3 (September): 195–203.

Ritz, J. R. {1955] (1969) Letter. *Times Literary Supplement*, May 6. Reprinted in *Gerard Manley Hopkins: 'The Windhover,'* ed. John Pick. Columbus, OH: Charles E. Merrill, 83–85.

Rooney, Ellen (2000) "Form and Contentment." *Modern Language Quarterly* 61.1 (March): 17–40.

Schneider, Elizabeth. [1960] (1969) "Hopkins' 'The Windhover.'" *The Explicator* XVIII (January): Item 773. Reprinted in *Gerard Manley Hopkins: 'The Windhover,'* ed. John Pick. Columbus, OH: Charles E. Merrill, 113–115.

Schoder, Raymond V. [1949] (1969) "What Does 'The Windhover' Mean?" *Immortal Diamond: Studies in Gerard Manley Hopkins*, ed. Norman Weyand (New York: Sheed and Ward). Reprinted in *Gerard Manley Hopkins: 'The Windhover,'* ed. John Pick. Columbus, OH: Charles E. Merrill, 30–43.

Sontag, Susan (1966) *Against Interpretation and Other Essays*. New York: Macmillan.

Tate, Allen (1940) "Miss Emily and the Bibliographer." *The American Scholar* 9.4: 449–460.

Tate, Allen [1951] (2008) "Is Literary Criticism Possible?", in *Praising It New: The Best of the New Criticism*, Ed. Garrick Davis. Athens, OH: Ohio University Press, 61–71.

Theile, Verena (2013) "New Formalism(s): A Prologue," in *New Formalisms and Literary Theory*, ed. Verena Theile and Linda Tredennick. London: Palgrave Macmillan, 3–28.

Vendler, Helen (2011) "Are These the Poems to Remember?" Review of *The Penguin Anthology of Twentieth-Century American Poetry*, ed. Rita Dove. *The New York Review of Books*. November 24.

Wellek, René (1978) "The New Criticism: Pro and Contra." *Critical Inquiry* 4.4 (Summer): 611–624.

Wellek, René and Austin Warren (1949) *Theory of Literature*. New York: Harcourt Brace.

Wilde, Oscar (1989) "Preface" to *The Picture of Dorian Gray*. *The Writings of Oscar Wilde*, ed. Isobel Murray. Oxford: Oxford University Press.

Wimsatt, W. K. and Monroe Beardsley (1954) *The Verbal Icon: Studies in the Meaning of Poetry*. Louisville: University of Kentucky Press.

Winters, Yvor [1943] (2008) "Preliminary Problems," in *Praising It New: The Best of the New Criticism*, ed. Garrick Davis. Athens, OH: Ohio University Press, 75–84.

Wolfson, Susan (1997) *Formal Charges: The Shaping of Poetry in British Romanticism*. Stanford, CA: Stanford University Press.

Woodring, Carl (1950) "Once More 'The Windhover.'" *Western Review* 15.1: 61–64.

3   The poem as event

We judge a work of art by its effect on our sincere and vital emotion, and nothing else. All the critical twiddle-twaddle about style, and form, all this pseudo-scientific classifying and analyzing of books in an imitation-botanical fashion, is mere impertinence and mostly dull jargon.

(Lawrence 1973: 18)

Nothing, of course, will ever take the place of the good old fashion of "liking" a work of art or not liking it; the more improved criticism will not abolish that primitive, that ultimate, test.

(James 1948: 15)

As we have seen, the New Critics wanted to rationalize and systematize the interpretive process. Wimsatt and Beardsley's intentional fallacy downplayed the author in order to put the text at the center of inquiry. The affective fallacy invalidated impressionistic or purely emotional responses to argue that a poem has an internally coherent meaning discernible using the correct critical method. In "Criticism, Inc.," the first item in John Crowe Ransom's proscriptions for literary criticism is: "Personal registrations, which are declarations of the effect of the art-work upon the critic as reader" (1938: 342). Ransom regards as "uncritical" any vocabulary "which ascribes to the object [the text] properties really discoverable in the subject [the reader]," such as *moving, exciting, entertaining, pitiful*—even to say a poem is *beautiful* is pushing it (1938: 342–343). In order to do criticism properly, one must discipline or suppress the unruly, reactive reader within. Statements such as "Othello's jealousy is so pitiful, it is painful to witness!" or "I really hate Iago!" cross the line because they confound a critical judgment with an emotional response—a *readerly* response—and so are anathema to the New Critical regime.

Yet I. A. Richards, who as we know exerted a major influence on the American New Critics and is usually hailed as the originator of close reading, *did* believe that the reader's responses should count in the literary encounter.[1] Indeed, his thoughts about the way critics talk about art present a wild twist on Ransom's prohibitions. For if Ransom says the critic must not "ascribe to the object properties really discoverable in the subject," Richards is reluctant to admit that objects even *have* properties. There is no verifiable meaning buried in the text, waiting for the critic to come and unearth it. The so-called objective critic, says Richards, is involved in a fallacy of his own, where he projects his reactions onto the work of art, then claims they belong to the work itself. "We continually talk as though things possess qualities," writes Richards, "when what we ought to say is that they cause effects in us of one kind or another" (1925: 21). Richards basically argues that in order for a critic to write anything about a work of art, he has to invent a vocabulary that expands on his personal response, to dress up his subjective feelings or psychological observations in the exalted robes of the critical act. He agrees with Ransom that it is inadequate *as criticism* to say, "This sonnet is beautiful." But for Richards, the problem is inherently one of language, not of critical acumen. People say an object is beautiful or harmonious or complete because something about it gives them satisfaction or pleasure, but very few people would claim that there is such a thing as "beauty" in the abstract that attaches to external objects.

> Whether we are talking about music, poetry, painting, sculpture, or architecture, we are forced to speak as though certain physical objects … are what we are talking about. And yet the remarks we make as critics do not apply to such objects but to states of mind, to experiences.
>
> (1925: 21–22)[2]

Richards insists that if we want to keep criticism from turning into the most banal kind of nit-picking, and if we also want to protect critics themselves from accusations of monasticism and snobbery, we have to be honest about the emotional and psychological dimensions of literary reading. In other words, we have to allow a critic to be, at the same time, a *reader*.

The formal analysis demanded by the New Critics and the widespread adoption of Brooks and Warren's textbooks (*Understanding Poetry* and *Understanding Fiction* went into multiple editions) formed a hegemony in English departments until the 1960s and 1970s, when critics and teachers came to recognize the role of the reader in the literary encounter. By the 1980s, important scholarly collections began to appear and *reader-response criticism* gained legitimacy as a critical and pedagogical approach. As I mentioned in Chapter 1 above, these reader-oriented theories were very diverse, and new thoughts about the role of the reader are still developing. "Reader-response criticism," Jane Tompkins wrote, "is not a conceptually unified critical position" (1980: ix), but has many strands, from its roots in structuralism in the 1960s to later developments in social psychology, psychoanalysis, and phenomenology in the 1970s, and up to discussions currently taking place in the emerging field of affect theory. There are many ways to go about setting up and taking apart the vital relationship between author, reader, and text. In this chapter, I bypass approaches that focus on the reader as a rhetorical structure within a text (i.e., narratological or structuralist procedures that identify the narratee, the ideal reader, etc.), and streamline the discussion by settling on a few critics who lean toward the sociological and psychological dimension of subjective close reading—that is, they are interested not in the implied reader who is constructed within the text, but in the flesh-and-blood reader who is holding the book and processing language.[3] Despite having slightly different methodologies and theories, this set of critics share the belief that the reader cannot be left out of the critical equation.

But before we engage these modern critics, I want to go back to nineteenth-century Oxford one more time, and to Matthew Arnold's dictum about "seeing the object as in itself it really is." In 1873, Walter Pater, a thirty-four-year-old Oxford professor, art critic, and essayist, published a collection of critical essays ostensibly about the great painters and poets of sixteenth- and seventeenth-century Europe, entitled *Studies in the History of the Renaissance*. It was immediately recognized as an arrant departure from the standards of critical objectivity, and generated a bit of controversy in intellectual circles (for a variety of reasons).[4] For in his Preface, and without naming him, Pater respectfully contradicted Arnold, his luminary elder colleague and distinguished Professor of Poetry at Oxford:

> "To see the object as in itself it really is," has been justly said to be the aim of all true criticism whatever, and in aesthetic criticism the first step towards seeing one's object as it really is, is to know one's own impression as it really is, to discriminate it, to realise it distinctly.... What is this song or picture, this engaging personality presented in life or in a book, *to me*? What effect does it really produce *on me*? Does it give me pleasure? and if so, what sort or degree of pleasure? How is my nature modified by its presence, and under its influence? The answers to these questions are the original facts with which the aesthetic critic has to do; and, as in the study of light, of morals, of number, one must realise such primary data for one's self, or not at all.
>
> (Pater 2010: 3, original italics)

In what may be the gentlest manifesto for subjective criticism ever written, Pater mildly contradicts Arnold's axiom: the critic's duty is not quite to study *the* object as it really is, but to study *one's* object as it really is. Monitoring one's personal impressions is the crucial "first step" in aesthetic criticism. Although Pater uses words such as "qualities," "facts," and "data," the turn away from the object toward the uniquely individual perceiver is definitive—and transgressive. For by implicitly refusing to honor the objective standards of the critical establishment, Pater initiated a more creative role for the critic. Indeed, the modernist discovery of subjectivity— the experimental novels of Woolf, Joyce, Faulkner, the art of Picasso, the writings of Sigmund Freud—might be said to have begun with Walter Pater, whose skepticism about objective epistemologies ushered in a new generation of writers and intellectuals who welcomed the invitation to explore their emotional reverberations and develop their own distinct forms of self-expression. Indeed, the work being criticized may not be more alluring than the intimate revelations of the mind it has stirred to form aesthetic reflections.[5]

The essays in *The Renaissance* are virtuosic examples of impressionistic writing, in which Pater offers as criticism the thoughts and feelings that came to him, a studious and sensitive man, under the provocations of a piece of music, a painting, a sculpture, or a poem. Sometimes called creative criticism, experimental criticism, or autobiographical criticism, this kind of writing is often taken up by people who are first and foremost poets or novelists, and so it can be a great pleasure to read (not that academic scholarship cannot also deliver pleasure, but of a different kind). It can also be quite challenging, since many creative critics don't follow the rules of expository writing or argumentation, and may decline to deliver a straightforward literary analysis. And this may be the point. Some early feminist critics, for example, deliberately set out to shatter what they saw as the patriarchal myth of objectivity, and so escape the regimen of a male-sanctioned academic methodology. Queer theory has also folded private reflections into public critique. There are many other examples of this type of critical performance from politically committed readers of the 1980s and 1990s (the queer theorist Eve Kosofsky Sedgwick even taught workshops on "Experimental Critical Writing" at Duke University), and highly esteemed scholars continue to argue for its legitimacy and pertinence, especially in light of cognitive and affect theory and fresh approaches to literature and psychoanalysis.[6] Later in this chapter we will explore what a set of gifted critics do with the enigmatic poetry of Emily Dickinson, a writer many people feel fascinated by, often for personal or hard to explain reasons.

But how is subjective criticism, sometimes called reader-response or reader-oriented criticism, tied to close reading, the mainstay of the objective approach? Both objective and subjective critics ask the reader to pay careful attention to the text and to think imaginatively about the author's choices without excessive recourse to historical or cultural contexts. A subjective critic would probably agree with the New Critics' concern that a lot of background information potentially distracts the reader from seeing what the poet created. Then again, too much stress on the poet's craft pulls the reader away from her own contribution to the process of making meaning. Where New Critics pay rigorous attention to how the poem communicates through its formal features and demand textual evidence for an interpretation, reader-response critics shift attention to what might be going on internally within the individual reader. Paraphrase, for instance, utterly heretical to Cleanth Brooks because it flattens out the work's structure and organic meaning, is to a subjectivist such as David Bleich a necessary stage in the reader's patterns of response and judgment. In Brooks's classroom, the question may be something like, "What is the central paradox in this section of the ode?" In Bleich's classroom, it might be, "What strikes you as the most important word in the poem?" The point is not to indulge the student's ego or to diminish the text as the object of study. The idea is to offer another route by which to arrive at knowledge other than the analytical—knowledge of a particular text, but also knowledge of the symbolic richness of our language, of our collective interest in literature, of our social and moral assumptions, of our emotional capacities, tastes, and potential.

Subjective criticism wants to authorize this alternative method of arriving at knowledge by encouraging the reader to become self-reflexive about what she is doing when she reads literature, and especially how she balances her desire to understand the text with any other internal motives she may have, aimed at other kinds of understanding. Bleich believes that reading literature "can produce new understanding of oneself—not just a moral here or a message there, but a genuinely new conception of one's values and tastes as well as one's prejudices and learning difficulties" (1975: 3–4). The goal of subjective criticism is not to explicate every line, but to focus on what most seizes the reader's attention, to be conscious of the personal associations we usually push to the back of our minds and use them to guide the interpretation we publish to others. The psychoanalytic critic Norman Holland describes this approach as reversing the methods of New Criticism: instead of sticking exclusively to the "words on the page" to get at the meaning of the text, we begin with the reader's response and discover the text from that special vantage point (Holland 1975: 12).

For some teachers and scholars, subjective criticism is too complaisant, a kind of anything goes way of dealing with literature. Do we really want to say that a text means anything a reader says it does? Is there no fixed meaning or purpose in the choices an author makes? A reader going through a divorce might argue that *Wuthering Heights* is a story about daft young lovers; another reader who has just become engaged will say the novel utters profound truths about erotic desire. Do either of these reactions take us closer to Emily Brontë's novel as a complete and autonomous work? It seems that interpretations could be endlessly varied, and some of them even a little bizarre, if all they are based on is the reader's predisposition. These are valid grounds for dissent. One may ask what distinguishes a professional critic's reading of *Blood Meridian* from anyone else's, other than a degree of erudition, if interpretations are based on personal taste or visceral responses. One could even argue that, given the popularity of on-line reviews from readers, cinema-goers, diners, music lovers, and every other kind of consumer who feels like giving a "thumbs down" or a "like" rating, there is more than ever a need for clear and dispassionate appraisal based on a set of criteria, or at least some benchmarks for excellence. The roles of the critic and of the reader, in this view, definitely *should* be distinct, since they are working on very different planes of meaning making—and of judgment.

Most (but not all) reader-response critics would argue that some interpretations will always be more defensible than others. Yet the central project of critical reading, from the subjective angle, is not proving one's interpretation is correct, but rather becoming more self-conscious about the reading experience itself and learning to think about the text as a means to new knowledge, and perhaps new insights. As Bleich puts it, "Subjective criticism assumes that each person's most urgent motivations are to understand himself, and that the simplest path to this understanding is awareness of one's own language system as the agency of consciousness and self-direction" (1972: 297–298). Getting at a writer's language opens a path into our own beliefs. So in subjective criticism, instead of accepting another reader's version of the novel's meaning—a teacher's or a literary critic's—each reader is encouraged to find her own way into the text, and so determine her own reasons for reading it.

But accurately articulating a response to a work of literature and pinpointing where and how it resonates is not a simple or speedy exercise. Some people would much rather memorize an instructor's Powerpoint presentation for an exam on Thoreau than write a paper on their impressions of *Walden*. Indeed, many people are much more comfortable with the quantitative sciences and subjects that use reliable rubrics than they are with the psychological and emotional demands of literary reading. Yet when readers attend seriously to the task of reflective reading, they take a major step toward owning the knowledge they believe is needed to lead a fulfilling life. In Bleich's words, "Knowing what one wants to know is the first conscious motive for developing knowledge" (1972: 134). A psychoanalytic critic, of course, would say we have *unconscious* motives as well as conscious ones, and I will look at psychoanalytic alternatives to Bleich's position briefly at the end of this chapter. But both positions agree that subjective criticism can be every bit as demanding as objectivity because these practices place the responsibility on the reader to find out *what she wants to know*—not only about how the poem or narrative is put together, which always enlarges the literary experience, but about her values, desires, and anything else she thinks she wants to gain from the event of reading.

I sometimes call it *bidding*. I mean the art or virtue of saying everything right *to* or *at* the hearer, interesting him, holding him in the attitude of correspondent or addressed or at least concerned, making it everywhere an act of intercourse—and of discarding everything that does not bid, does not tell. I think one may gain much of this by practice.

(Hopkins 1955: 160)

Can reader-response criticism be an effective model for rigorous close reading? Can subjective critics teach other readers what's verifiably happening *within* a text? To present these questions for debate, I would like to go back to the poetry of Gerard Manley Hopkins for a moment. As we know, Hopkins's difficulty and his linguistic inventiveness interested the formalist New Critics, who were keen on understanding his imagery and his innovations with rhyme and meter. Yet individual readers have for many years gone to Hopkins's poetry for personal reasons—for emotional strength or pleasure, or for consolation. The small group of friends to whom he showed his verse in the late nineteenth century certainly recognized its transformative power, and later readers have offered testimonials to the profound effect of his poems on their beliefs, feelings, and life choices.[7] The way these readers experience Hopkins's work seems to meet the poet's idea of *bidding*, cited above—the hope that his readers would enter into the poem's spirit as in a personal conversation. So to test whether subjective reading can be as close and discerning as the objective critiques we read in Chapter 2 above, I would like to offer an excerpt from an interpretation of "The Windhover" by Amanda Freeman, a graduate student in a seminar I taught on reading practices. Freeman wanted to write a professional critical essay without, in Sedgwick's words, losing touch with her own "writerly energies" (1998: 104). The result is an engaging experiment in reader-response criticism.[8] I suggest going back to Hopkins's poem before getting into the following critique.

The "heart in hiding": "The Windhover" and reader-response criticism

Amanda Freeman

Since the first time I encountered this poem, probably in high school, the word "windhover" seemed a rather unnecessarily obscure title. A helpful gloss in an anthology clarified that by the term "windhover" Hopkins meant kestrel, which only compounded the confusion. Either way, the subject in question was clearly a bird's skilled battle against the rolling, buffeting currents of air.

About a month ago, however, I happened to see part of a BBC documentary series on *The Life of Birds*. Halfway through an episode titled "Mastery of Flight," David Attenborough's smooth voice directs our attention to what appears to be a small dot hovering over the wave-crashed shore of an island. As the camera moves closer, we see that the stationary speck is actually a bird—a kestrel, Attenborough informs us delightedly. Since the bird hunts by sight, it hovers in place for long stretches of time in order to scan the landscape below for prey. The kestrel faces a headwind with beak down and sharp eyes alert, barely moving as the air currents pass over its brown wings and support its flight. Only when the wind dies down slightly must it beat its wings leisurely and reveal the white-and-black-speckled feathers underneath, still waiting, biding its time. When at last it spots movement below, the kestrel cranes its head and turns with the wind, bunching its wings close to its body and extending its claws as gravity carries its motionless body towards the ground.

Until I chanced upon this less-than-one minute segment in a lengthy avian documentary, the physical motion of Hopkins's windhover had visually meant very little to me. Suddenly, however, a sort of puzzle took shape in my mind as the word choices began to make sense: the bird's "riding/Of the rolling level underneath him steady air," its reigning upon the rein of a "wimpling wing," its sweeping "smooth on a bow-bend," its "rebuffing" the wind, were phrases that illustrated the precise and masterful moves not of all birds in flight, but of the kestrel, king of the air. In its stillness it seems to sit upon a throne, "dauphin"-like, surveying its domain while riding the boisterous "big wind" like an unruly horse. Only a casual and kingly motion of its wings reveals the "dappled" underside and indicates any effort—until the bird "buckles." Suddenly it turns, folds its wings inward and collapses, "buckles," as if it were a puppet on strings. The visual of the kestrel's flight is accurate and complete; I now understand its movements and I can see its flight through the words of the poem.

And yet, this knowledge has not changed my perception of the poem. The impact of these lines was quite as strong before I was familiar with the kestrel's flight as it is now that I understand the bird's ability to hover; for the alliteration, the word choice, the rolling rhythm, the enjambment and the cluster of incessant images and metaphors, do not so much create a visual image in my mind as enact the motion and emotion. The key word is "caught." Why not "saw"? "Witnessed"? "Glimpsed"? Though "caught" may simply mean "caught sight of," the omission highlights the action and ownership implied by the verb. No matter how royal the kestrel appears in air, no matter how freely it flies, the poet has captured in language some of its grace and recreated its flight with words. The bird's beauty and power do not diminish in the process; rather, they increase. The poem does not seek merely to describe a bird's flight pattern, but to share the windhover's soaring spirit and infuse the bird with a more profound and personal significance than it could hitherto claim.

Before the poet caught sight of it, the bird was sovereign only of the territory it could physically cover, and its rule was one of "brute beauty" and fear: eat or be eaten. Now, its realm has extended in typically Hopkins-ian fashion to embrace a rounder, more fully dimensional sphere of meaning that includes both the physical and the spiritual. The bird has become both king and captive, master and minion, and is far more powerful in its captivity and servility than it was as monarch. The bird's significance increases as it assumes a role not only within its limited territory, but within the grander scheme of nature itself: as "morning's minion" and "kingdom of daylight's dauphin," the kestrel accepts its place within a larger plan that endows its every movement with more meaning than if it remained dictator of one isolated province.

Moreover, the bird is now both captive and master of the human heart. Caged in verse, it now paradoxically traverses a wider space than it ever could have on its own wings. It is "caught" in language; but in this captivity it achieves untold heights of influence and immortality. With every reading of this poem, the bird's wings beat back to life and it relives and reenacts over and over again the "ecstasy" of its mastery of flight and of the human heart. This new flight may be confined to immaterial spaces— imprisoned on the page until read, forced to breathe only through the sound of the lines and restricted to a life that pulses only with the heartbeat of a human reader—but through this ephemeral existence, the bird achieves the ability to stir not just one heart, but thousands, time and time again. Beginning with its glorious exposure as heir to the kingdom of morning and dappled dauphin of the dawn, continuing into the round rustle of the alliterative "r's" and the cool sound of the successive "s's" that vividly recreate the smooth roll of the bird's flight, and concluding with the boldly proclaimed "b's" of "bow-bend," "rebuffed" and "big," the bird's victorious battle against the elements comes to a close and stirs the heart of the hearer with unspeakable yearning.

"My heart in hiding/Stirred for a bird,—the achieve of, the mastery of the thing!" At these lines, the very roots of our souls stir in painful awakening. We ache with desire and strain with longing; but, of course, it is not the bird we truly yearn for. In fact, this whole time, the bird's flight has been of minor importance. The poet's heart may have stirred for the pure strength and majesty of the kestrel's perfect mastery of a particular skill and its seemingly utter freedom in air; but our hearts stir more at the unadulterated poetic perfection of the lines than at the image of the bird in flight. The power of the octave culminates in the resonating "r's" of the words "stirred for a bird" that reverberate in our ears and rouse our hearts. The language approaches the orgasmic with relentless splendor, and before we grasp the meaning of every word or realize what precisely we desire, we know that our hearts hunger for something—perhaps the freedom, the "mastery" of a bird in flight, or the linguistic skill, the "achieve of" the poet. Whatever we yearn for, we know only that it promises absolute ecstasy.

And then—"buckle." At the height of desire, at nearly the pitch point of joy, the sestet causes us to pause. Instead of soaring to the heights of happiness with the uninhibited freedom of a bird on the wing, we plummet downward with the kestrel as it forsakes its throne and drops to earth. And despite a sense of disappointment and frustration, we are told that the "fire" of this descent is "a billion/Times told lovelier." Why? How?

In a sense, perhaps, the kestrel is more glorious at its most "dangerous" in pursuit of prey than in its aforementioned ecstatic flight. Similar downward, to-some-degree-deathly motions in nature have the same effect: the blade of a plough mercilessly cuts through and overturns "plough down sillion" to reveal a soft, dark, earthy shimmer; and "blue-bleak embers" burst with a beauty like fireworks when they fall to the ground and "gash gold-vermilion." The workings of nature are more striking, more intimidating and shocking, when they are "barbarous" in their beauty.

But if this were all, the poem would be sadly anticlimactic. Both the ecstatic and the barbarous are beautiful—how privilege one over the other? Why is the buckling bird a "billion"—billion!—"times told lovelier" in its descent than in its deft riding of the rolling air? The lilt and cadence of the lines remains quite as moving and eloquent, but the tone has changed; the underlying emotion is no longer euphoria, but subdued joy and realization. The rhythm and images no longer rise and build to a single, rapturous climax—they break and pause repeatedly, the pace halting, punctured with every punctuation mark and interrupted by arresting words such as "buckle," "fall," and "gall."

Here, I am reminded of a video I saw once of a young girl reciting "The Windhover" for a national poetry competition. Her voice is sweet and her expression elated; she exclaims every word with heartfelt passion and charming sincerity, her emphasis elegant and eloquent until the end. In the last line, the girl stresses a word that surprised me: "themselves." She pronounces the word in a tone of surprise and wonder, her inflection rising with the end of the word almost as if it were a question: "them*selves*," she sighs in awe. The weight of the word seemed almost jarring to me at the time and, to be quite honest, rather distasteful. The proper accent would seem to rest on "gall," would it not? "Fall, *gall* themselves, and gash gold-vermilion." With a shrug, I charitably attributed her mistake to inexperience and ignorance.

As I reflect on this poem now, I believe that this girl's choice of accent reveals a far deeper insight than I realized. To "fall"—well, we know what the word "fall" signifies. To "gall"—the Oxford dictionary reveals that the verb "gall" means to irritate or make sore by rubbing. Neither definition exactly suits Hopkins's use of the word; the context of the falling embers and the ensuing word "themselves" seems to indicate that by "gall" he means that the embers "dash" or "hurl" themselves against a surface in a self-destructive fashion. The wording implies an unusual sense of agency in the situation; the embers seem to purposefully fling themselves from the fire to the floor in a way that echoes the kestrel, the "chevalier's," voluntary buckling, as if of armor for battle. And what of the "plough down sillion"? Does it willingly meet the plow blade as well? Perhaps—the image of the sharp blade accentuates the painful aspect of buckling and galling, no matter how deliberate the action. If their fall promises suffering, then, why do the bird and the flame seem to accept, even embrace it?

And now, in this shattered sestet, we discover the poem's spiritual dimension. Without it, the pain of loss would indeed be unbearable: the bird abandons its throne, the blade cuts cruelly through the virgin soil, the embers of the fire fall and die, and with them would die our hopes and desires, our dream of achieving a state of heavenly bliss. The beauty of the barbarous would be only the sad splendor of the dying—a last, bittersweet burst of brilliance before the end—if the epigraph of the poem did not endow this act of "falling," "galling," "buckling" with new hope and meaning. We do not fall to die; we fall to live.

We fall to live, the poet claims, because our moments of pain and loss are as meaningful as our most joyful memories. The majesty of a bird at the peak of its flight seems enviable; but, the poet declares, it is nothing compared to the act of willing, loving sacrifice. We are significant not only in our successes, but also in our failures; our laughter and our sorrows, our victories and our disappointments, can be equally worthwhile if we make them so. In fact, the poet assures us, we are far more beautiful in times of hardship than prosperity. The phrase "grace under pressure" comes to mind: unusual and out of context as Hemingway's phrase may seem in this discussion, it aptly describes that moment when, instead of bending and breaking, we stand tall and accept pressure with dignity, nobility, even joy. If we fall, it is not because we have been pushed involuntarily to our knees; it is because we willingly accepted our burden.

As I see it, the true glory of "The Windhover" lies not simply in the pain of sacrifice, but in the act of giving. Our most noble human actions, and paradoxically, what Hopkins would call our most divine moments, involve a gift of self. In this letting go, we achieve the "lovelier" glory of self-giving that the magnificence of the princely, even prideful "daylight's dauphin" lacked. Dirt turns light, blue turns gold, Christ gives all, humanity reaches happiness through self-sacrifice. When we give of ourselves, we gain the most.

This close reading begins and ends with a personal anecdote, but the critic never loses sight of the text. In reaching for a meaningful experience of Hopkins's vision of the kestrel in flight, Freeman moves more and more deeply into the movement and language of the poem, almost as though she is working toward a union with the poet's attitudes and beliefs. In this critique, we stay close to the sound and sense of Hopkins's words (notice that this subjective critic also uses a dictionary), but the explication does not seek to wring the poem of its affective impact in order to dig out Hopkins's objective meaning or syntactical cleverness. Instead, the sonnet's meaning is created in the reader's attentive appraisal of her responses to Hopkins's imagery.

To someone trained in the methods of New Criticism, cultural studies, or New Historicism, subjective criticism may come across as self-indulgent, and even a little pointless. These critics might object that the permissiveness of reader-response criticism disqualifies it as literary scholarship, the purpose of which is to produce new knowledge of texts, authors, and literary contexts—not new knowledge of the critic's feelings, sex life, or family traumas. But subjective close reading by well-informed and careful readers may open up texts in new and startling ways. In this view, the text is not an unchanging object, stable artifact, or verbal icon, but something animate and malleable that the reader helps to create or bring into existence, as in Freeman's wonderful critique of "The Windhover." Indeed, she acknowledges and affirms the role of the reader in bringing the bird's flight and Hopkins's poem to life: though "caught" in language, "with every reading ... the bird's wings beat back to life and it relives and reenacts over and over again the 'ecstasy' of its mastery of flight and of the human heart." And the reach of the poem is potentially infinite, for "not just one heart, but thousands, time and time again," may be quickened with shared joy whenever the poem is fully experienced.

Amanda Freeman's reading of the "The Windhover" is clearly not a simple outpouring of feeling or unprocessed reactions. She works through the entire text, asks questions about it, and arrives at a judgment about its possible meaning through a sensitive analysis of Hopkins's language alone. She models a fair methodology for subjective criticism, which might look something like this. First, a reader takes the time to register the ideas, emotions, or train of connections generated by the act of reading. Second, he studies the text *in detail*, working to locate the passages, words, images, expressions that seem to structure his response. Finally, and what's often hardest, he must find the language to effectively communicate his responses to others within a shared context—to make accessible his understanding of the text within an interpretive frame, whether in a class, an on-line community, or a scholarly journal.[9] For although reader-oriented criticism affirms the potential for self-knowledge in the reading experience, responsive reading and subjective criticism are still social practices. The critics and thinkers I turn to now advocate engaged, immersive, or reflexive reading and criticism not only for personal enrichment, but for social and pragmatic purposes.

> [W]e learn through feeling; we cannot suppress our own idiosyncrasy without impoverishing it. But as time goes on perhaps we can train our taste; perhaps we can make it submit to some control.
>
> (Woolf 1989: 268)

The difficulty of finding the grounds for one's response to a text, "to know one's own *impression* as it really is," is the challenge of subjective interpretation. How does a reader turn her impressions into valid literary criticism, work that would interest others and contribute to an understanding of the text? We are back at the problem of standards and judgment. Does the subjective critic abdicate her role as a judge of literary worth and as an instructor of literary value? Some psychoanalytic critics would say yes: the encounter with literature may be too deep and intimate to require justification. But other scholars who defend the subjective paradigm argue that judgment is imperative, because values are unavoidable in all human inter-actions. It may also be argued that one criterion of evaluative judgment (perhaps even the most important criterion) is the quality of the response a work generates. In his book *Art Matters*, Peter de Bolla looks at three works of art—a painting by abstract expressionist Barnett Newman, Glenn Gould's recording of Bach's *Golberg Variations*, and the poem "We Are Seven" by William Wordsworth—in order to explore the possibilities of articulating specifically *affective* responses to art. For although "we have a full armory at our disposal for talking about, describing, and analyzing the sense or meaning of poetry," we are poorly equipped when it comes to our emotional responses (de Bolla 2009: 16). De Bolla's strategy is to use what he can identify as a "feeling" as a basis for further elaboration:

> In proceeding this way, a map or architecture of my experience will begin to emerge, and what I take to be the specifically *aesthetic* [i.e., affective] aspects of my responses will become more evident. It is on the basis of the descriptions of these responses that a discriminatory evaluation of artworks becomes possible: if my response to a particular work is uniform, monotonous, weakly felt, or trivial I feel confident in assigning to it a lower *aesthetic value* than to one that elicits a varied, sustained, polyphonic, or deeply felt response.
>
> (de Bolla 2009: 17, original italics)

De Bolla, a professor of cultural theory and aesthetics at Cambridge Univer-sity, is careful to explain that the task he has set for himself is quite challeng-ing; it may take a person many years of practice before she can fully grasp or become attuned to certain works of art. So it is certainly legitimate to ask what an individual needs to know in order to appreciate a piece of music or a poem. But it's also important to ask how much knowing things may get in the way of patiently seeing, hearing, and reading. De Bolla insists that we can only know how much background or special training we need by *first attend-ing to our affective responses* (2009: 22).

If literary critics must judge, and thereby help others toward knowledge, it is vital to establish some kind of criteria for what kind of knowledge is being sought. A good critic asks, "What do I want to know?" Formalists may want knowledge that will illuminate the way the poem's metaphors communicate shifting ideas. Marxist critics may want knowledge of the economic and ideological forces that are traceable in the work, or that pro-duced it. For these scholars, a subjective response may be irrelevant. If someone wants to interpret *Their Eyes Were Watching God* as a social document of the 1930s or as part of an anthropological study of the Amer-ican blues, she will push her personal responses to the periphery and zero in on the purpose for her reading. In the same way, scholars who use computer-generated maps to find out how a literary genre developed, or track the use of particular words in Dickens's novels using big data and algorithms, have other ends in mind than their personal reading experience.[10] This kind of research can certainly teach a great deal about an author's linguistic habits and the emergence of different styles in a given historical moment, and subjective critics do not reject these epistemological goals—indeed, they commend innovations in the digital humanities that help us to understand the history of readers and reading. But unless this research leads back to the literary experience—the reader's meeting with the work itself—it does not qualify as literary *interpretation*. Such research diverts attention from the primacy of the creative exchange between the reader and the work of art, and so forfeits participation in helping the reader know the text experientially. But why is this more important than or as important as objective or more quantifiable forms of knowing?

The twentieth-century American philosopher John Dewey asserted that works of art have been valued in all human societies because people's experience of art intensifies other modes of experience. We have many kinds of experience, usually classified as work or as leisure, but most people know when they are fully present in an experience, when they are doing something with complete attention or creative commitment. The "esthetic experience is experience in its integrity," writes Dewey, freed from anything that tries to subordinate or redirect it (1934: 274). When I am immersed in reading a novel (or building a bookcase, cooking a soufflé, or playing the violin) I unconsciously filter out intruding thoughts in order to sink into the experience of processing words, forming pictures in my head, dwelling in the world the novelist has invented. The argument of Dewey's *Art as Experience*, published in 1934, is that aesthetic experience is important not because it is segregated from daily life, set aside for moments of contemplation in libraries and museums and concert halls, but because it is continuous with and deeply affects "the practice of living" (1934: 10). The critic, then, is an important person, charged with the task of promoting the active process of grasping the art experience. The critic's work, says Dewey, is about "the re-education of perception" (1934: 324–325). In this view, the role of the critic is not to rank good poems and bad poems according to a fixed standard, or to explain the economic conditions that propel literary production, or to graph reader demographics. It is to assist people to tune in to their own potential as readers—to help them to be more awake and percipient, to be better experiencers.

Dewey was writing in the 1930s, when the pace of contemporary life was accelerating and technological efficiency prevailed. In the twenty-first century, the speed and handiness of communication devices and the ubiquity of the internet may be making it harder and harder for people to sink into an authentic experience—of literature, or of almost anything else.[11] So it may not be a frivolous exercise for a critic to stop and think about what happens subjectively when he reads a poem or a novel, or for a teacher to ask students to respond candidly in writing or discussion to their reading of a text. The goal is not just to break the ice or solicit likes and dislikes.

It's to heighten awareness of the literary experience, to help readers to see the poem not as a consumable artifact or an assignment, but as an event in their lives. And there *is* judgment implied in this work. Dewey writes, "The material out of which judgment grows is the [text], the object, but it is this object as it enters into the experience of the critic by interaction with his own sensitivity and his knowledge" (1934: 309–310). To write good subjective criticism requires discernment and intelligence, as well as emotional receptivity. As Walter Pater wrote in his Preface to *The Renaissance*, the ultimate aspiration is to become the kind of person who is capable of *having* singular impressions in the first place, instead of being a passive consumer who swallows whatever the culture tells her to, or a dismissive person who says, "I don't know anything about poetry."[12] *Everyone* registers an impression to the stimulus of reading, listening to music, or looking at works of art. But we have to learn how to handle our aesthetic responses patiently and self-critically. Dewey writes that to "define an impression signifies a good deal more than just to utter it. Impressions … are the antecedents and beginnings of all judgments." For when we undertake to define an impression, we have started to analyze it, and that process circles back to the grounds on which the impression rested—the story, the film, the poem (Dewey 1934: 304–305).

Dewey reminds us of something we all know intuitively: intellectual work begins with experiences, with striking impressions of the people and things we encounter in the world. It can be quite perplexing to make sense of the variable impressions we each have, even on an ordinary day. When we encounter a sophisticated work of art, a poem, a painting, a symphony, or a film, it may be extremely difficult to order, process, and assimilate our responses. But it is important to attempt to do this, since that is the process whereby one comes to know one's object—the poem, story, or play that is the stimulus for one's impressions.

Recall that in *Practical Criticism*, Richards studied the difficulties his Cambridge students encountered when faced with unfamiliar verse. He wanted to comprehend where they go astray—what confused them about figurative language, or why a poet's tone seemed so hard to locate. In one section of the book, he identified the students' tendency to fall back on conventional responses when reading poetry (1929: 228). Why did so many students think in clichés or repeat the truisms of their society, instead of grappling with the poems on their own? Why were their responses careless, sentimental, or obtuse? Reading poetry clearly disturbed students' routine ways of thinking, but the voices of different cultural authorities kept competing with their own experience; they did not know how to process and express their reactions sincerely and originally. Richards believed that the formal study of literature could assist young people in the daunting task of reorganizing their minds. Reading poetry, "our chief means by which subtle ideas and responses may be communicated," Richards thought, could teach students to nourish a many-sidedness that might help them, in the long run, to climb back up from the "levelling down" of the repetition and conformity that dominates modern people's lives (1929: 235). As Dewey would put it, the *experience* of art may help them to see and hear over the confusion and din of the modern world, and so be in shape for "active and alert commerce" with its many and surprising people, objects, and events (Dewey 1934: 19).

The work of Dewey and Richards, both advocates of progressive education in the 1930s and 1940s, resonated powerfully with the American scholar and educator Louise Rosenblatt. In 1938, she published what is generally acknowledged as the first work of scholarship on reader-response criticism, *Literature as Exploration*. In this work and those that followed, Rosenblatt offered a unique theory of the dynamic reciprocity of the reader and the text, one that sought to acknowledge the two-way exchange of the reading experience.[13] Like Dewey and David Bleich, Rosenblatt believed that in any literary encounter there is always a human being who is choosing, consciously or unconsciously, and so bringing forth discrete meanings. For Rosenblatt, both reader and text come together to create an experience, called "the poem." The task for all readers, she argues, is to *evoke* the work by developing a *stance* toward it.

> Books are to be call'd for, and supplied, on the assumption that the process of reading is not a half-sleep, but, in the highest sense, an exercise, a gymnast's struggle; that the reader is to do something for himself, must be on the alert, must himself or herself construct indeed the poem, argument, history, metaphysical essay—the text furnishing the hints, the clue, the start or frame-work. Not the book needs so much to be the complete thing, but the reader of the book does (Walt Whitman).[14]

Rosenblatt and the New Critics started on the same path in the pre-war years. Both deplored, in her words, "the neglect of literature as an art resulting from the traditional preoccupation with literary history and 'the message' of the work" (1995: 289). But they parted company in their very different understandings of the nature of art. Where the New Critics treated the poem as an autonomous entity that could be objectively analyzed, Rosenblatt believed that the poem is delivered, created, or performed in the event of reading. Three ideas are central to her theory of reader-response.

First, Rosenblatt believed that when someone reads a poem or a novel, it is an experience that is being lived through—it is a *new* experience, "an event in time ... an occurrence, a coming-together ... of a reader and a text" (1962: 126). A competent critic can summarize what happens in *Othello*, paraphrase "The Raven," or explain the technical brilliance of either of these works in a way that enhances a reader's appreciation of them. But no one can supply the *experience* of reading these works or predict their potential resonance for someone else. No one can read the poem for you, as Rosenblatt puts it, because your personality, your memories and associations, your physical state and your mood at the time of reading all contribute to this new experience in your life. The poem is not an iconic object or an ideal entity, but the product of the mutual involvement of the reader and a certain kind of writing:

> There is no such thing as a generic reader or a generic literary work; there are only the potential millions of individual readers of the potential millions of individual literary works. A novel or a poem or play remains merely inkspots on paper until a reader transforms them into a set of meaningful symbols. The literary work exists in the live circuit set up between a reader and a text: the reader infuses intellectual and emotional meaning into the pattern of verbal symbols, and those symbols channel his thought and feelings. Out of this complex process emerges a more or less organized imaginative experience. When the reader refers to a poem, say "Byzantium," he is designating such an experience in relation to a text.
>
> (1995: 24)

Like Richards, Rosenblatt here suggests that when people refer to works of literature, what they are really talking about are *acts of reading*. Phenomenological critics have delved into what it feels like to process language and mutually create with an author a world of the imagination—and I will touch on those ideas a bit later, for they have an important place in subjective close reading. Rosenblatt's concept differs slightly from the phenomenologists', though, in that she sees the reader as only one half of the creative process, and she sees *every* reader as exceptional in his or her individuality.[15] In her transactional theory of reading, the meaning is not *in* the text or *in* the reader, but is a product of a complex two-way process (1995: 27). In Rosenblatt's formulation, the reader + the text = the poem.

Rosenblatt is well aware that the transactional theory she advocates may come across as unmethodical, fanciful, overly psychological—as not objective! But she replies that the verbal symbols we process when we read are not only subjective stimuli; they have a public existence, as well. We can always turn away from our response and investigate what gave rise to it:

> The "close reading" of the New Critics centered on the text. *The transactional view also assumes close attention to the pattern of signs. But it assumes an equal closeness of attention to what that particular juxtaposition of signs stirs up within each reader.*
>
> (1993a: 137, original italics)

In other words, in subjective close reading, we are called upon to test our evocation for its inner coherence and relevance to the text—to reference the words that exist both on the page and in our minds, imaginations, and memories.

The second concept running through Rosenblatt's work is that the reader's mental and emotional orientation and bearing to *any* work of written communication helps to determine its status and its meaning.[16] She identifies two positions. What she calls the *efferent* stance (from the Latin *efferre*, to carry away) is primarily involved with analyzing and summarizing what the reader wants to retain after reading—what to do in a tornado, travel directions, gardening tips, the rules of golf, dog training techniques, recipes, navigational tools, building a database, learning a language. In these situations, the reader's attention tends to be focused outward, on how the information in the reading material will be put to use. In the *aesthetic* stance, on the other hand, the reader is focused on what is happening during the act of reading. She "listens to herself" while she reads, pays attention to associations, questions, ideas that words and their referents arouse (Rosenblatt 1993a: 25). Note that not all features of a text will penetrate the reader's experience. Rosenblatt refers to the phenomenon of "selective attention": when we read aesthetically, some features of a text will "have a sharp impact, others will be glossed over or stay on the outer fringes of consciousness" (1993a: 167). Also, the same text may be read efferently and aesthetically—we might scan a poem in order to understand its meter, or just focus on the emotions it awakens.

Rosenblatt definitely sees that the author's manipulation of connotation and denotation, syntax, context, and genre can direct the reader's stance toward the text—readers do react to something concrete on the page. The term *stance* is important because it suggests a readiness to respond to the work in a particular way on the continuum of efferent or aesthetic reading—the stance is the way a reader "swings between two poles" of meaning, in Annie Dillard's words, and it's an apt visual metaphor for the mind's flexibility (Dillard 1996: ix). Many texts are susceptible to being read both ways, just as we adapt different attitudes, some even simultaneously, toward events in real life. "We don't have the cognitive, the referential, the factual, the analytic, the abstract on one side and the affective, the emotive, the sensuous on the other," claims Rosenblatt. "Instead, both aspects of meaning—which might be termed the public and the private—are always present in our transactions with the world" (1993b: 383). Indeed, Rosenblatt's rejection of the dualistic model of perception (thought/feeling, cognition/emotion, knowledge/experience) echoes T. S. Eliot's queries about the objective/subjective split, and anticipates the work of Eve Sedgwick and others in their turn to affect in the 1990s, an approach that recognizes the role of less conscious motives in our experiences with culture, art, and politics.

The aesthetic stance is requisite in the literary encounter—it is the mode of entry. A poem or a novel demands of the reader an attitude of presence, of being with the text for the duration of the reading. When someone reads a work of imaginative literature aesthetically, he does not automatically screen out matter he isn't going to use, as he might when trying to navigate a website. Instead, he pays attention to many things at once—to the particular words in their particular arrangement, to sounds, images, and patterns, even to the physical time and place in which the reading occurs, and so concentrates, almost intuitively, "on the complex structure of experience that he is shaping and that becomes for him the poem" (Rosenblatt 1993a: 26). Unlike John Crowe Ransom's edict separating the critic from the reader, or any number of other theoretical approaches that break up a text and then rearrange it according to a pre-existing filter or code, Rosenblatt urges critics of all persuasions to recognize the personal commitments and desires that enter the reading experience.[17] She says straightforwardly, "the critic must begin by being a reader. Paradoxically, the contrary is also true: the reader must be a critic" (1993a: 137). I take this to mean that the *reader* must accept her responsibility to pay attention to "the second stream of response," that mode of listening, sorting, and selecting that is the provenance of criticism (1993a: 137). But the *critic* must equally recognize that her formal analysis of a text has its roots in the reading experience itself.

Indeed, to study a text in its social contexts, as historians or sociologists might do, or as a document to be correlated with other evidence concerning the structure of language, or as items in an author's biography, may produce valuable knowledge, and Rosenblatt in no way denigrates such interests. But, she argues, when these concerns predominate, the student or scholar is functioning not as a literary critic, but as a linguist, a historian, a biographer. "The term 'literary critic' should be reserved for one whose primary subject is his aesthetic transaction with the text; he reflects on the work of art he has evoked" (1993a: 162). She also notes that classification and analysis of the elements of the text can produce interesting data, but may neglect the work itself, the actual aesthetic event: we become so interested in the frame, we fail to notice the picture. For Rosenblatt, the raw data that really matter are "individual personal encounters with texts" (1993a: 174–175).

One benefit of Rosenblatt's approach is that she invites readers to recognize possible biases before they harden into a creed. As we'll see in the next section, reader-response theory welcomes the element of surprise. To be sure, some readers are more experienced than others, and so better at making sense of their reading encounters. But Rosenblatt advocates a democracy of readers—there should be no "naïve" readers trailing behind experts, because *every* reader ventures into the comparative unknown when he enters into the literary transaction. Even if someone sits down to reread a poem or novel for the fifth or tenth or twentieth time, every reading is a potentially new experience. Instead of stultifying readers and students with authoritative pronouncements, say the subjectivists, literary critics and teachers might model the process of mentally registering the literary transaction in all its strangeness before they launch into more sophisticated discussions of form or externalizations of the work's place in history.

These first two concepts—the reader/text transaction and the efferent/aesthetic stance—are linked to the third important argument in Rosenblatt's work. At the very start of her career, Rosenblatt insisted on the intersections of literature, psychology, and the social sciences. She believed that the study and teaching of literature, using the transactional model, could enlarge readers' understanding of themselves, of the changing world, of human values, and of the social and political responsibilities of individuals in a modern democracy. Indeed, she argued that "literary experiences might be made into the very core of the kind of educational process needed in a democracy" (1995: 261). Reading literature with genuine involvement and a commitment to the experience itself may help people to participate imaginatively in how other people choose to live, liberating them from stale or narrow patterns of thought. For Rosenblatt, reading aesthetically and practicing subjective criticism does not imply navel-gazing or cutting oneself off from any reasonable discussion about a literary work. On the contrary, this practice demands self-ordering and self-criticism. For in this deliberate positioning, the text is not primarily a sovereign object, an historical fact, or a political tool. Nor is it seen simplistically as a form of therapy or as a clue to the reader's subconscious—the poem is not a Rorschach inkblot or a free-association exercise (but it *may* have personal and psychological significance, as I'll discuss). And a novel or play is not a random assortment of symbols, as deconstructionists might claim. It is a work of art created by an individual employing language, a socially produced medium of human communication. Thus close reading in the transactional approach takes into account the social dimension, for the reader is "engaged in a creative process at once intensely personal, since the poem is something lived through, and intensely social, since the text ... can be shared with others" (Rosenblatt 1962: 126). An aesthetic experience is always more than aesthetic; it is human, value-laden, social. Following Richards and John Dewey, Rosenblatt believes that experiencing literature actively and personally may help people grow into "critically minded, emotionally liberated individuals who possess the energy and the will to create a happier way of life for themselves and others" (1995: 262).

> If I read a book and it makes my whole body so cold no fire can warm me I know *that* is poetry. If I feel physically as if the top of my head were taken off, I know *that* is poetry. These are the only way I know it. Is there any other way?
>
> (Dickinson 1986: 474/L342a)

> One sheds one's sicknesses in books—repeats and presents again one's emotions, to be master of them.
>
> (Lawrence 1981: 90)

Like Gerard Manley Hopkins, Emily Dickinson published only a few poems during her lifetime. Also like Hopkins, Dickinson has attracted close inspection from formalist critics, and almost all of the New Critics emphatically supported her status as a major American poet. When Thomas H. Johnson's three-volume edition of her poems was published by Harvard University Press in 1955, John Crowe Ransom hailed the event as the long-overdue restoration of one of America's greatest poets (1963: 88). Austin Warren praised Dickinson's pliant use of meter and her inventiveness, asserting that her "use of language is almost unfailingly meditative and precise" (1963: 105). Cleanth Brooks and Robert Penn Warren used Dickinson's poems to teach students about tone and imagery in *Understanding Poetry*. Allen Tate enthusiastically praised "the verbal excitement" of her style, her feeling for language and use of tension, her "intellectual toughness," which, like Nathaniel Hawthorne's, demonstrates "a hard, definite sense of the physical world" (1963: 16, 27). If some of these eminent men of letters were uneasy with her gender or the domestic aspects of her work—John Crowe Ransom, for example, patronized her as "a little home-keeping person"—they also admired her astonishing originality, intelligence, and control of her craft. She was "a key writer for New Critical methods," according to Lena Christensen, and indeed it was the New Critics who consolidated her work as worthy of inclusion in the American literature canon (Christensen 2008: 35). Later critics, notably Helen Vendler, Sharon Cameron, and Cristanne Miller, also focused on formal matters in Dickenson's poetry—on her rhetorical strategies and repetitive patterns, her troubling imagery and enigmatic use of names, her verbs and epigrams, her eccentric punctuation and difficult syntax. It's almost impossible for critics to stay away from matters of form and language when they write about Dickinson's "riddling, elliptical poetry" (Miller 1987: 1).

Yet Emily Dickinson, again like Hopkins, has had a broad following among readers who are drawn to something more entrancing than her precise word choice and careful puns. Readers are curious about Dickinson's take on the world, her sentient questionings of death and love, nature and God. Scholars who have read her poems dozens of times have confessed that what attracts them to her work is deeper than a fascination with her meter and her puzzling lexicon. In the mid-twentieth century, some feminist literary critics openly embraced the identificatory power of Dickinson's poetry, or her ability to speak to their own dreams and frustrations. Partly they were reacting to the New Critics' coolly objective or proprietary approach to Dickinson, their cultural nostalgia and paternalism. These younger critics wanted to express their sense that Dickinson's imagery, linguistic disruptions, and verbal hesitations contained a rebelliousness that resonated with their own psychological and political realities. Because these scholars were trained to be close readers, they analyzed features of Dickinson's vocabulary or her carefully managed tone with great skill. But in a sense, they also wanted to *feel close* to Dickinson, to honor her particular vision, learn how the constraints of her life as an unmarried woman in nineteenth-century New England shaped her poetry, understand her comprehension of life from a woman's point of view. Unapologetically, some feminist critics set out to read Dickinson personally—almost protectively—because to them her poetry addressed dilemmas and concerns that still mattered to contemporary women.[18]

Three landmark works by feminist critics from the 1970s and 1980s stand out in their creative mingling of attentive close readings of Dickinson's texts with personal involvement in the critical act: Adrienne Rich's essay, "Vesuvius at Home: The Power of Emily Dickinson" (1976); Sandra M. Gilbert and Susan Gubar's chapter on Dickinson in *The Madwoman in the Attic* (1979); and Susan Howe's *My Emily Dickinson* (1985).

These critics' original, and even impassioned, readings of Dickinson's poetry attest to the vitality of literary scholarship when it is freed from the straitjacket of strict objectivity. More historically attuned to Dickinson's position as a woman writer than their New Critical predecessors, and with much more biographical information to go on, they read the poetry with acute attention to themes of violation or desire, to splintered meanings and subtle inflections in tone. Their analysis is driven not only by an intellectual fascination with the poet's verbal genius. It is also guided by personal curiosity about Dickinson's life, and searching wonder at the labor that went into writing those brilliant, puzzling 1,789 poems.[19] I would like to present a subjective approach to one perplexing poem that has generated more criticism than any other in Dickinson's body of work. Susan Howe makes this "singularly haunting" poem the focus of her entire book (2007: 35); Gilbert and Gubar note its "deadly vocabulary," an expression of the poet's "murderous energy" and "Satanic ferocity" (1979: 608–609). It is the poem at the center of Adrienne Rich's thoughts about Dickinson, as well.

Rich begins "Vesuvius at Home" by describing a pilgrimage she has made to Emily Dickinson's house in Amherst, Massachusetts—a place that raises questions about Dickinson's life and the power of her poetry. Standing in Dickinson's corner bedroom, walking around the hedge of cedar trees surrounding the house, then driving back to Boston, Rich begins a train of thought that takes in the confined spaces of Dickinson's life and the immensity of her genius, the "unorthodox, subversive, sometimes volcanic propensities" of the poet and the sentimental image (perpetuated by a masculine literary establishment) of the "fragile poetess in white" (1979: 166). Throughout the essay, Rich weaves reflections about Dickinson's life and their shared identity as women and poets with brief readings of over twenty poems, exploring the energy in Dickinson's writing, her willfulness, her pride, and what Rich calls her "daemon—her own active, creative power" (1979: 170). Before she arrives at the poem that is at the root of her relationship with Dickinson's verse, Rich offers some personal history. When she was a girl and beginning seriously to write poetry, Dickinson was a confusing role model, a figure who affirmed that "there was a range

for psychological poetry beyond mere self-expression," yet whose circum-
scribed life "[whispered] that a woman who undertook such explorations
must pay with renunciation, isolation, and incorporeality" (1979: 168).
Blending self-narrative with literary criticism, Rich confesses:

> There is one poem ... I have mused over, repeated to myself, taken
> into myself over many years. I think it is a poem about possession by
> the daemon, about the dangers and risks of such possession if you are
> a woman, about the knowledge that power in a woman can seem
> destructive, and that you cannot live without the daemon once it has
> possessed you.
>
> (1979: 172–173)

Now here is the poem.

> My Life had stood – a Loaded Gun –
> In Corners – till a Day
> The Owner passed – identified –
> And carried Me away –
>
> And now We roam in Sovreign Woods –
> And now We hunt the Doe –
> And every time I speak for Him
> The Mountains straight reply –
>
> And do I smile, such cordial light
> Upon the Valley glow –
> It is as a Vesuvian face
> Had let its pleasure through –
>
> And when at Night – Our good Day done –
> I guard My Master's Head –
> 'Tis better than the Eider Duck's
> Deep Pillow – to have shared –
>
> To foe of His – I'm deadly foe –
> None stir the second time –
> On whom I lay a Yellow Eye –
> Or an emphatic Thumb –
>
> Though I than He – may longer live
> He longer must – than I –
> For I have but the power to kill,
> Without – the power to die –
>
> (Dickinson 1998: FR/764)

Here is a portion of Adrienne Rich's reading:

> Here the poet sees herself as split, not between anything so simple as
> "masculine" and "feminine" identity but between the hunter, admit-
> tedly masculine, but also a human person, an active, willing being, and
> the gun—an object condemned to remain inactive until the hunter—
> the *owner*—takes possession of it. The gun contains an energy capable
> of rousing echoes in the mountains and lighting up the valleys; it is
> also deadly, "Vesuvian;" it is also its owner's defender against the
> "foe." It is the gun, furthermore, who *speaks for him.* If there is female
> consciousness in this poem it is buried deeper than the images: it exists
> in the ambivalence toward power, which is extreme. Active willing and
> creation in women are forms of aggression, and aggression is both
> "the power to kill" and punishable by death. The union of gun with
> hunter embodies the danger of identifying and taking hold of her
> forces, not least that in so doing she risks defining herself—and being
> defined—as aggressive, as unwomanly, ("and now we hunt the Doe")
> and as potentially lethal. That which she experiences in herself as
> energy and potency can also be experienced as pure destruction. The
> final stanza, with its precarious balance of phrasing, seems a desperate
> attempt to resolve the ambivalence; but, I think, it is no resolution,
> only a further extension of ambivalence.... The poet experiences
> herself as a loaded gun, imperious energy; yet without the Owner, the
> possessor, she is merely lethal. Should that possession abandon
> her—but the thought it unthinkable: "He longer *must* than I." The
> pronoun is masculine; the antecedent is what Keats called "The Genius
> of Poetry."
>
> (1979: 173–174, original italics)

Rich's brilliant reading is considerably influenced by her identity as a poet
who has struggled to assert her voice in a culture where women have historically had to conceal their creative energies or channel them into socially
acceptable roles. She sees, too, that the struggle is often within: the image
of the gun, in her reading of the poem, represents Dickinson's ambivalence
toward the power of her gift, which can release her into psychic freedom
but also engender intense or destructive emotions, such as rage, depression,
and social and spiritual isolation.

Rich's reading, radical and original when it first appeared in 1976, is
undertaken in a spirit of speculation and discovery as much as of formal
argument. In a summary paragraph, she writes:

> I do not pretend to have—I don't even wish to have—explained this
> poem, accounted for its every image; it will reverberate with new tones
> long after my words about it have ceased to matter. But I think that
> for us, at this time, it is a central poem in understanding Emily

Dickinson, and ourselves, and the condition of the woman artist, particularly in the nineteenth century.

(1979: 173–174)

Unlike a New Critic, Rich does not try to "account for every image" or
insist that her reading is the only correct one. Indeed, she respects the
poem's integrity as a work of art that will communicate different things to
different readers, long after her words about it have been forgotten. Yet
she implies that this poem has special relevance for readers with similar
needs to her own. When she writes, "for us, at this time, it is a central
poem for understanding Emily Dickinson, and ourselves," Rich evokes a
community of readers who care about Emily Dickinson—perhaps other
feminist literary critics or aspiring poets, or her contemporaries, living
through the excitement of the women's movement in the United States in
the 1960s and 1970s.

Though she is a good close reader of the poem, Rich is not merely interested in "understanding Emily Dickinson" (as she says) in a kind of
detached, New Critical way, in order to produce knowledge of the mechanics of this lyric's linguistic ambiguities. What is equally important to her
is bringing the poem into relevance with her life, and with the lives of other
readers. This can be a vital component of the reading experience. Felski
has written about the importance of *recognition* in the literary encounter:
"Reading may offer a solace and relief not to be found elsewhere, confirming that I am not entirely alone, that there are others who think or feel like
me." She goes on to explain that these moments of recognition are not
restricted to solitary reading, but may also crystallize "an awareness of
forming part of a broader community" (Felski 2008: 33). This is exactly
what happens in the process of Rich's response to Dickinson—as she
herself affirms, "The poetry of extreme states, the poetry of danger, can
allow its readers to go further in our own awareness, take risks we might
not have dared; it says, at least: 'Someone has been here before'" (Rich
1979: 182).

Skeptics of Rich's emphasis on gender and aggression in the poem might
argue that she is letting herself get carried away by a theory of feminine
creativity that simply resonates with her personally. Her interpretation is
too bound to the assumptions of 1960s feminism, whereas it should be tied
a little more tightly to the poem—to Dickinson's tone, for example, which
rather than being "precarious" might be described as quite direct, even
exuberant, an expression of "robust equality," as another scholar prefers
to see it (Farr 1991: 243). These are fair objections to a work of criticism
that interweaves readings of poems with other topics and forms of
expression—self-narration, travelogue, commentary on the American literary canon, an argument for women's autonomy. Indeed, none of the
poems cited by Rich are anatomized the way we saw "The Windhover"
taken apart in Chapter 2 above, and the style is a little meandering and

diffuse. Still, partly because she was responding to changing currents in literary study, but also, I think, because her own voice comes through with great daring and commitment, Rich's provocative essay has become a canonical work of literary criticism (and is worth reading in its entirety). Because she is willing to attach Dickinson's story to her own, Rich may have found something in "My Life Had Stood – a Loaded Gun" that a strictly objective critic, tracking a single, non-enigmatic interpretation, might miss.

Can literary criticism blend analysis and attachment, the cognitive and affective elements of reading and critique? Some highly respected Dickinson scholars, along with well-known poets and writers, have tried to achieve that balance, often describing their experience rereading Dickinson over the years as an interpersonal relationship.[20] Her poetry has been studied against personal experiences of depression, divorce, grief, and sexual love, as well as of war, politics, and the events of 9/11. Critics trace their discovery of Dickinson's verse in the language of a spiritual or emotional journey, as well as an intellectual one. In other words, these scholars do not only read Dickinson defensively, looking for symptoms of rage or suffocation in a patriarchal plot to thwart female creativity (though some of them do this, too).[21] They also read Dickinson's poetry of pain, longing, or loss as potentially curative for them.

Eve Kosofsky Sedgwick has called this approach *reparative reading*. Like Felski, who has defended ordinary motives for literary reading, such as recognizing oneself in a literary text or reading for pleasure and enchantment, Sedgwick is responding to the culture of suspicious reading and ideologically driven critique that has dominated English studies for the past several decades. Her essay, "Paranoid Reading and Reparative Reading," first published in 1997, has drawn new interest from a range of scholars, especially those working in queer theory and psychology, literature and medicine, and the emerging field known as affect studies.

Reparative reading draws on the ideas of the psychoanalyst Melanie Klein, who has discussed a child's or adult's development from a paranoid position toward the world—one which is marked by anxiety, fear, or envy—toward one in which those emotions are reassembled and put to positive use (Sedgwick 2003: 128). In translating this model of psychoanalysis to literary and cultural criticism, Sedgwick identifies five features or assumptions of paranoid theory: (1) it sees everything as already known and there are no surprises; (2) it grants no immunity, all texts are implicated; (3) it is strongly tautological (so a critic may argue that everything can be understood in terms of surveillance, and therefore surveillance is everywhere); (4) it is pessimistic; and (5) it views knowledge in terms of exposure and demystification. This style of criticism is often tied to the critic's liberatory politics, and because Sedgwick has seen the energy and radical insight brought to bear on literature from queer, feminist, and Marxist scholars, she would never advocate eliminating paranoid hermeneutics. But she does question why this practice has become so imperative in contemporary criticism. Why do critics always begin with unmasking a text, with "the detection of hidden patterns of violence and their exposure," or the contemptuous assumption that the text knows nothing (2003: 143)? She wants to encourage a critical practice that could take its place beside paranoid or suspicious reading, one which would permit openness to affective responses, to an expression of need, or to a desire for connection.

The problem, Sedgwick argues, is not that critics do not read from the reparative position, for we do, all the time—affective reading is just as attached to concepts of freedom, justice, and survival as ideologically driven readings, and just as eager for knowledge of the world and of human actions. But we lack a critical vocabulary of reparative reading, as well as some good critical models of reparative *writing*. "The vocabulary for articulating any reader's reparative motive toward a text or a culture has long been so sappy, aestheticizing, defensive, anti-intellectual, or reactionary that it's no wonder few critics are willing to describe their acquaintance with such motives," she says (2003: 150). Yet if critics embrace such practices, offers Sedgwick, we may learn "the many ways selves and communities succeed in extracting sustenance from the objects of a culture" (2003: 150–151).

Literary critics must acknowledge that people read for many reasons: to enter a different world, to bask in the beauty of language, to identify with a voice or a character, to learn about a certain time and place. Literature might be used to assist us in navigating our way through life's uncertainties and problems, or to express thoughts that otherwise we would not know how to access. Indeed, therapeutic reading goes on all the time, as does therapeutic writing; every year dozens of memoirs are published about surviving the death of a loved one or struggling with terminal illness, and how many blogs and websites exist to help people cope with disease and loss? As Ann Jurecic writes in *Illness as Narrative*, a book indebted to the work of Felski and Sedgwick, paying attention to "care of the self, attention, recognition, and repair point to the possibility of redefining the relationship of writers and readers to the books in their hands and the worlds they inhabit" (Jurecic 2011: 17).

What follows are two examples of literary criticism that hold onto personal or reparative motives for reading while also focusing on the textual encounter. Cindy MacKenzie and Suzanne Juhasz, experienced Dickinson scholars, each uniquely observes herself reading—or, more accurately, rereading—along the lines Rosenblatt has described: they closely follow their cognitive and emotional responses to the movement and structure of Emily Dickinson's verse, to her odd vocabulary or multiple meanings. They watch themselves as they read her poems, asking themselves questions about what puzzles them, and in the process come to realize something about their past assumptions or ingrained reading habits. They also record surprise that poems they have studied for years could look so strange and unfamiliar.

MacKenzie recounts what happened when she returned to Dickinson's poetry after going through a painful divorce. She reads several poems closely, and then steps back from her analysis to study what she has learned about both Dickinson's craft, her own reading practices over time, and her need for companionship and encouragement. She knows lines from many poems by heart ("There is a pain – so utter"; "Pain – has an Element of Blank"; "After great pain a formal feeling comes"; "Pain – Expands the Time"), and acknowledges that these and many more poems offered her the "liquid Word to make [my] sorrow less" because of the truth they expressed. But she senses something more is taking place than consolatory utterances. These are *poems*, not snippets of greeting card verse. So Mac-Kenzie's attention shifts to the reading process:

> I began to be aware of a certain pattern in Dickinson's writing: the compelling first lines that would pull me into the poem, trusting that I would find some kind of answer, some kind of anodyne to alleviate my pain, but then the poem would become more and more esoteric, often moving toward incomprehensibility. With time, I have come to see this as a deliberate method in that we follow the poet from the point of our present reality—feelings of acute pain—to an inward spiritual search of ourselves. Hardly aware at the time of what was happening, thinking that I was simply trying to "figure the poem out," I was actually doing something of far more personal signifi-cance: that is, I was executing a rigorous self-examination of all the dark corridors the wound of divorce had forced me to enter. I began to understand that while the divorce itself was a distinct and painful rupture in my life, Dickinson's view of that rupture as a wound around which deeply significant meanings accrue began to lead me slowly toward accepting it.
>
> (2007: 51–52)

Reading Dickinson's poetry from a position of uncertainty and vulner-ability (instead of paranoia or mastery) brought this critic into contact with the significance of the structure of Dickinson's poems. She was able to see that entering the poem and feeling blocked or confused by its devel-opment paralleled a psychic journey: Dickinson makes the reader fill the gaps between one solitary word and another as a means "to find the trace in the words to which we can bond" (2007: 56). MacKenzie concludes that the poet's rhetorical strategies are tied to the reader's need to find utterance for pain. In analyzing her responses, the critic develops a greater awareness of Dickinson's faith in the power of words and in the material-ity of language, which Dickinson invites her readers to connect to in times of need.

Suzanne Juhasz, a prominent Dickinson scholar and founder of the *Emily Dickinson Journal*, also reflects on the project of rereading Dickinson's poetry after a career devoted to studying her work. Her essay, "A Life with Emily Dickinson: Surprise and Memory," is centered on the excitement of rediscovery. Like MacKenzie, Juhasz admits that Dickinson's poetry "has become a part of my daily life, in some ways a part of my consciousness" (2012: 82). Retired from university teaching, she decides to reread all of Dickinson's 1,789 poems to see "the sort of responses that I would have to the poems *now*. I expected that there would be surprises, because surprise, I always think, is at the essence of a Dickinson poem" (2012: 83). And she *is* surprised, even a bit dismayed, at the sheer difficulty of reading shorter poems she had never studied closely before. It is instructive to see a good critic self-consciously work through to a poem's meaning, as in Juhasz's opening volley to this poem:

> Our share of night to bear –
> Our share of morning –
> Our blank in bliss to fill,
> Our blank in scorning –
>
> Here a star, and there a star,
> Some lose their way!
> Here a mist – and there a mist –
> Afterwards – Day!
> (1998: FR/116)

Juhasz writes:

> An initial reading of this poem raises more questions than it answers. What does "share" mean? Or "bear"? "Or "blank"? Or "bliss"? Or "scorning"? each of these words is clear on its own, but I do not see how they are operating here. When I get to the second stanza, I follow it more easily, although I do not understand why the "star[s]" are personified—how a star can "lose" its way. Stanza two seems to describe how day happens after night, but I do not know what it has to do with stanza one. And I really have no idea what the first stanza means. I am unsettled and surprised by the ways in which the poet uses familiar words in unusual ways that I do not immediately understand. Any conclusion now would be my guess, my creation, and have little to do with the words before me. Therefore, I need to start again and go more slowly.
>
> (2012: 83)

This could be an interior monologue by one of the New Critics! Juhasz is aware that it would be irresponsible to invent an interpretation that does not stay true to "the words before [her]." So she starts again, as the most meticulous objective critic would do, and teases out possible meanings for *bear, blank, bliss, morning,* and *stars*. Five paragraphs later, she is able to say,

> Now I have an idea about how the stanzas are related. Although stylistically different, they both deal with the experience of night and day, or, if this natural process can be viewed symbolically, with the process of life itself. Thus I will say that the poem as a whole describes first human participation in life and then activities or phenomena in nature. The quality of human experience, relentlessly required to make choices, to take on responsibilities, seems to be contrasted with nature's more elemental processes. Poor humans. And yet, as a conscientious reader I must account for the fact that the stars are granted agency, *like* humans. Therefore the notion that human life is one thing, nature is another, is ultimately too simplistic. Maybe God is the missing link, He who grants different roles to those who are ultimately all His creatures. Nice idea, but I made it up to make sense of this ambiguity; God is never mentioned in the poem. Readers frequently try to erase or solve such ambiguities, especially to provide a conclusion, but I find it better to acknowledge and try to work with them.
>
> (2012: 84)

Juhasz, again like a New Critic, is tolerant of the poem's ambiguities, yet she has to confess she doesn't know exactly what this particular poem *means*. She recognizes why she has struggled with its obliqueness, for in its use of commonplace words that don't seem to fit together it resembles other Dickinson poems she feels she understands much better. Though she hasn't cracked the poem, she's learned a bit more about how it works; her difficulties now make sense to her, based on her other experiences reading Dickinson—and she seems content with this limited knowledge.

We might complain that this critic's reflections on the reading process do not help us understand the poem any better than before we read her commentary (I recommend reading Juhasz's essay in full, though, to see what she comes up with). Yet her puzzlement gets our own imagination working so that we might take up the problem of interpretation based on her opening gambit. I had never seen this poem before I found Juhasz's essay. I agree that it seems to be a commentary on human existence, but I read it as about each person's struggle to make sense of a random and meaningless situation, the muddle of finding oneself in the world, without rhyme or reason. The exclamation points and the sing-songy, childish, almost ironical sound of "Here a star, and there a star" and "Here a mist – and there a mist –" suggest to me that the speaker doesn't take a tragic view of the confusion we bear upon going to sleep, waking up, and filling the blank hours of consecutive days with the gamut of exhausting emotions. But does "Afterwards – Day!" express encouragement or mockery? Is "Afterwards" our awakening in death, "Day" when our bewilderment is finally over? Or is "Day" not death, but hope or spiritual enlightenment?

Throughout the essay, Juhasz also recalls classes she's taught and conferences she's attended over the years that have become intertwined with Dickinson's verse. She even returns to her critical fascination with one poem she has analyzed in three different books, over three decades, producing a mini-scholarly memoir about how changing critical fashions made her notice new possibilities for interpretation. As she tells these stories, Juhasz realizes that surprise was not the only aspect of Dickinson's poetry that her journey through the poems revealed (2012: 89). She describes a crucial insight about reading's two-way process. Because she has worked on Dickinson for a long time, "certain poems have contexts that create a narrative surrounding my pleasure in the words alone. Sometimes what I think of as *'the poem'* has become an *event* that is composed of both the *words* and my *experiences* with them" (2012: 89–90, my italics). What Juhasz describes in this perceptive comment is precisely Rosenblatt's transactional theory of reader-response! The reader's *experience* + the poet's *words* = "Our share of night to bear." The *event* of reading and the critic's reflection on the reading experience over time have brought the poem into being.

> I always say, my motto is "Art for my sake."
> (Lawrence 1979: 491)

The resurgence of interest in the reading experience, reparative reading, and what has been called *bibliotherapy* are signs that reader-response theory and subjective criticism are no longer deemed trivial, mushy, or anti-intellectual. Questions about reading and subjectivity—the function of memories, anticipation, attachment and other mental and emotional states—are gathering momentum in many different areas of inquiry. These investigations of human emotion have been newly analyzed and energetically debated in both the humanities and social sciences under the general term *affect theory*. But the affective turn, as it's been called, is not simply a return to reader-response theory—it is not concerned principally with the reading process, for example, or with a reader's explanation of his experiences with a story or poem. Like New Formalism, affect theory is more an orientation to literature and culture than a single methodology, and it is much more interdisciplinary.

For our purposes, we can say that affect theory antagonistically engages the New Critics, especially the injunction against personal feeling in literary criticism, enshrined in Wimsatt and Beardsley's affective fallacy. Affect theory is also a reaction to social constructivist and language theories that have dominated literature, philosophy, and cultural studies for four decades. Poststructuralists working on subjectivity and culture, for example, distanced the physical, material existence of actual readers for fear of being labeled essentialist—that is, of reducing complex cultural influences to "natural" or biological situations that are beyond the reach of human intervention, and so of political activism and change. Now, however, scholars are rethinking the linguistic turn, in which virtually every probe into culture, philosophy, politics, social studies, art, literature, psychology, and anthropology begins and ends with language systems. They want to bring the experience of embodiment back to the discussion, and especially the experience of affective life—what it *feels* like to move through time, to be in the world, to act, think, and respond to stimuli. These scholars are also interested in how cognitive science has categorized and theorized affective states, and the ways our culture maps our emotional lives. They are working within the intersections of neuroscience, media studies, biotechnology, philosophy, art, feminism, queer theory, popular culture, and psychology.

Of course, philosophical interest in the emotions is not a new development. From the ancient Greeks to Descartes, Kant, and Darwin, major thinkers have asked how we should understand the relationship between rational thought and unruly feelings such as love, lust, jealousy, anger, and fear. What seems to be happening now, though, is that a set of well-established questions about human feeling and cognition are being applied to cultural and media studies, and those methodologies have overflowed into English and textual studies generally. Scholars studying this development have identified several intellectual strands, each with slightly different goals. One set of approaches involves theories of human and non-human bodies in fields such as cybernetics, artificial intelligence, robotics, and bio-engineering. These critics analyze corporeality and the "affectional line" between the living and the non-living. Other strands include the more human-centered aims explored in social psychology, as in the naming or categorizing of major affective structures in a culture, such as shame or disgust, and in politically engaged works focused on race, class, gender, and queerness. There is, in addition, an interest in opening up our understanding of those identities by shifting the focus from discourse to affective encounters with cultural objects such as technology, music, public spaces, animals, etc. Other vectors are oriented toward neuroscience, and deploy brain imaging to study affect in relation to cognition and an array of social stimuli.[22]

At this point in time, the affective turn seems more at home in the social sciences, media studies, and cultural studies than it does in English—although the field of cognitive cultural studies, as it's been named, also partially explores the lived experience of reading. Recent works of literary criticism have also embraced psychology's "theory of mind" to account for how the mind makes sense of patterns (such as texts), and how fiction helps us to understand our ability to make inferences about what other people are feeling and thinking.[23] Lisa Zunshine, a leading scholar in this field, has argued in *Why We Read Fiction: Theory of Mind and the Novel*, that we read novels because

> the sustained representation of numerous interacting minds ... feeds the powerful, representation-hungry complex of cognitive adaptations whose very condition of being is a constant social stimulation delivered either by direct interactions with other people or by imaginary approximation of such interactions.

More simply, our "evolved cognitive capacity for mind-reading" makes the reading of fictional narratives both a pleasure and good mental and social exercise for our real-world interactions (Zunshine 2006: 10–11).

Dissenters have argued that their feelings of attachment, identification, and empathy when they read *The Portrait of a Lady* or *King Lear* are deep-seated and real, and cannot be satisfactorily explained as a theory-of-mind mechanism! But Zunshine has anticipated such objections, replying simply that the data aren't all in, that "we are a long way off from grasping fully the levels of complexity" that go into engaged reading (2006: 164). She even implies that you're kidding yourself if you think you *don't* read fiction because it gives an intense and pleasurable "workout" for your cognitive adaptations.

Like other scholars working on reading and neural science, such as Nicholas Dames and Alan Richardson, Zunshine has introduced provocative concepts about how and why we read. These scholars' methods of analysis, though, show that there is still reluctance to locate the substance and meaning of a literary work in the reading experience itself. As Paul B. Armstrong has observed, "much of the most interesting work on literature and cognitive science is historical, comparing ... how psychologists in the Romantic or Victorian periods understood consciousness with how the novelists and poets defined it," or else it applies the work of neurohistorians in order to draw paradigms for reading (2011: 88). Questions about reading and feeling are being addressed with new enthusiasm, yet historicism, cultural context, and the circumvention of the actual reading experience seem to prevail.

A few influential scholars have lately asked how we might begin to amplify our interpretive strategies, or at least modify how we talk about reading literary works in order to do justice to the rich texture and affective density of the reading experience. Troubled by the predominance of grammatical methodologies and of readings based on theories of social power, these critics have sought to refocus attention on what occurs within the consciousness of the reading subject. Because our responses are usually mysterious and opaque even to ourselves, we're liable to distort the integrity of the literary work. But as Stephen Best and Sharon Marcus argue, ideological readings produce distortions as well. For "even if we cannot exhaustively explain what causes our responses, we can strive to describe them accurately," and it is okay if those responses are not always right on the money (2009: 18). Best and Marcus have asked critics to stop looking eagerly for hidden meanings and pay more attention to "what lies in plain sight but often eludes observation" (2009: 18). They call this *surface reading*, arguing that it's often constructive to read for what is evident and apprehensible in a text, or for what strikes us as interesting or sounds true. A good close reader may concentrates on what she understands about a work, not only on what eludes her or seems buried beneath the surface.

Other contemporary scholars have proposed a re-examination of the mid-twentieth century *phenomenologists* who set out to describe the active and dynamic character of the reading process in all its strangeness. In "Phenomenology of Reading," Georges Poulet (1969: 57) tried to comprehend how reading a work of literature seems to bring into existence "a second self." A book is merely an object, he argued, like a vase or a table, until someone begins to read it. But by a weird alchemy, when the consciousness of the author begins to interpenetrate that of the reader, it really seems that the reader is thinking the thoughts of another. When we read immersively, as we ought to read, says Poulet, "without mental reservation ... with the total commitment required of any reader," our comprehension "becomes intuitive," and we actually experience the feelings proposed to us in the book we are reading (1969: 57). Poulet concedes that we do need outside information such as biographical or critical matter to understand a book, but

> this knowledge does not coincide with the internal knowledge of the work.... At this moment what matters to me is to live, from the inside, in a certain identity with the work and the work alone. It could hardly be otherwise. Nothing external to the work could possibly share the extraordinary claim which the work now exerts on me.
>
> (1969: 58)

A few years later, the German theorist Wolfgang Iser wrote that the dual subjectivity Poulet describes is inevitably colored by the reader's personality. The "true meaning" of any text is inseparable from the reader's anticipation and his memories of the text (if he has read it before), and so the reading experience, the "gestalt" of the text, is going to be subject to the reader's illusions and desires. A truly good work of literature, one "worth its salt," requires a reader to exert her imagination—it has, inevitably, gaps and indeterminacies a reader has to fill in to get the text's meaning. She has to "shade in the many outlines" suggested by the author's words and sentences, each of which opens up a horizon that has the potential to be completely changed by the next word, the next sentence (Iser 1972: 281, 283).

The connections a reader automatically forms between the lines, so to speak, may seem very real to him. This is how literary texts "transform reading into a creative process that is far above mere perception of what is written. The literary text activates our own faculties, enabling us to recreate the world it presents ... it is the coming together of text and imagination" (Iser 1972: 283–284). Iser says that because this process of continual modification is almost unconscious, it resembles how we gather experience in life: "the 'reality' of the reading experience can illuminate basic patterns of real experience" (1972: 286). Literary reading mirrors the complex process of sorting through the innumerable phenomena we chance to perceive in everyday life.

My summary of phenomenology is drastically simplified here, but the point is that the Geneva School critics, as they were called, differed radically from their American and French counterparts, the New Critics and the structuralists. They did not see the goal of literary criticism either as a type of objective knowledge or as a way to systematize language. Criticism is simply another way to understand being and human consciousness, and in this respect it is actually like literature itself. Why are some contemporary critics interested again in phenomenologies of reading? In fact, the scholars I have in mind—Rita Felski, Charles Altieri, Frank Farrell, and Sedgwick— never explicitly urge a return to the Geneva School critics. What they seem to be reaching for is an approach to literature that acknowledges the particular and affective qualities of the reading experience, its intimacy and waywardness, the psychological, and maybe even metaphysical, importance that we attach to making sense of literature. These critics often stress the intersubjective nature of close, immersive reading. The philosopher Frank Farrell is particularly strong on this point, arguing that to dissolve the reading experience into patterns of social power or grammatical schemas diminishes literature's dynamism. In his defense of a more phenomenological approach, Farrell writes:

> There is an implicit phenomenological stance, a general way of taking the world to be meaningful that is expressed in the sequence and rhythms of words, in the descriptions of physical space, in the overall style of engagement with the objects brought into view. The space of the literary text remains one where that life of the self, its fundamental way of setting itself in relation to the universe ... are being enacted in a particular fashion, not only in the lives of the characters but also in the very process of writing and reading.
>
> (Farrell 2004: 9–10)

The "literary space," insists Farrell, relies on "self-to-world patterns" that demand our personal investment. So instead of distancing himself from the reading experience in order to externalize a poem's significant features or prove that a novel intervenes in systems of power, the critic should step closer to the text, and attend more deliberately to the truths, insights, disturbances, and pleasures it offers him.

The American critic Charles Altieri has also given serious thought to the importance of affect in our treatment of literature. He gravitates toward phenomenology because he believes there are innate forms of knowing, "some kind of intuition or noncritical judgment" that register the power of a poem's evocations (2003: 34). These inchoate ways of knowing invite interesting questions about how we are changed because of our response to a poem, or what desires get expressed because of our reading. For Felski, the promise of phenomenology for literary studies is that it gives a more expansive account of aesthetic experience. "Phenomenology ... allows us to do justice to the widespread conviction that works of art can enrich our understanding of the world" (2009). The mood of absorption that occurs when we are under the spell of a novel, she says, may color the particular experience of pleasure or contribute to our mental awakening. If we allow ourselves to pay attention to such quasi-hypnotic states, we may find different sorts of meanings emerge from the text we hold before us.

For some critics, this emphasis on intuition, imagination, and immersion is a little whimsical and esoteric—just a mystical way to talk about what goes on in our brains when we read a novel. Others, especially within cultural studies, are uneasy with the assumption that the aesthetic, or what Farrell calls the space of literature, occupies a special category in human experience. They feel that works of art are continuous with other forms of social discourse, and have no intrinsic force, no special spiritual or metaphysical access to truth, knowledge, or reality. I appreciate and partly share this assumption. Yet I also believe that contemporary literary theory should take into account the fact that works of art, especially literature, uniquely inhabit a cherished in-between space in most people's lives—a space between the boredom and repetition of everyday routine and the inchoate wishes, regrets, and dreamscapes of the private self. I suspect the unease I experience when I am kept away from solitary, immersive reading time is a kind of psychic deprivation—or perhaps I should say imaginative hunger. For as Iser observes, the indeterminacy of literary texts is what enables readers to exert their imaginations. As we attend to the words before us, we are often casting around in our minds for images that will vivify the scene the author has created, for devices to *picture* what we're reading.

The scholar Elaine Scarry has studied minutely the process by which writers incite readers to bring forth mental images that resemble their own real-world perceptions. In *Dreaming by the Book*, Scarry examines how great authors stretch, fold, and tilt language in order to get readers to "see" the phenomena of their invented world—flowers, faces, birds in flight, human movements, even fabrics and textures. How does it happen, she asks, that words in a book acquire "the vivacity of perceptual objects" (1999: 5)? How is it that we can so easily visualize the speed of Achilles or feel the cloth of Emma Bovary's dress? Scarry's close readings include many fascinating examples, including this one:

> And brilliant Achilles tested himself in all his gear,
> Achilles spun on his heels to see if it fit tightly,
> See if his shining limbs ran free within it, yes,
> And it felt like buoyant wings lifting the great captain.

Scarry asserts that Homer's epic relies on what she calls "a steady surge of ignitions," language that flares, lights, fires, sparks and seems to lift up the warrior's heavy armor in one conveyance of agility and lightness. The poet knew how important it was to get mental pictures *to move*, because motion carries "a mimesis of aliveness," so necessary to our imagining (1999: 87). Lighting conveys motion in this poem, and is often sharply specified, either dropping vertically, shooting across horizontally, originating in someone's body, or surrounding him in a golden cloud. These radiant words "glide across the mental retina" so that the reader both feels and witnesses the movements of these gleaming figures (Scarry 1999: 88). This is one reason why Homer is a great epic poet: he is able to give us a verbal transcription of images as they come full-blown to his mind, and so allow the reader to reconstruct them in her imagination (1999: 244). We can all think of images that have remained with us after reading a novel, even if we've forgotten the writer's actual language. But if we return to the text and reread the *exact words* chosen by the author, we begin to see how they have combined to stimulate our imagination, and our emotional response—breathlessness, fear, awe, giddiness, delight. This kind of close reading seeks to explain qualities of the literary imagination, the workings of poetic language at the confluence of authorial direction and readerly imagining.

Close subjective reading requires close listening, too. When we read a narrative, we imaginatively stage its aural as well as pictorial effects—we "hear" a narrator's voice or the special intonations and accents of certain characters' speech. This experience may be deepened when we read poetry and really seem to inhabit the voice of the poem, a process which begins by sounding out the words, hearing them mentally, forming them physically in our mouths, feeling them in our bodies. Charles Altieri has suggested that this initial "sounding out" should develop into what he calls "voicing." This amplification is one of the most important effects of reading lyric poetry with full engagement:

> For there is no better access to other identities, or to who we become because we can take on other identities, than giving ourselves over to a range of speaking voices. Then we are not watching characters on a screen or a stage; we are actually becoming the voices through which they live.
>
> (2001: 262)

In close reading, it becomes possible to appreciate how a sense of who we are may be modified by entering into articulations of different experiences and ideas. Reading poetry and fiction may "sharpen our awareness of the intricate ways we feel our attention and care becoming contoured to other existences" (2001: 270).

But why does it matter that I can "see" the marsh mists in *Great Expectations* or "hear" the warmth in Keats's "To Autumn"? After all, those are just images and echoes in my private, dream-like repertoire of images, and we cannot reliably generalize about knowledge, psychology, or literature from my idiosyncratic responses. Have neuroscience, sociology, and ethnography surpassed phenomenology in analyzing what happens to people when they read literature? Perhaps. But in my view, cognitive science and brain imaging can only supply a flat, reductive picture of human emotion, one that doesn't take into account the degrees to which people answer back to their feelings, or sort through the changes that occur in their impressions of a text over time. Sociology, similarly, can only calculate the surface of people's experience; questionnaires and interviews "are not especially conducive to capturing the experiential density of what is involved in reading a book or watching a film," says Felski (2009). There are more layers to the reading experience than social or scientific theories can account for.

On the other hand, it's certainly fair to argue that phenomenological, reparative, or affective readings are liable to serious errors of misreading. For instance, there might be very little attention given to the author's political motives or his social critique. Intent on examining our emotional responses, we may miss a poet's formal experimentation, a novelist's narrative innovations. Furthermore, foregrounding personal response may lead readers to project their wishes or frustrations onto a totally innocent poem, or perform all kinds of ego-centered maneuvers to get the text to confirm one's own experiences of love or sex or grief. We do have to be cautious about indulging our private fantasies! Yet in its best practice, close reading that is sensitive to affective response and to the workings of the imagination may acutely refocus a text's formal features, and demand that we attend minutely to the author's choices.

Affective or phenomenological reading is not simply about releasing one's feelings. We begin to understand and isolate specific ways the novel or poem structures our affective response in its descriptive and verbal energy. By looking closely at our subjective feelings about this or that word or situation we may better appreciate the achievements of the creative imagination. So I would say that we *do* gain aesthetic appreciation by attending to our emotional responses to works of art. There are other values, as well, identified by Altieri as "a self-reflexive feeling of one's own capacity for intensity, a sense of involvedness in which we feel our personal boundaries expanding … and a sense of the psyche's plasticity as it adapts itself to various competing imaginative demands" (Altieri 2011: 267). The capacity for *intensity*, the sense of *involvedness*, and psychic *plasticity*: this critic's resplendent language points to the revitalizing capacities of affective close reading—the dynamic freedom for self-making wrought by reading's demanding intimacies.

> It is as though a poem gave the reader as he left it a single, new *word*, never before spoken and impossible to actually enunciate, but self-evident as an active principle in the reader's consciousness henceforward.
>
> (Crane 2006: 163)

> The proof of a poem is not that we have never forgotten it, but that we knew at sight that we never could forget it.
>
> (Frost 2007: 88)

I want to end this chapter with a few words about psychoanalytic criticism, and in particular one branch of psychoanalysis known as *object-relations theory*. The British psychologist D. W. Winnicott used the term *transitional object* to describe those common, ubiquitous things a child takes up—a toy, doll, teddy bear, or blanket—to fill the space between his newly realized autonomous identity and his ongoing attachment to his mother. This ritual-ized, transitional space of "play" is an important stage in the child's develop-ment because he is testing the boundaries of selfhood: he is learning to be independent and is becoming aware that his thoughts and experiences have a separate existence, while at the same time he still needs to feel a dependable sense of unity with his mother. Instead of undergoing a sudden, traumatizing separation, the child uses a toy that is both "me and not me" to help him adjust to these scary, emerging new boundaries.

In a healthy infancy, a child secure in her mother's nearby presence will relax into a state of absorption in her playing and pretending. In Winni-cott's theory, this is a crucial stage in a person's complex negotiations between the inner self and the outer world, and can establish the pattern of someone's relationship with people and things well into adulthood. Everyone requires transitional objects and intermediate spaces in their adult lives because we are always being challenged to relate our subjective, inner experiences to an ever-changing environment. Art, music, and literature may have a special status in people's lives, then, because for Winnicott, "the intermediate quality of transitional objects between fantasy and reality fore-shadows that of works of art, which likewise partake simultaneously of reality and illusion" (Rudnytsky 1994: xii). Any experience of "play" that allows us to temporarily lose a sense of self—reading a novel, listening to a symphony, coloring a picture, taking a photograph—opens the door a little wider for inner perception, when we can project meaning onto an object without letting our conscious thoughts take control. A person who cannot enter into this type of experience, or who simply has had no practice with mental absorption, according to the psychoanalyst Christopher Bollas, "will have less psychic vocabulary ... and so a diminished internal world when he returns to being the complex self" (1992: 23).

As the above epigraphs by Hart Crane and Robert Frost suggest, people seem to recognize moments when they arrive at some truth about themselves assisted by the transitional object, whether it be a new word, a poem, a song, or something else. We are offered a more creative relationship to the world, and "we know it deeply, yet it is exceptionally difficult to describe" (Bollas 1992: 60–61). Bollas, for instance, relates that he chose to write his doctoral dissertation on Herman Melville's *Moby-Dick*. Why *Moby-Dick*? It was "an intuitive choice," he thinks, "based on my knowing (yet not knowing why) that this book—rather than, say, Hawthorne's *The Scarlet Letter*—would bring something of me into expression" (1992: 57). Many years later, he recalls two separate experiences, when he was nine and eleven, both extremely frightening, that seem to explain how *Moby-Dick* was needed to help him to detect and confront some of the unconscious meaning of the book for him (1992: 57–59). Of course, this doesn't mean that everyone has repressed a traumatic memory. But this personal, psychological function of reading is seldom addressed in departments of English—this occurrence and recurrence of texts we favor, knowing but not knowing the reason for our choices. Someone may respond powerfully to stories and films about physical survival, or feel the need to reread *Jane Eyre* every two years. Why do you choose to write your paper on one theme rather than another, feel disturbed or attracted by the worlds of Haruki Murakami or Willa Cather or Salman Rushdie? We are all inhabited by ghostly knowledge that may transform how we experience the self and the world when evoked by a work of art—a story, a sonnet, a song, a beloved film.

Literary works, some critics have suggested, may have special relevance to this psychic project, for ultimately it is language that takes over the role of the doll or the blanket as the intermediary between self and world. And though getting lost in a book can *feel* like a dream, the book is always a product of a specific culture, and its reader inescapably bound to his own time and place. Reading a novel or seeing a play may intervene importantly in someone's interactions with his society—its norms, institutions, stereotypes, and assumptions. In this sense, the work of literature functions as a transitional object to the culture, a point of contact with a specific external reality that can reduce the violence of an encounter that may be overwhelming.

Frank Farrell writes,

> One of the cultural tasks we face now is to shape literary rituals that will train us in setting ourselves in relation to a universe whose operations are not designed to make human life turn out well, or even make it significant in the larger picture.
>
> (2004: 189)

It is interesting to think of reading literature as a ritualistic space in our lives. Whether someone decides to formally study *Macbeth* or pleasurably read Dickens, as he works through a text's language he is "patiently acknowledging the world as it is … how fragile things are in the way they emerge into view, remain stably there for our seeing, and then dissolve" (Farrell 2004: 214). When we read closely, when we are wholly present, but also relaxed and receptive, we may be permitted a glimpse of the intensity of human experience, and we may even feel its intensity—that is one way reading mirrors the phenomenon of being. At the same time, we have to recognize the limits of our conscious knowing and the comparative briefness of our reading time.

Against the cultural studies bent of affect theory, and unlike critics who lean toward cognitive science, phenomenological and psychoanalytic critics want to emphasize the strangeness of the reading experience and individual subjective responses. Rather than examine only or primarily a text's diagnosable structural features or its social underpinnings, these critics want to pay due heed to the interiority of reading, those intangible responses that share as much with intuition as with cognition. Close reading belongs to this school of criticism, too, for the critic has to pay attention to and ponder these internalizations—to see the work's images and listen to its voices as they bounce from author to text, text to self, and self to world.

Notes

1　Some of the New Critics were ambivalent about Richards, admiring much of his theory but holding back on the psychological emphasis of his work. See Ransom, *The World's Body*, "A Psychologist Looks at Poetry" (1938: 143–165).

2　John Dewey wrote that Richards overlooks the fact that the work of art—a picture, for example—possesses certain properties that stimulate the perceiver: vibrations of light, pigments on canvas, the interaction of molecules, etc. An art object *does* belong to the physical world. Dewey agrees, though, that "beauty" is "a short term for certain valued qualities" (1934: 250–251).

3　Wayne Booth, as we'll see in Chapter 4 below, belongs in both the rhetorical and the sociological camps. His book, *The Rhetoric of Fiction* (1961), analyzed the verbal strategies that locate the reader in the text, but he was also interested in the moral effects of texts on real readers.

4　The notorious "Conclusion" to *The Renaissance* was construed by some as an invitation to young men to embrace a life of sensual indulgence.

5　Pater's chapter on Leonardo da Vinci's *La Gioconda* (the *Mona Lisa*) contains one of the most famous passages of subjective criticism ever written, prose so extraordinarily lush and original that the poet William Butler Yeats called it the first modern poem; he rearranged Pater's sentences into verse form for his edition of *The Oxford Book of Modern Verse*, published in 1936.

6　A representative sampling of close readings from this more experimental angle can be found in Benson and Connors (2014)

7　Thomas Merton, for instance, the twentieth-century author and religious mystic, wrote that he came to his vocation after reading Hopkins's poetry. British psychoanalyst D. W. Winnicott reported that one of his patients "lived from poem to poem," often quoting Hopkins from memory to explain her feelings. See Bump (1989/1990: 65–70).

8　I would like to thank Amanda Freeman for permission to use this excerpt from her seminar paper.

 9 David Bleich has a slightly different three-part phase of registering reader response: perception, affective response, and associative response. Associative response is the most complex, and brings the reader closest to "the larger process of critical judgment" (1975: 48).

10 As in Franco Moretti's *Distant Reading* (2013), and books such as Matthew Jockers's *Macroanalysis* (2013) and Stephen Ramsay's *Reading Machines* (2011).

11 A *New York Times* editorial describes how many people don't even bother to have an experience, but form their judgments through second-hand opinions and media feeds. See "Faking Cultural Literacy," Karl Taro Greenfield, May 24, 2014.

12 Matthew Arnold called such people Philistines—that smug, closed-minded set who dismiss the value of poetry and art because they don't understand it or don't see its practical use.

13 In her later work, Rosenblatt developed her ideas in light of postmodernism. Though she was anti-foundationalist (someone who is skeptical of absolute truths or certainties), she could not accept the poststructuralist idea that language is a self-contained system, author and reader "simply conduits," as she puts it, "for arbitrary codes, conventions, and genres" (1993: 381). Although she has some ideas in common with cultural critics, she is somewhat wary of the view that literary works indoctrinate readers into the dominant ideology.

14 Walt Whitman, *Democratic Vistas* (http://xroads.virginia.edu/~hyper/Whitman/vistas/vistas:html).

15 Rosenblatt believes this trend is condescending toward the "common or ordinary or general reader ... who chooses to devote part of life's short span to the kind of experience called literary—to aesthetic reading—doing this not as a professional but for personal satisfaction" (1993: 138). Rita Felski seconds the position that the non-specialist, non-academic reader should not be dismissed in our conversations about literary theory and reader response.

16 Similarly, David Bleich argues that a work becomes literature based on a subjective decision to read it *as* literature. He uses the example of the Bible, which some people read as literature, some as history, and some as a divinely inspired truth.

17 Rosenblatt discusses French structuralism and deconstruction, especially the work of Roland Barthes, in *The Reader, the Text, the Poem* (1993: 165–175).

18 Feminist theory broke new ground by inviting personal inflections into literary criticism. For an overview of New Criticism's contributions to Dickinson studies and the reaction from feminists in the 1970s, see Christensen (2008: Chapter 1).

19 Adrienne Rich, Sandra Gilbert, and Susan Howe are themselves highly regarded poets.

20 For example, Ruefle (2012); McLane (2012); and Ryan (2006). See also MacKenzie and Dana's (2007) edition, which includes essays by both scholars and poets.

21 Check out Camille Paglia's chapter on Dickinson, flamboyantly titled "Amherst's Madame de Sade," in *Sexual Personae* (1991)

22 In my tentative foray into this expanding field, I found certain authors were often mentioned as foundational, though their work may be applied differently depending on the critic's disciplinary focus: Baruch Spinoza, Søren Kierkegaard, Gilles Deleuze, Felix Guattari, Silvan Tomkins, Paul Ekman, Antonio Damasio, Daniel Gross, Daniel Lord Smail, Brian Massumi, Sarah Ahmed, William E. Connolly, Eve Kosofsky Sedgwick, Ruth Leyes, Lauren Berlant, Sianne Ngai. See also Gregg and Seigworth (2010) and Clough and Halley (2007).

23 See Zunshine (2010) and Leverage et al. (2010).

References

Altieri, Charles (2001) "Taking Lyrics Literally: Teaching Poetry in a Prose Culture." *New Literary History* 32.2 (Spring): 259–281.

Altieri, Charles (2003) *The Particulars of Rapture: An Aesthetics of the Affects.* Ithaca, NY: Cornell University Press.

Armstrong, Paul B. (2011) "In Defense of Reading." *New Literary History* 42.1 (Winter): 87–113.

Benson, Stephen and Claire Connors, eds. (2014) *Creative Criticism: An Anthology and Guide.* Edinburgh: Edinburgh University Press.

Best, Stephen and Sharon Marcus (2009) "Surface Reading: An Introduction." *Representations* 108.1 (Fall): 1–21.

Bleich, David (1972) *Subjective Criticism.* Baltimore, MD: Johns Hopkins University Press.

Bleich, David (1975) *Readings and Feelings: An Introduction to Subjective Criticism.* Urbana, IL: National Council of Teachers of English.

Bollas, Christopher (1992) *Being a Character: Psychoanalysis and Self Experience.* New York: Hill and Wang.

Bump, Jerome (1989/1990) "Reader-Centered Criticism and Bibliotherapy: Hopkins and Selving." *Renascence* 42.1–2 (Fall/Winter): 65–86.

Christensen, Lena (2008) *Editing Emily Dickinson: The Production of an Author.* London: Routledge.

Clough, Patricia Ticineto and Jean Halley, eds. (2007) *The Affective Turn: Theorizing the Social.* Durham, NC: Duke University Press.

Crane, Hart (2006) *Complete Poems and Selected Letters*, ed. Langdon Hammer. New York: The Library of America.

Dana, Barbara and Cindy MacKenzie, eds. (2007) *Wider than the Sky: Essays and Meditations on the Healing Power of Emily Dickinson.* Kent, OH: Kent State University Press.

De Bolla, Peter (2009) *Art Matters.* Cambridge, MA: Harvard University Press.

Dewey, John (1934) *Art as Experience.* New York: Perigee Books.

Dickinson, Emily (1986) *The Letters of Emily Dickinson*, ed. Thomas H. Johnson. Cambridge, MA: Harvard University Press.

Dickinson, Emily (1998) *The Poems of Emily Dickinson: Variorum Edition*, ed. Ralph W. Franklin. Cambridge, MA: Harvard University Press.

Dillard, Annie (1996) *Mornings Like This: Found Poems.* New York: HarperCollins.

Farr, Elaine (1991) *The Passion of Emily Dickinson.* Cambridge, MA: Harvard University Press.

Farrell, Frank B. (2004) *Why Does Literature Matter?* Ithaca, NY: Cornell University Press.

Felski, Rita (2008) *Uses of Literature.* Malden, MA: Blackwell.

Felski, Rita (2009) "Everyday Aesthetics." *Minnesota Review* 71/72 (Winter/Spring).

Frost, Robert (2007) *The Collected Prose of Robert Frost*, ed. Mark Richardson. Cambridge, UK: Cambridge University Press.

Gilbert, Sandra M. and Susan Gubar (1979) *The Madwoman in the Attic: The Woman Writer and the Nineteenth-Century Literary Imagination.* New Haven, CT: Yale University Press.

Gregg, Melissa and Gregory Seigworth, eds. (2010) *The Affect Theory Reader*. Durham, NC: Duke University Press.

Holland, Norman (1975) *Five Readers Reading*. New Haven, CT: Yale University Press.

Hopkins, Gerard Manley (1955) *The Letters of Gerard Manley Hopkins to Robert Bridges*, ed. Claude Colleer Abbott. Oxford: Oxford University Press.

Howe, Susan [1985] (2007) *My Emily Dickinson*. New York: New Directions.

Iser, Wolfgang (1972) "The Reading Process: A Phenomenological Approach." *New Literary History* 3.2: 279–299.

James, Henry (1948) *The Art of Fiction and Other Essays*, ed. Morris Roberts. Oxford: Oxford University Press.

Jockers, Matthew L. (2013) *Macroanalysis: Digital Methods and Literary History*. Urbana: University of Illinois Press.

Juhasz, Suzanne (2012) "A Life with Emily Dickinson: Surprise and Memory." *The Emily Dickinson Journal* 21.2: 80–94.

Jurecic, Ann (2011) *Illness as Narrative*. Pittsburgh, PA: University of Pittsburgh Press.

Lawrence, D. H. (1973) *Selected Literary Criticism*, ed. Anthony Beal. New York: Viking.

Lawrence, D. H. (1979) *The Letters of D. H. Lawrence*, ed. James T. Boulton. Vol. I. Cambridge, U.K.: Cambridge University Press.

Lawrence, D. H. (1981) *The Letters of D. H. Lawrence*, ed. James T. Boulton. Vol. II. Cambridge, U.K.: Cambridge University Press.

Leverage, Paula, Howard Mancing, Richard Schweickert, and Jennifer Marston William, eds. (2010) *Theory of Mind and Literature*. Lafayette, IN: Purdue University Press.

MacKenzie, Cindy (2007) " 'It ceased to hurt me': Emily Dickinson's Language of Consolation," in *Wider than the Sky: Essays and Meditations on the Healing Power of Emily Dickinson*, ed. Cindy MacKenzie and Barbara Dana. Kent, OH: Kent State University Press, 47–59.

McLane, Maureen N. (2010) "My Emily Dickinson/*My Emily Dickinson*," in *My Poets*. New York: Farrar Straus Giroux, 193–204.

Miller, Cristanne (1987) *Emily Dickinson: A Poet's Grammar*. Cambridge, MA: Harvard University Press.

Moretti, Franco (2013) *Distant Reading*. London: Verso.

Paglia, Camille (1991) *Sexual Personae: Art and Decadence from Nefertiti to Emily Dickinson*. New Haven, CT: Yale University Press.

Pater, Walter [1873] (2010) *Studies in the History of the Renaissance*. Oxford: Oxford University Press.

Poulet, Georges (1969) "Phenomenology of Reading." *New Literary History* 1.1: 53–68.

Ramsay, Stephen (2011) *Reading Machines: Toward an Algorithmic Criticism*. Urbana: University of Illinois Press.

Ransom, John Crowe (1938)*The World's Body*. New York: Scribner's.

Ransom, John Crowe [1956] (1963) "Emily Dickinson: A Poet Restored," in *Emily Dickinson: A Collection of Critical Essays*, ed. Richard B. Sewall. Englewood Cliffs, NJ: Prentice-Hall, 88–100.

Rich, Adrienne (1979) "Vesuvius at Home: The Power of Emily Dickinson," in *On Lies, Secrets and Silence: Selected Prose 1966–1978*. New York: W. W. Norton, 157–185.

Richards, I. A. (1925) *Principles of Literary Criticism*. New York: Harcourt Brace.

Richards, I. A. (1929) *Practical Criticism*. New York: Harcourt Brace.

Rosenblatt, Louise M. [1938] (1995) *Literature as Exploration*. New York: Modern Language Association.

Rosenblatt, Louise M. (1962) "The Poem as Event." *College English* 26.2 (November): 123–128.

Rosenblatt, Louise M. [1978] (1993a) *The Reader, The Text, The Poem: The Transactional Theory of the Literary Work*. Carbondale: Southern Illinois University Press.

Rosenblatt, Louise M. (1993b) "The Transactional Theory: Against Dualisms." *College English* 55.4 (April): 377–386.

Rudnytsky, Peter, ed. (1994) *Transitional Objects and Potential Spaces: Literary Uses of D. W. Winnicott*. New York: Columbia University Press.

Ruefle, Mary (2012) "*My* Emily Dickinson," in *Madness, Rack, and Honey: Collected Lectures*. Seattle: Wave Books, 143–182.

Ryan, Michael (2006) "My Favorite Poet." *The Emily Dickinson Journal* 15.2: 38–39.

Scarry, Elaine (1999) *Dreaming by the Book*. Princeton, NJ: Princeton University Press.

Sedgwick, Eve Kosofsky (1998) "Teaching 'Experimental Critical Writing,'" in *The Ends of Performance*, ed. Peggy Phelan and Jill Lane. New York: New York University Press, 104–115.

Sedgwick, Eve Kosofsky (2003) *Touching Feeling: Affect, Pedagogy, Performativity*. Durham: Duke University Press.

Tate, Allen [1932] (1963) "Emily Dickinson," in *Emily Dickinson: A Collection of Critical Essays*, ed. Richard B. Sewall. Englewood Cliffs, NJ: Prentice-Hall, 16–27.

Tompkins, Jane (1980) "Introduction," in *Reader-Response Criticism: From Formalism to Poststructuralism*, ed. Jane Tompkins. Baltimore, MD: Johns Hopkins University Press, ix–xxvi.

Warren, Austin [1957] (1963) "Emily Dickinson," in *Emily Dickinson: A Collection of Critical Essays*, ed. Richard B. Sewall. Englewood Cliffs, NJ: Prentice-Hall, 101–116.

Woolf, Virginia [1932] (1989) "How Should One Read a Book?," in *The Second Common Reader*, ed. Andrew McNeillie. New York: Harcourt, 258–270.

Zunshine, Lisa (2006) *Why We Read Fiction: Theory of Mind and the Novel*. Columbus: The Ohio State University Press.

Zunshine, Lisa, ed. (2010) *Introduction to Cognitive Cultural Studies*. Baltimore, MD: Johns Hopkins University Press.

4 The ethical turn

Although literature is one thing and morality a quite different one, at the heart of the aesthetic imperative we discern the moral imperative.

(Sartre 1988: 67)

You are perfectly free to leave that book on the table, but if you open it you assume responsibility for it.

(Sartre 1988: 56)

As we know by now, the New Critics believed that the content of a literary work—a poem's or a novel's apparent message, or the author's stated intentions or implied views—was secondary to a consideration of its artistic form. As Cleanth Brooks wrote in *The Well Wrought Urn*, "The classic difficulty involved in lumping aesthetic judgments in with moral judgments is, of course, that one thus ties aesthetic values to a moral system: poetry tends to become the handmaid of religion or philosophy" (1947: 239). This attitude misunderstands the value of poetry, argued Brooks, which lies in its status as an aesthetic object. Does the poem sharply illustrate some side of human existence, or portray mundane reality with profound verisimilitude? Perhaps, and it's lovely if it does, but these are tangential concerns for the formalist. Objective criticism is about cultivating a reader's awareness of the poetic uses of language and the ways in which great poets coax meaning from structure, metaphor, paradox, ambiguity, irony. Questions about morality and ethics do not strictly belong to the critical enterprise.

Yet some contemporaries of the New Critics declared straightforwardly that literature *must* be studied as ethical discourse and as a comment on human possibilities. Kenneth Burke famously said that literary works should be categorized and studied as "equipment for living" (1998: 597). I. A. Richards says throughout *Principles of Literary Criticism* that our experiences with literature have social importance because they are communicable to others. Reuben Brower connected his work as a literary critic to the cultivation of a democratic attitude, since reading literature is practice in discriminating among different values (2013: xx). Perhaps the most influential work along these lines was a collection of essays called *The Liberal Imagination*, published in 1950 by Columbia University's Lionel Trilling. Trilling debunked the New Critics' defense of the self-contained autonomy of poetry, arguing forcefully that no aesthetic theory can make the ideas of great authors other than what they are intended to be: "ideas relating to action and to moral judgment" (1957: 279). Literary criticism is wrong to shelter poetry and fiction from ideas, whether about personal relationships, politics, religion, or human society. Indeed, even the form of a literary work—a five-act tragedy, an epistolary novel, a lengthy ode—is designed to lead the mind to certain conclusions. "Literature," Trilling famously declared, "is the human activity that takes the fullest and most precise account of variousness, possibility, complexity, and difficulty" (1957: xiii). Literary reading and criticism entail, indeed necessitate, an ethical awareness from the start, because these activities fundamentally involve a mode of conduct, an attitude toward the work and by extension toward other people and our social organization. Even though Trilling and other mid-century critics were never grouped together as "ethical critics," their commitment to engage literature's relation to the real world and with important social and political questions (and during the Cold War with questions about democracy and human freedom) established a trajectory quite apart from New Critical formalism. Literature, ethics, and criticism are simply entwined, because reading well and writing responsibly involve decision-making and judgment. As I. A. Richards wrote at the conclusion of *Practical Criticism*, "The lesson of all criticism is that we have nothing to rely upon in making our choices but ourselves" (1929: 329).

It would seem that these astoundingly intelligent critics would have become role models for the politically engaged theorists of the 1960s and 1970s. Critics committed to feminism, Marxism, or postcolonial theory were motivated by the highest principles: to listen to the voices of the oppressed, to grant dignity to literature written by less privileged or almost entirely disenfranchised groups of people, to expose myths of personal freedom as instruments of power. They cared deeply about survival, honesty, inclusion, respect, and diversity. Yet most of these critics purposefully distanced themselves from the liberalism of Trilling's generation, and what later came to be called ethical criticism. Some scholars felt puritanical connotations adhered to the term, which sounded uncomfortably censorious. (Queer theorists, for example, were loath to introduce moral claims into their writing, since labels of immorality and deviance had been the very weapons used against gays.) There was also, perhaps, a lingering feeling that ethical criticism deals with the obvious or surface features of a text—the dilemmas of characters, the presentation of moral predicaments, dramatizations of vice or frailty—and so had a tendency to be reductive or preachy. Ethical criticism was also thought to privilege fiction over poetry, and literary realism over more avant-garde or abstract forms of art. It was fine to talk about ethics in Victorian novels, but for many postmodern writers language and narrative experimentation seemed much more central than moral issues.

Many politically informed critics were also influenced by poststructuralism and social constructivists, such as Foucault, who challenged the idea of a stable subject position and called into question the whole category of "the human." These theorists rejected the Enlightenment idea of individual moral agency, and argued that subjectivity is an artificial construct, made from culture and language. The reader, the characters, the author herself are part of a fluid system of signs, identity is a linguistic performance, subjectivity is the product of social discourses. I hasten to add that some of these critics *did* incorporate ethics into their theories about the way literature works.[1] But generally speaking, theories about the indeterminacy of language and a text's radical openness to all kinds of meaning shut down arguments for a "right reading" in an ethical sense. The project of interpretation at this time was not interested in what was apprehensible as moral commentary or mimesis (what could be represented believably as social or psychological reality), but focused on the open-endedness of the text, what the literary work didn't know or concealed.

This approach sometimes borrowed the logic of psychoanalysis, apparent in the title of Frederic Jameson's wave-making *The Political Unconscious*, published in 1981. Jameson, a Marxist critic, insisted that it was time to reconsider what has passed under the name of ethical criticism since the mid-twentieth century, and analyze just how that term operates within capitalist and patriarchal ideologies. Jameson argued that because so-called humanism is grounded on certain universals (such as "human nature"), ethical projects are linked with a belief in something permanent about "human experience," the idea that we can acquire and broadly apply "wisdom" about our personal situations and relationships (1981: 59). But these ethical values are in reality not universal and permanent. They are historically and institutionally determined, the product of group solidarity or class cohesion (1981: 59). Thus the whole concept of ethics relies on exclusion and the invention of an alien "Other." The binary opposition of good and evil upon which ethics rests is one of the fundamental forms of ideological thought in Western culture, argued Jameson, nothing more than a cover-up for the power interests of dominant groups—men, capitalists, imperialists, heterosexuals, whites (1981: 88). Ethics changes nothing; it's a category that has been evoked to conceal inequities and maintain the status quo of social power. Only political readings can reveal the workings of power and of history, only the unmasking of moral categories can lead to revolutionary social change. Criticism should not bother to analyze the *manifest* (surface) content—Dickens's moral intention, for example, in dramatizing Pip's remorse—but should focus on the *latent* (buried) collective and ideological meaning, the work's "political unconscious." The literary critic, therefore, should labor to transcend the ethical in the direction of the political (1981: 60).

When Jameson ignored ethical assertions on the face of the text in order to penetrate its ideological mystifications, ethics was subsumed into socio-political realities. He showed that beliefs and traditions people had come to take for granted (Judeo-Christian morality, the Western literary canon) were thoroughly conditioned by a particular historical time and its power relations. And I think we must concede that ethics *can* be ideological, unconsciously sexist or bourgeois or hetero-normative. But for Jameson, ethics were only and always a mask for ideology. By the 1990s, some critics could not accept the totalizing nature of his theory, especially when they recalled their own multi-layered experiences reading the works of great writers. Important literary theorists began strongly to urge that teachers and critics renew questions about the relationship of literary works to human values.[2] Are there ways to understand literature's ethical content outside of the workings of ideology? Can literature offer genuine moral insight? Should literary critics introduce ethical categories and moral concepts into their analyses of literary works? Does the very act of reading literature contain an ethical relationship?

In 1983, a highly regarded academic journal, *New Literary History*, published a special issue devoted to these kinds of questions, with essays by distinguished literary critics and philosophers. It was followed five years later by a similar cluster on literature in the philosophy journal *Ethics* and by major studies by moral philosophers, including Richard Rorty, Stanley Cavell, and Martha Nussbaum.[3] These philosophers made a conscious shift away from the purely linguistic and analytic models of moral inquiry that had been dominant for decades, arguments that are based on the slipperiness of terminology, or "the meaning of meaning." They began to ask questions about how ethics operate personally and concretely, in our day-to-day transactions with others, as private individuals and public citizens living under specific social and political conditions. They felt that linguistic analysis and abstract theoretical propositions alone could not do justice to the density of our ethical lives—could not offer a "thick" description of the messiness of most people's moral decisions and their feelings about their ethical choices. Summaries, abstract propositions, and generalizations are necessary to philosophical argument, but a novel shows us human life in its individualized detail and specificity. Some philosophers began to look to novels, not for dramatizations of a priori moral propositions, but for new contributions to moral knowledge. Novels take up essential questions about human life and conduct non-systematically, and so involve not only the reader's intellect but also her intuition, emotion, memories, and beliefs. Certain works of literature, claimed Nussbaum, "are indispensable to a philosophical inquiry in the ethical sphere: not by any means sufficient, but sources of insight without which the inquiry cannot be complete" (1990: 23–24).

This *narrative turn* in philosophy, as it came to be called, coincided with a similar redirection of interest in English departments toward the real-world and moral consequences of literary study, what was called the *ethical turn*. Crucial works by Wayne Booth, Tobin Siebers, James Phelan, Adam Zachary Newton, and David Parker argued that English criticism should reclaim literary categories that had been relegated to the dustbin by the combined effects of poststructuralism and the hermeneutics of suspicion, questions about fictional characters, point of view, authorial intention, and the presentation of moral ideas in literature. Their works were followed by a wave of scholarly books, collected editions, and major essays on literature and ethics. Indeed, theorists have attempted to explain, define, and validate an ethical approach to literature for over four decades, and they continue to try to work out an inclusive methodology, one that would embrace philosophy, politics, pedagogy, and the experiences of ordinary readers. In a sense, ethical criticism is the most multiform and versatile among the three approaches to close reading I have presented in this book, and so its conflicts and petitions will be the hardest for me to describe (especially as a non-philosopher). Let's say that the crux of ethical criticism goes back to the idea of *intersubjectivity* discussed in Chapter 1 above—the interpersonal, self-to-other, social dimension of reading literature. Ethical criticism assumes that a close reading of a work of literature is always an encounter with *alterity*—a meeting with another consciousness and another world, whether it's the style, voice, or narrative space of the text itself, or the mind of its actual author. Because close reading calls for a response to the "otherness" of literature, it is always a form of ethical conduct. As the existentialist philosopher Jean-Paul Sartre expressed it, literature and all works of art make an appeal to the reader's freedom—to his powers of acceptance or refusal, to listening or not, to talking back or turning away (Sartre 1988: 56–57). Ethical criticism thus asks us to accept the reciprocal nature of literary reading—to step closer to literature's capacity to involve us in complex moral situations and present ideas about how we should live our lives.

To some, ethical criticism seems to trade in bromides and generalizations. There's also a worry that it can slide into universal claims that merely reassert unconscious ideological assumptions, as Jameson argued. Yet often we turn to literary examples, says J. Hillis Miller, not to help us formulate universal rules, but because "we may learn from [fiction] how much on our own we are when we are in a shrewd situation and must make an ethical decision" (2001: 217). Literature helps us see how many-sided moral life almost always is by showing how people live and feel from the inside, without reducing them to flat moral statements. Reading a novel may also provide space in a busy day for reflection about how different people respond to life's problems—to marital strife, worldly desire, fear of death, intellectual defeat, family rivalries, growing old. People are invited to think through these life situations a little more acutely and honestly when they are not presented theoretically, but in the complex particularity of Anna Karenina's desperation, Gatsby's delusions, Pip's remorse. The Czech novelist Milan Kundera wrote that the novel is "an imaginary paradise of individuals," where no one is absolutely right or absolutely wrong, but "everyone has a right to be understood" (1986: 159). Thus the spirit of the novel is *complexity*: "Every novel says to the reader: 'Things are not as simple as you think'" (Kundera 1986: 18–19).

General claims are, in a sense, unavoidable. Yet ethical critics strive to steer clear of proscriptive judgments based only on their own values, which they see as evolving, capable of being revised by another reading of the work at a different time. It's true that ethical critics do not idealize Matthew Arnold's virtue of disinterestedness the way objective critics may. Yet Arnold was an ethical critic if there ever was one, and a true liberal in his faith in the value of open-minded and rational discussion; he believed fervently that great works of literature could ennoble and animate modern people, address their confusion, and contribute to their moral development. The late revival of ethical criticism may be driven by a similar belief that engaging in ethical problems is a central mission of the humanities, and that English departments should reclaim the value of literature and reading for civic education. For when we really weigh a text's implicit arguments, mull over the author's viewpoint, and think about the implications of the world and the people she has placed before us, our mind has gone out to meet another's perspective, and we are troubled to assess and understand the view of life we temporarily inhabit as readers.

Some ethical criticism argues that literary readers and critics should be made aware of the ethical contract reading entails, and be held accountable to it. Close reading under this approach means that the reader is never exempt from making judgments and choices—we must figure out on our own if we believe a character's actions are cowardly or defiant, if the world the author has shown us is just or evil, if we understand, accept, or reject the ethical perspective implied in the story that's being told, and in the way it is told. And we can only sort out these important matters by close reading—giving our attention to the work itself, getting inside the story, living through the story as if it were our own.

There are several strands to the ethical turn, and most scholars who have attempted to trace this movement's trajectory have acknowledged its great diversity of thought. The ethical turn now incorporates thinkers from many traditions and backgrounds, converging to form what Michael Eskin has called "a burgeoning subdiscipline" in literary studies (Eskin 2004: 557).[4] In this chapter, I drastically limit my treatment to some controlling ideas and the work of a few influential critics. Although they may have different focuses, these ethical critics are united in agreeing that the first step in ethical criticism is to *assent* to the reading (rather than suspect or resist the text). The second step is to make sure of one's interpretation, to conscientiously explicate the text's operations—to do a good close reading!

The last important step is to form a judgment or develop an argument about the text according to certain moral criteria. *What* criteria are perhaps the most difficult determination for ethical criticism. For a conscientious and sensitive critic does not want to read literature as a prescriptive list of acceptable or unacceptable ideas. That kind of legalistic, policing attitude violates the plurality of artistic expression and intellectual inquiry. An ethical critic who happens to be a Christian *may* find reasons not to recommend Margaret Atwood's *The Handmaid's Tale*, but it shouldn't be because the author's implied atheism contradicts his faith, just as an atheist shouldn't assume *Paradise Lost* has nothing to offer because it presents a Christian worldview. But should a black reader be open-minded about offensive language in *Huckleberry Finn*? Should a Jewish reader set aside his discomfort with some of T. S. Eliot's poetry? Should a woman be untroubled by the perceived misogyny in *The Taming of the Shrew*? An ethical critic is compelled to grapple with these types of questions and responses. Importantly, she does not simply assert her opinion about a novel or a film based on her own beliefs; she also must publicly interrogate the basis of that judgment and those beliefs in light of what the text says or implies. As Booth puts it, "every reader must be his or her own ethical critic" (1988: 237). As we will see, when a reader is honest about her judgments, ethical criticism can be extremely difficult and sometimes uncomfortably self-revealing.

It's important to grasp that ethical critics are not interested in measuring a novel's value against a moral scale; they are concerned with the communicative situation of reading. Ethical criticism is rooted in the space of narrative itself. As James Phelan puts it, narratives always entail "somebody telling somebody else on some occasion and for some purpose(s) that something has happened" (2005: 18). And unlike abstract moral rules, the precise and singular identity of these "somebodies" and "somethings" is almost endlessly varied and complexly layered—a story could have a narrative structure of "somebody telling us that somebody is telling somebody else that something happened" or "somebody telling somebody else (who may or may not be present to the speaker) or even himself or herself on some occasion for some purpose..." etc. (Phelan 2005: 20, 162). Ethical critics and philosophers who've taken the narrative turn tend to agree that, when it comes to ethics, the value of literature over philosophy is its infinite variations on these acts of telling, on its concrete particularity. So, like the New Critics and the subjectivists, ethical critics are not concerned with sweeping claims about literary movements, historical contexts, or the development of a genre. What is important is the point of contact between reader and text—the attentiveness of close reading.

It's appropriate, then, that in this last chapter we read a few literary works in their entirety. All of my examples will be works of fiction, for although ethical critics have certainly taken poetry as their subject, both literary scholars and philosophers have argued persuasively that stories have always been fundamental to the way human beings comprehend the world. "No human being, literate or not, escapes the effects of stories," says Wayne Booth, "because everyone tells them and listens to them" (1988: 39). "For human beings, the pull of stories is primal. What oxygen is to our bodies, stories are to our emotions and imagination," asserts Marshall Gregory (2009: 19). And although we may sometimes decide not to listen to some stories, most of the time we accept the invitations stories extend to us, almost every day of our lives. This is undoubtedly because narratives offer great pleasure. Yet stories also go a small way toward satisfying our craving for a deeper understanding of ourselves and others. Fiction, in Gregory's words, can "liberate our minds and hearts from the limitations of the everyday" (2009: 22), creating an opening for new kinds of knowledge and a more elaborated experience of our world.

> There is one point at which the moral sense and the artistic sense lie very near together; that is, in the light of the very obvious truth that the deepest quality of a work of art will always be the quality of the mind of the producer.
>
> (James 1948: 21)

> Poetry is closer to rhetoric than we today are willing to admit.
>
> (Trilling 1957: 281)

The American literary critic Wayne Booth, who died in 2005, is perhaps the best-known and most influential promoter of ethical criticism in North America. He was a vastly erudite scholar, with books and essays on authors as different as Chaucer and Freud, Austen and Derrida. He was also an eloquent spokesperson for teaching as a vocation, and a lifelong defender of liberal arts education.

Booth was trained at the University of Chicago in the 1940s, by the so-called Neo-Aristotelians (also called the Chicago School). These critics wanted to establish a different critical methodology from that of the New Critics, one based on Aristotle's *Poetics*. They emphasized genre, plot, and the structure of a literary work, rather than nuances of language, such as paradox, irony, and ambiguity. They were also intensely interested in *rhetoric*, the art of persuasion, which Aristotle thought was always connected to the project of virtue.

In 1961, Booth published a groundbreaking work called *The Rhetoric of Fiction*, where he argued with great skill and suggestiveness that all narratives have designs upon our moral selves. He analyzed the nature of a novel's "invitations" through both the ideas expressed in the text and its rhetorical features, studying in particular the manipulation of perspective and types of narration: dramatized, personal, impersonal, reliable, and unreliable. Booth believed that the presentation of the author's "official self," what he called the *implied author*, had a central moral function in the literary work. He creatively reimagined an argument going back to Plato: that a poem or a story is itself an act, a *doing*—something created by someone, deploying certain techniques, in order to produce certain effects on real people in the political sphere (1968: 113).

Novelists great and small are adept at using rhetorical strategies power-fully, subtly, and imaginatively, and readers or critics who think they have the mental power to resist the ethical influences of literature are probably less immune than they believe. "Perhaps," writes Booth,

> we underestimate the extent to which we absorb the values of what we read. And even when we do not retain them, the fact remains that insofar as the fiction has *worked* for us, we have lived with its values for the duration: we have been *that kind of person* for at least as long as we remained in the presence of the work.
>
> (1988: 41, original italics)

So when Booth refers to ethics in literature, he means something much larger than setting up moral standards or making up a list of good and bad books. He is interested in *what kind of person* we become when we meet the mind of a particular author—the "character" or "person" or "self" that is in the process of being known and shaped in the act of reading. "From ancient Greece to the present," he writes, "the word 'ethos' has meant something like 'character' or 'collection of habitual characteris-tics,'" and we express our ethos, our character, by our choices and habits. "Ethical criticism attempts to describe the encounters of a story-teller's ethos with that of the reader or listener," he claims (1988: 8). So Booth's concept of ethical criticism relies strongly on the communicative dimension of reading literature, its effects in the world, and especially on the idea of building character. Reading literature and writing criticism are human-centered practices for Booth, and the implications of these activities for human conduct is at the root of all his work.

The Company We Keep: An Ethics of Fiction, published in 1988, con-tinued the rhetorical project of *The Rhetoric of Fiction*, and is Booth's most sustained and developed treatment of ethical criticism, a book he spent almost ten years writing. At over 500 pages, it is a capacious, lively, and still influential study of the value and challenge of ethical criticism. I won't be able to do justice to the abundance of Booth's intelligence and the breadth of his examples here, but a couple points are key to his argument. First, Booth argues that we should revive the nineteenth-century metaphor of *friendship* for the relationship that exists between readers and books. For just as when we meet a new person in life, we size up the value for us of the books we encounter, calculating the possibility for knowledge, trust, delight, excitement, or wisdom. Booth cites Aristotle's concept of three kinds of friendship: friendships of pleasure and delight, friendships of per-sonal profit or gain, and friendships of virtue, or of "a kind of company that is not only pleasant or profitable, in some immediate way, but is also ... good for its own sake" (1988: 175). The three kinds almost always overlap, and they do not need to be thought of hierarchically, but for Booth, the third kind clearly represents the fullest form of companionship because it is a "relation of virtue with virtue," a mutually helpful and permanent relationship that improves the quality of both people's lives—it is the best kind of company, the company we keep (1988: 174).

Booth claims "the implied authors of *all* stories," from the most elevated to the most mundane, "purport to offer one or another of these friendships" (1988: 174). Furthermore, every reader judges herself as she judges the offer of friendship, for her response to the offer is always on a continuum of affirmation or withholding—in other words, it is never passive, but always a mode of active volition, as the reader assents or not to the text's "pattern of desiring" or its "spectrums of quality." Booth identifies seven levels of engagement proffered by every work of fiction, and goes on to explain precisely how they operate in all of our literary judgments. The following passage, a nice example of Booth's style, fleshes out the friendship metaphor. I've placed the seven levels italicized in square brackets:

> In our living friends, we find these same variables. Some of them offer a lot of whatever they are good at; others offer precious gems though few [*quantity*]. Some dominate the conversation, or try to, while others offer to play an equal role, and yet others ask *us* to dominate [*reciprocity*]. Some open themselves to a bold and potentially healing intimacy, revealing our own depths or depths we never dreamed of, while others politely preserve our illusions ... [*intimacy*]. Some wake us up or scare us off by the intensity and pace of their offering, while others are satisfied with a steady or slack pace that may console or bore us [*intensity*]. Some are sufficiently coherent to make us feel that we are dealing with a whole person, a solid character, while others feel shallow or devious, flabby or unreliable [*coherence*]. Some companions fit our old ways like old comfortable shoes and others are *so* "other" as to shock, shatter, and either destroy or re-mold us [*distance*]. And finally, some offer us only one kind of pleasure or profit while others range over many of life's values [*range of kinds*].
>
> (1988: 179–180)

Booth argues that almost every conceivable reworking of these seven variables has, at one time or another, been set down as the critical benchmark for great literature. But in fact, readers seek a balance among all these features, weighing and measuring their worth according to what's best for them at the time, based not on general rules or categorical imperatives, but on their expanding literary experiences and their ongoing conversations with others.

Booth takes the novel *Jaws*, Peter Benchley's 1974 bestseller, as a test case of readerly judgment. The *intensity* of the book may be high if Booth succumbs to reveling in the bloodshed, and the *intimacy* and *reciprocity* depend on whether or not Booth thinks Benchley believes in what he's doing or is a cynical hack. But *Jaws* is a friend that lets him down chiefly on the level of its *range*. The novel wants him to fear what is "other" without understanding it, to mold his ethos into a limited, bifurcated shape of "victims" and "villains" (1988: 202–204). Even if he is titillated by a sentence like, "They fumbled with each other's clothing, twined limbs around limbs, and thrashed with urgent ardour on the cold sand," the future rewards of continuing to read are not worth it to Booth. The novel asks him to both fear and desire scenes of spectacular bloodshed, to hope for death for characters who don't matter, and safety for the good guys, who don't matter much more (1988: 203). If he assents to the ethical vision of *Jaws*, he will become *"that kind of desirer* with precisely the kinds of strengths and weaknesses that the author has built into his structure" (1988: 204, original italics). So, because Booth doesn't like who he is or what's expected of him ethically when he's reading *Jaws*, he puts it aside after the first few chapters.

Is Booth's evaluation of *Jaws* narrow-minded? After all, the book sold over twenty million copies! His judgment runs the risk of making ethical criticism seem aloof and scolding, as if he is determined to spoil the reader's pleasure. What's wrong with reading for sheer entertainment, or for the satisfactions offered by a suspenseful, well-constructed plot? An ethical critic would reply that there's nothing wrong with being hooked by *Jaws*, or by any other novel you choose to read, but you should be minimally aware of the structuring of your desires while you are reading (or watching); suspense-filled entertainment is not innocent of ethical force. Booth's practice of ethical critique helped him to determine that the implied author of *Jaws* was not a good friend for him, not someone he wanted to dwell with for the time being, thereby foreclosing opportunities to meet better, more helpful friends, who "demonstrate their friendship not only in the range and depth and intensity of pleasure they offer, but finally in the irresistible invitation they extend to live during these moments a richer and fuller life than I could manage on my own" (1988: 223).[5]

Some critics have taken issue with Booth's friendship metaphor, finding it obsolete or simplistic—indeed, Charles Altieri suggests that sometimes we value texts because they are challenging, highly interesting *enemies* that spur our engagement (2001: 38). But even this accepts provisionally the interpersonal dimension to our appraisal of a novel or story. Some thirty years after *The Company We Keep*, contemporary theorists readily equate textual encounters with human encounters. According to Lawrence Buell, the idea of reading as "a scene of virtual interpersonality that enacts, activates, or otherwise illuminates ethical responsibility may ... prove one of the most significant innovations of the literature-and-ethics movement"

(1999: 13). Probably the most influential philosopher in contemporary ethical criticism has been Emmanuel Levinas, whose writings on the ethical significance of the face-to-face encounter in real life have been frequently applied to literary encounters. "One faces a text as one might face a person," according to Adam Zachary Newton, "having to confront the claims raised by that very immediacy, an immediacy of contact, not of meaning" (1995: 11).

Ethical criticism is not about bullying a work of art into moral submission. But judgment is not optional—in fact, a negative judgment, such as Booth's on *Jaws*, can reveal the ways in which unwelcome, even damaging, ethical invitations may be presented rhetorically as funny, suspenseful, or harmlessly diverting. In his book, *Shaped by Stories*, Marshall Gregory, another Chicagoan, does a close reading of a well-known and much loved comic story by James Thurber, author of *The Secret Life of Walter Mitty*, to explain how a reader enters into an implied author's ethical vision under the guise of mere entertainment. The story first appeared in *The New Yorker* magazine, in 1942. Here it is in full.

The Catbird Seat

James Thurber

Mr. Martin bought the pack of Camels on Monday night in the most crowded cigar store on Broadway. It was theatre time and seven or eight men were buying cigarettes. The clerk didn't even glance at Mr. Martin, who put the pack in his overcoat pocket and went out. If any of the staff at F & S had seen him buy the cigarettes, they would have been astonished, for it was generally known that Mr. Martin did not smoke, and never had. No one saw him.

It was just a week to the day since Mr. Martin had decided to rub out Mrs. Ulgine Barrows. The term "rub out" pleased him because it suggested nothing more than the correction of an error—in this case an error of Mr. Fitweiler. Mr. Martin had spent each night of the past week working out his plan and examining it. As he walked home now he went over it again. For the hundredth time he resented the element of imprecision, the margin of guesswork that entered into the business. The project as he had worked it out was casual and bold, the risks were considerable. Something might go wrong anywhere along the line. And therein lay the cunning of his scheme. No one would ever see in it the cautious, painstaking hand of Erwin Martin, head of the filing department at F & S, of whom Mr. Fitweiler had once said, "Man is fallible but Martin isn't." No one would see his hand, that is, unless it were caught in the act.

Sitting in his apartment, drinking a glass of milk, Mr. Martin reviewed his case against Mrs. Ulgine Barrows, as he had every night for seven nights. He began at the beginning. Her quacking voice and braying laugh had first profaned the halls of F & S on March 7, 1941 (Mr. Martin had a head for dates). Old Roberts, the personnel chief, had introduced her as the newly appointed special adviser to the president of the firm, Mr. Fitweiler. The woman had appalled Mr. Martin instantly, but he hadn't shown it. He had given her his dry hand, a look of studious concentration, and a faint smile. "Well," she had said, looking at the papers on his desk, "are you lifting the oxcart out of the ditch?" As Mr. Martin recalled that moment, over his milk, he squirmed slightly. He must keep his mind on her crimes as a special adviser, not on her peccadillos as a personality. This he found difficult to do, in spite of entering an objection and sustaining it. The faults of the woman as a woman kept chattering on in his mind like an unruly witness. She had, for almost two years now, baited him. In the halls, in the elevator, even in his own office, into which she romped now and then like a circus horse, she was constantly shouting these silly questions at him. "Are you lifting the oxcart out of the ditch? Are you tearing up the pea patch? Are you hollering down the rain barrel? Are you scraping around the bottom of the pickle barrel? Are you sitting in the catbird seat?"

It was Joey Hart, one of Mr. Martin's two assistants, who had explained what the gibberish meant. "She must be a Dodger fan," he had said. "Red Barber announces the Dodger games over the radio and he uses those expressions—picked 'em up down South." Joey had gone on to explain one or two. "Tearing up the pea patch" meant going on a rampage; "sitting in the catbird seat" means sitting pretty, like a batter with three balls and no strikes on him. Mr. Martin dismissed all this with an effort. It had been annoying, it had driven him near to distraction, but he was too solid a man to be moved to murder by anything so childish. It was fortunate, he reflected as he passed on to the important charges against Mrs. Barrows, that he had stood up under it so well. He had maintained always an outward appearance of polite tolerance. "Why, I even believe you like the woman," Miss Paird, his other assistant, had once said to him. He had simply smiled.

A gavel rapped in Mr. Martin's mind and the case proper was resumed. Mrs. Ulgine Barrows stood charged with willful, blatant, and persistent attempts to destroy the efficiency and system of F & S. It was competent, material, and relevant to review her advent and rise to power. Mr. Martin had got the story from Miss Paird, who seemed always able to find things out. According to her, Mrs. Barrows had met Mr. Fitweiler at a party, where she had rescued him from the embraces of a powerfully built drunken man who had mistaken the president of F & S for a famous retired Middle Western football coach. She had led him to a sofa and somehow worked upon him a monstrous magic. The aging gentleman had jumped to the conclusion there and then that this was a woman of singular attainments, equipped to bring out the best in him and in the firm. A week later he had introduced her into F & S as his special adviser. On that day confusion got its foot in the door. After Miss Tyson, Mr. Brundage, and Mr. Bartlett had been fired and Mr. Munson had taken his hat and stalked out, mailing in his resignation later, old Roberts had been emboldened to speak to Mr. Fitweiler. He mentioned that Mr. Munson's department had been "a little disrupted" and hadn't they perhaps better resume the old system there? Mr. Fitweiler had said certainly not. He had the greatest faith in Mrs. Barrows' ideas. "They require a little seasoning, a little seasoning, is all," he had added. Mr. Roberts had given it up. Mr. Martin reviewed in detail all the changes wrought by Mrs. Barrows. She had begun chipping at the cornices of the firm's edifice and now she was swinging at the foundation stones with a pickaxe.

Mr. Martin came now, in his summing up, to the afternoon of Monday, November 2, 1942—just one week ago. On that day, at 3 PM, Mrs. Barrows had bounced into his office. "Boo!" she had yelled. "Are you scraping around the bottom of the pickle barrel?" Mr. Martin had looked at her from under his green eyeshade, saying nothing. She had begun to wander about the office, taking it in with her great, popping eyes. "Do you really need all these filing cabinets?" she had demanded suddenly. Mr. Martin's heart had jumped. "Each of these files," he had said, keeping his voice even, "plays an indispensable part in the system of F & S." She had brayed at him, "Well, don't tear up the pea patch!" and gone to the door. From there she had bawled, "But you sure have got a lot of fine scrap in here!" Mr. Martin could no longer doubt that the finger was on his beloved department. Her pickaxe was on the upswing, poised for the first blow. It had not come yet; he had received no blue memo from the enchanted Mr. Fitweiler bearing nonsensical instructions deriving from the obscene woman. But there was no doubt in Mr. Martin's mind that one would be forthcoming. He must act quickly. Already a precious week had gone by. Mr. Martin stood up in his living room, still holding his milk glass. "Gentlemen of the jury," he said to himself, "I demand the death penalty for this horrible person."

The next day Mr. Martin followed his routine, as usual. He polished his glasses more often and once sharpened an already sharp pencil, but not even Miss Paird noticed. Only once did he catch sight of his victim; she swept past him in the hall with a patronizing "Hi!" At five-thirty he walked home, as usual, and had a glass of milk, as usual. He had never drunk anything stronger in his life—unless you could count ginger ale. The late Sam Schlosser, the S of F & S, had praised Mr. Martin at a staff meeting several years before for his temperate habits. "Our most efficient worker neither drinks nor smokes," he had said. "The results speak for themselves." Mr. Fitweiler had sat by, nodding approval.

Mr. Martin was still thinking about that red-letter day as he walked over to the Schrafft's on Fifth Avenue near Forty-sixth Street. He got there, as he always did, at eight o'clock. He finished his dinner and the financial page of the *Sun* at a quarter to nine, as he always did. It was his custom after dinner to take a walk. This time he walked down Fifth Avenue at a casual pace. His gloved hands felt moist and warm, his forehead cold. He transferred the Camels from his overcoat to a jacket pocket. He wondered, as he did so, if they did not represent an unnecessary note of strain. Mrs. Barrows smoked only Luckies. It was his idea to puff a few puffs on a Camel (after the rubbing-out), stub it out in the ashtray holding her lipstick-stained Luckies, and thus drag a small red herring across the trail. Perhaps it was not a good idea. It would take time. He might even choke, too loudly.

Mr. Martin had never seen the house on West Twelfth Street where Mrs. Barrows lived, but he had a clear enough picture of it. Fortunately, she had bragged to everybody about her ducky first-floor apartment in the perfectly darling three-story red-brick. There would be no doorman or other attendants; just the tenants of the second and third floors. As he walked along, Mr. Martin realized that he would get there before nine-thirty. He had considered walking north on Fifth Avenue from Schrafft's to a point from which it would take him until ten o'clock to reach the house. At that hour people were less likely to be coming in or going out. But the procedure would have made an awkward loop in the straight thread of his casualness and he had abandoned it. It was impossible to figure when people would be entering or leaving the house, anyway. There was a great risk at any hour. If he ran into anybody, he would simply have to place the rubbing-out of Ulgine Barrows in the inactive file forever. The same thing would hold true if there were someone in her apartment. In that case he would just say that he had been passing by, recognized her charming house, and thought to drop in.

It was eighteen minutes after nine when Mr. Martin turned into Twelfth Street. A man passed him, and a man and a woman, talking. There was no one within fifty paces when he came to the house, halfway down the block. He was up the steps and in the small vestibule in no time, pressing the bell under the card that said "Mrs. Ulgine Barrows." When the clicking in the lock started, he jumped forward against the door. He got inside fast, closing the door behind him. A bulb in a lantern hung from the hall ceiling on a chain seemed to give a monstrously bright light. There was nobody on the stair, which went up ahead of him along the left wall. A door opened down the hall in the wall on the right. He went toward it swiftly, on tiptoe.

"Well, for God's sake, look who's here!" bawled Mrs. Barrows, and her braying laugh rang out like the report of a shotgun. He rushed past her like a football tackle, bumping her. "Hey, quit shoving!" she said, closing the door behind them. They were in her living room, which seemed to Mr. Martin to be lighted by a hundred lamps. "What's after you?" she said. "You're as jumpy as a goat." He found he was unable to speak. His heart was wheezing in his throat. "I—yes," he finally brought out. She was jabbering and laughing as she started to help him off with his coat. "No, no," he said. "I'll put it here." He took it off and put it on a chair near the door. "Your hat and gloves, too," she said. "You're in a lady's house." He put his hat on top of the coat. Mrs. Barrows seemed larger than he had thought. He kept his gloves on. "I was passing by," he said. "I recognized—is there anyone here?" She laughed louder than ever. "No," she said, "we're all alone. You're as white as a sheet, you funny man. Whatever has come over you? I'll mix you a toddy." She started toward a door across the room. "Scotch-and-soda be all right? But say, you don't drink, do you?" She turned and gave him her amused look. Mr. Martin pulled himself together. "Scotch-and-soda will be all right," he heard himself say. He could hear her laughing in the kitchen.

Mr. Martin looked quickly around the living room for the weapon. He had counted on finding one there. There were andirons and a poker and something in a corner that looked like an Indian club. None of them would do. It couldn't be that way. He began to pace around. He came to a desk. On it lay a metal paper knife with an ornate handle. Would it be sharp enough? He reached for it and knocked over a small brass jar. Stamps spilled out of it and it fell to the floor with a clatter. "Hey," Mrs. Barrows yelled from the kitchen, "are you tearing up the pea patch?" Mr. Martin gave a strange laugh. Picking up the knife, he tried its point against his left wrist. It was blunt. It wouldn't do.

When Mrs. Barrows reappeared, carrying two highballs, Mr. Martin, standing there with his gloves on, became acutely conscious of the fantasy he had wrought. Cigarettes in his pocket, a drink prepared for him—it was all too grossly improbable. It was more than that; it was impossible. Somewhere in the back of his mind a vague idea stirred, sprouted. "For heaven's sake, take off those gloves," said Mrs. Barrows. "I always wear them in the house," said Mr. Martin. The idea began to bloom, strange and wonderful. She put the glasses on a coffee table in front of the sofa and sat on the sofa. "Come over here, you odd little man," she said. Mr. Martin went over and sat beside her. It was difficult getting a cigarette out of the pack of Camels, but he managed it. She held a match for him, laughing. "Well," she said, handing him his drink, "this is perfectly marvellous. You with a drink and a cigarette."

Mr. Martin puffed, not too awkwardly, and took a gulp of the highball. "I drink and smoke all the time," he said. He clinked his glass against hers. "Here's nuts to that old windbag, Fitweiler," he said, and gulped again. The stuff tasted awful, but he made no grimace. "Really, Mr. Martin," she said, her voice and posture changing, "you are insulting our employer." Mrs. Barrows was now all special adviser to the president. "I am preparing a bomb," said Mr. Martin, "which will blow the old goat higher than hell." He had only had a little of the drink, which was not strong. It couldn't be that. "Do you take dope or something?" Mrs. Barrows asked coldly. "Heroin," said Mr. Martin. "I'll be coked to the gills when I bump that old buzzard off." "Mr. Martin!" she shouted, getting to her feet.

"That will be all of that. You must go at once." Mr. Martin took another swallow of his drink. He tapped his cigarette out in the ashtray and put the pack of Camels on the coffee table. Then he got up. She stood glaring at him. He walked over and put on his hat and coat. "Not a word about this," he said, and laid an index finger against his lips. All Mrs. Barrows could bring out was "Really!" Mr. Martin put his hand on the doorknob. "I'm sitting in the catbird seat," he said. He stuck his tongue out at her and left. Nobody saw him go.

Mr. Martin got to his apartment, walking, well before eleven. No one saw him go in. He had two glasses of milk after brushing his teeth, and he felt elated. It wasn't tipsiness, because he hadn't been tipsy. Anyway, the walk had worn off all effects of the whiskey. He got in bed and read a magazine for a while. He was asleep before midnight.

Mr. Martin got to the office at eight-thirty the next morning, as usual. At a quarter to nine, Ulgine Barrows, who had never before arrived at work before ten, swept into his office. "I'm reporting to Mr. Fitweiler now!" she shouted. "If he turns you over to the police, it's no more than you deserve!" Mr. Martin gave her a look of shocked surprise. "I beg your pardon?" he said. Mrs. Barrows snorted and bounced out of the room, leaving Miss Paird and Joey Hart staring after her. "What's the matter with that old devil now?" asked Miss Paird. "I have no idea," said Mr. Martin, resuming his work. The other two looked at him and then at each other. Miss Paird got up and went out. She walked slowly past the closed door of Mr. Fitweiler's office. Mrs. Barrows was yelling inside, but she was not braying. Miss Paird could not hear what the woman was saying. She went back to her desk.

Forty-five minutes later, Mrs. Barrows left the president's office and went into her own, shutting the door. It wasn't until half an hour later that Mr. Fitweiler sent for Mr. Martin. The head of the filing department, neat, quiet, attentive, stood in front of the old man's desk. Mr. Fitweiler was pale and nervous. He took his glasses off and twiddled them. He made a small, bruffing sound in his throat. "Martin," he said, "you have been with us more than twenty years." "Twenty-two, sir," said Mr. Martin. "In that time," pursued the president, "your work and your—uh—manner have been exemplary." "I trust so, sir," said Mr. Martin. "I have understood, Martin," said Mr. Fitweiler, "that you have never taken a drink or smoked." "That is correct, sir," said Mr. Martin. "Ah, yes." Mr. Fitweiler polished his glasses. "You may describe what you did after leaving the office yesterday, Martin," he said. Mr. Martin allowed less than a second for his bewildered pause. "Certainly, sir," he said. "I walked home. Then I went to Schrafft's for dinner. Afterward I walked home again. I went to bed early, sir, and read a magazine for a while. I was asleep before eleven." "Ah, yes," said Mr. Fitweiler again. He was silent for a moment, searching for the proper words to say to the head of the filing department. "Mrs. Barrows," he said finally, "Mrs. Barrows has worked hard, Martin, very hard. It grieves me to report that she has suffered a severe breakdown. It has taken the form of a persecution complex accompanied by distressing hallucinations." "I am very sorry, sir," said Mr. Martin. "Mrs. Barrows is under the delusion," continued Mr. Fitweiler, "that you visited her last evening and behaved yourself in an—uh—unseemly manner." He raised his hand to silence Mr. Martin's little pained outcry. "It is the nature of these psychological diseases," Mr. Fitweiler said, "to fix upon the least likely and most innocent party as the—uh—source of persecution. These matters are not for the lay mind to grasp, Martin. I've just had my psychiatrist, Dr. Fitch, on the phone. He would not, of course, commit himself, but he made enough generalizations to substantiate my suspicions. I suggested to Mrs. Barrows, when she had completed her—uh—story to me this morning, that she visit Dr. Fitch, for I suspected a condition at once. She flew, I regret to say, into a rage, and demanded—uh—requested that I call you on the carpet. You may not know, Martin, but Mrs. Barrows had planned a reorganization of your department—subject to my approval, of course, subject to my approval. This brought you, rather than anyone else, to her mind—but again that is a phenomenon for Dr. Fitch and not for us. So, Martin, I am afraid Mrs. Barrows' usefulness here is at an end." "I am dreadfully sorry, sir," said Mr. Martin.

It was at this point that the door to the office blew open with the suddenness of a gas-main explosion and Mrs. Barrows catapulted through it. "Is the little rat denying it?" she screamed. "He can't get away with that!" Mr. Martin got up and moved discreetly to a point beside Mr. Fitweiler's chair. "You drank and smoked at my apartment," she bawled at Mr. Martin, "and you know it! You called Mr. Fitweiler an old windbag and said you were going to blow him up when you got coked to the gills on your heroin!" She stopped yelling to catch her breath and a new glint came into her popping eyes. "If you weren't such a drab, ordinary little man," she said, "I'd think you'd planned it all. Sticking your tongue out, saying you were sitting in the catbird seat, because you thought no one would believe me when I told it! My God, it's really too perfect!" She brayed loudly and hysterically, and the fury was on her again. She glared at Mr. Fitweiler. "Can't you see how he has tricked us, you old fool? Can't you see his little game?" But Mr. Fitweiler had been surreptitiously pressing all the buttons under the top of his desk and employees of F & S began pouring into the room. "Stockton," said Mr. Fitweiler, "you and Fishbein will take Mrs. Barrows to her home. Mrs. Powell, you will go with them." Stockton, who had played a little football in high school, blocked Mrs. Barrows as she made for Mr. Martin. It took him and Fishbein together to force her out of the door into the hall, crowded with stenographers and office boys. She was still screaming imprecations at Mr. Martin, tangled and contradictory imprecations. The hubbub finally died out down in the corridor.

"I regret that this happened," said Mr. Fitweiler. "I shall ask you to dismiss it from your mind, Martin." "Yes, sir," said Mr. Martin, anticipating his chief's "That will be all" by moving to the door. "I will dismiss it." He went out and shut the door, and his step was light and quick in the hall. When he entered his department he had slowed down to his customary gait, and he walked quietly across the room to the W20 file, wearing a look of studious concentration.

Marshall Gregory asserts that the ethical vision of "The Catbird Seat" is driven by Thurber's tone and his heightened use of metaphors to shape the reader's attitudes, which turn on the desire to see meek Mr. Martin triumph over threatening and obnoxious Mrs. Ulgine Barrows. Mr. Martin is a recognizable type, the tiny bureaucrat who has no identity outside of the system, a character often satirized but seldom made into the hero of the narrative (which is Thurber's genius). To get the reader to root for Mr. Martin, whose smoldering, murderous violence is another comic stroke, Mrs. Barrows must be guilty of a heinous crime, or at least something that affirms for the reader that she is asking for it. Gregory asserts that Thurber's *style* makes it clear what she's guilty of: "She is guilty of not being a human being, she is guilty of being bestial, and, most of all, she is guilty of being an 'uppity' woman in a man's world" (Gregory 2009: 133).

First of all, her name is a condemnation of her deficient femininity: "Ulgine" is a hideous word which on the page looks anagrammatically like "ugly" and could be (mis)pronounced that way. Her surname is the word for a castrated male pig, a "barrow pig" (surely not an innocent decision for Thurber, who went to an agricultural college in Ohio in the early part of the twentieth century). Gregory asserts that the character's name deprives her of both her humanity and her sex—she's "an unnatural monster," who stands before the reader saturated with unpleasant associations before we know anything about her opinions, character, or conduct (2009: 133). Furthermore, Thurber hammers home her animal nature in "her quacking voice and braying laugh" (a cross between a duck and an ass) and in a series of other demeaning descriptions: she "romped now and then like a circus horse," she "snorted and bounced out of the room," she *bawls*, she *brays*, and she has "great popping eyes" that remind the reader of a frog.

Besides being bestial and unsexed, Mrs. Barrows is a destroyer who wields the tools of men: "She had begun by chipping at the cornices of the firm's edifice and now she was swinging at the foundation stones with a pickaxe." Mr. Martin thinks, "the faults of the woman *as a woman* kept chattering on in his mind like an unruly witness," suggesting, says Gregory, that Mrs. Barrows's sins are not that she is loud, aggressive, and opinionated, but that *women* are wrong to be this way (2009: 136). Thurber takes for granted that the reader will assent to this opinion, because he has established sympathy for poor Mr. Martin's position; readers *do* laugh at Mrs. Barrows and want Mr. Martin to win out so completely that she'll never threaten him again. If Mrs. Barrows were a man, argues Gregory,

Mr. Martin's scheming might tell against his character, because men are permitted to be loud and aggressive. But it is doubly humiliating for Mr. Martin to lose his precious filing system to a forceful woman, and so she must be punished for overreaching. Also, because even large, "braying" women are prone to hysteria and mental instability, it only takes a phone call to Dr. Fitch for Mr. Fitweiler to conclude that Mrs. Barrows is having a "nervous breakdown." The men readily close ranks against her. "Nothing in the story suggests," urges Gregory, "that Thurber has anything but complacent confidence that his readers will overwhelmingly agree with his misogynistic, mean, belittling joke" (2009: 137).

Gregory concedes that this widely anthologized story is an example of brilliantly effective comic writing. He sees that Thurber's plot is very skillfully constructed, that in its lively and humorous style, its compact characterization, and its tightly condensed presentation of conflict, climax, and resolution, "The Catbird Seat" is a very artfully written story, and a funny one. Yet for Gregory, the ethical vision that informs Thurber's artistic brilliance makes it deeply troubling: "in the end, my approval of the art of the story is undermined by my realization that to yield to this art is to yield to the misogynistic message unfolding inside it" (2009: 140). Still, he conscientiously tests the fairness of his response. Is he being "dour, puritanical, and humorless," denouncing as immoral a story he simply dislikes? Doesn't Thurber have a right to satirize any target he wants? Chaucer poked fun at the Wife of Bath, Shakespeare at shrewish Katherine Minola, Jane Austen at Lady Catherine de Bourgh—why should Thurber be condemned for his portrait of an obnoxious woman? Gregory says the difference in Thurber's treatment of human frailty is that Mrs. Barrows's faults are not individualized, but assigned to her on the basis of received ideas—sexist ideas—about women's social role. The problem with Thurber's treatment is that he

> ridicules Mrs. Barrows's character not by portraying an obnoxious character who happens to be a woman, but by relying on ready-made anti-woman stereotypes as the grounds of his criticism. He doesn't work to *earn* our antipathy. Instead he draws brilliantly but with intellectual laziness and ethical malice on many centuries of standing antipathy toward "uppity" women.
>
> (Gregory 2009: 135)

Thurber exploits, and so reinforces, sexist stereotypes, thereby inviting readers to feel contempt for Mrs. Barrows and all women "who are strong enough and driven enough to be called 'uppity' by those who want all women to meet traditional expectations of subservience" (2009: 135).

Gregory concludes that his judgment isn't final, and he invites further conversation, insisting that in ethical criticism "discussion is needed, *not* in order for one view to win out over all others but in order for us to learn what we think is important" (2009: 122). Indeed, another reader might see the story as a satire of the bland, obedient conformity represented by Mr. Martin and his co-workers, which cannot contain or comprehend the energy of Mrs. Barrows, with her colorful language and larger-than-life personality. Other readers might object that Gregory is applying twenty-first-century ideas about women's roles to a story written in the 1940s, and that to appreciate Thurber's brilliance requires both more imagination than Gregory is able to conjure, and more social and cultural contexts. Is it possible to read "The Catbird Seat" as a satire of timid, silly *men* who don't know how to handle confident, authoritative women? Or should we argue that looking at gender misses the real target of satire, which may be the genre of American pulp or *noir* crime fiction that was so popular in the 1940s? The answer to these sorts of queries would require another close reading of the story, more analysis of Thurber's style and tone—and more critical discussion.

I'd like to give one more example of ethical criticism along the same lines, borrowed from James Phelan's *Experiencing Fiction*. Phelan was Booth's student at Chicago, and he has written many books and articles about narrative theory and rhetorical approaches to reading fiction. The short story that follows, by the American writer Ambrose Bierce, was published in 1899.

The Crimson Candle

Ambrose Bierce

A man lying at the point of death called his wife to his bedside and said:

> "I am about to leave you forever; give me, therefore, one last proof of your affection and fidelity, for, according to our holy religion, a married man seeking admittance at the gate of Heaven is required to swear that he has never defiled himself with an unworthy woman. In my desk you will find a crimson candle, which has been blessed by the High Priest and has a peculiar mystical significance. Swear to me that while it is in existence you will not remarry."

The Woman swore and the Man died. At the funeral the Woman stood at the head of the bier, holding a lighted crimson candle till it was wasted entirely away.

Phelan uses this story to explore seven theses about narrative judgment. They are, briefly: (1) judgment comes at the intersection of narrative sense-making, ethics, and aesthetics; (2) these three kinds of judgments almost always overlap; (3) narrative judgments emerge from the inside out, because individual narratives establish their own ethical standards; (4) we judge not only the characters and their actions, but implicitly the ethics of the implied author; (5) individual readers evaluate individual narratives in different ways; (6) aesthetic judgments also emerge from the inside out, from the choices made by the individual author; (7) individual readers' ethical and aesthetic judgments influence each other.

Phelan tests his theses in an analysis of Bierce's story. For one thing, a lot of interpreting is going on: the man interprets a religious principle, the wife interprets his instructions, and the reader interprets both interpretations, forming an ethical judgment of the man, the woman, and the implied author of the story. Is the husband's interpretation controlling, selfish, and possessive? If so, do we condone the wife's interpretation of her oath? If, says Phelan, we decide the wife "has found a valid loophole in her promise, we may say that it is an ethically just fulfillment of that promise" (Phelan 2008: 10). If not, we would find her guilty of breaking her promise, for she certainly knew she was not honoring the spirit of his instructions—it even looks like some kind of private vengeance. Yet even with that reservation, we could still make a positive ethical judgment of her decision to burn the candle because it represents "an appropriate response to her husband's ethically deficient actions of misinterpreting the principle for his selfish ends," his assumption that she is there to do his bidding, both in life and death (Phelan 2008: 10).

Ethical judgment comes from inside out, not from outside in. Like Thurber's in "The Catbird Seat," Bierce's *stylistic* choices reveal his underlying ethical principles and guide our judgment—in this case, that the husband is authoritative and unloving. Phelan (2008: 11) points out that the man

> does not make requests; he issues commands. He "calls" his wife to his bedside, and delivers a series of additional imperatives: "give me one last proof"; "swear that you will not remarry." The ethical subtext of his speech ... is "because I am your superior and my fate matters more, you should do what I command regardless of the personal consequences for you."

We also have to make an ethical judgment of the wife. Because Bierce leaves her twist on the man's injunction to the very end, our judgment is linked to the pleasure we experience in the ending's kick (2008: 11–12). With the last sentence, we are also implicitly invited to extrapolate on the nature of the marriage itself, which was probably not a very happy one for the wife. Her subversive act at the funeral suggests that she was not too crazy about the "holy religion," either.

Phelan makes several other points about "The Crimson Candle." He notes, for instance, that the narrator restricts his involvement to simply reporting the action, coyly assuming the reader will side with him. Yet individual readers may evaluate the implied author's presentation in quite different ways.

Bierce's handling of the characterization and the progression, with its emphasis on the husband's selfishness and the wife's brilliant manipulation of her promise, may receive the total approval of some readers, while it may make others uneasy about the way Bierce treats the husband. For these readers, including me, the issue is not that Bierce may be unfair to his own creation but rather that he delights in exposing the husband's ultimate futility. I discover that this delight borders on a gleeful embrace of the impotence conferred by death that I find emotionally chilling and ethically deficient.

(2008: 13)

Before reading Phelan's take on the story, this view would not have occurred to me. I read the story in the context of nineteenth-century patriarchy, and felt the wife's rebellion was vindicated by the husband's selfishness. Now I see the story in a different light, and I am a little troubled by my callousness toward the dying man. Phelan's aim, though, is not to convince me that his evaluation of the underlying ethics in "The Crimson Candle" is correct, but to initiate "productive dialogue about ethics" (2008: 13). And, potentially, he has done just that. The story has made me think about when a promise looks like blackmail, what violations of honor are allowed in order to keep our self-respect, and how love becomes distorted by unequal power or obedience to religious authority.

A similar dialogue should ensue when we make aesthetic judgments about the crafting of the story, which is also an "inside out" procedure—we don't start with a list of certified and approved formal features for short fiction, but use our experience with many texts and our best guess of an author's ambitions to come up with some evaluation of the work's success or failure. Ethical judgments and aesthetic judgments go hand in hand. For example, if "The Crimson Candle" had a more engaging narrator who guided our opinions more surely, Phelan perhaps would not be bothered by the futility of the husband's wish. If the story were less like a parable or a fable, the reader would have more to go on in his evaluation of the characters' actions and psychology. So our judgment of the story's ethics are tied to the way Bierce chooses to tell the tale. Overall, Phelan judges Bierce's story as so-so, both ethically and aesthetically. The values it suggests are sound but conventional, and the aims of the tale are pretty simple: "to construct a pleasurable reversal narrative involving tyrannical husband and apparently submissive wife." Yet Phelan admires Bierce's compact storytelling, and how the tale gets readers involved on many ethical levels (2008: 14–15). Like "The Catbird Seat" for Gregory, "The Crimson Candle" is not the pinnacle of literary achievement. Yet both critics acknowledge the storyteller's rare skill. Indeed, Phelan and Gregory exhibit their own ethos in their readings, one that embraces intellectual humility, respect for the sheer labor that goes into creating a work of art, and open-mindedness about other points of view.

Ethical criticism emphasizes that if a reader is called upon to sacrifice some of her ethical values in order to be amused for a few hours by a story or a film, or even to experience the more sophisticated enjoyment of a work's aesthetic components, she should be cognizant of the choice she is making. We cannot pretend that when we assent to an author's ethos we have not been invited to reflect on or to change our own. It's true that, in their zeal to determine ethical criteria, some critics have to monitor a tendency to over-generalize or lay down the law; ethical criticism has been liable to accusations of censorship, or to the universalizing impulses that lead to homogeneity and prejudice. Yet I would argue that ethical criticism, as performed by these particular critics, affirms that almost every text's value is relative, because every reader will bring to the work different expectations. "Rhetorical reading ... stops short of ever declaring any one reading as definitive and fixed for all time," says Phelan. "But it assumes that one significant value of reading narrative is the opportunity it offers to encounter other minds—that of the author who has constructed the narrative and those of other readers also interested in shared readings" (2005: 19). So Wayne Booth would never say that no one should read *Jaws*. Marshall Gregory would not ban "The Catbird Seat" from high school English classes. For who can say what other readers might take away from the time they have spent with these narratives? There is, in Booth's phrase, a *"plurality* of goods" in our reading experiences (1988: 115, original italics); it is the ethical critic's job to clarify and express his reasons for embracing or rejecting what the text has to offer.

This is the other important point made in *The Company We Keep*: our readings of literature are not private but communal, and should be shared with others. Booth invented the word *coduction* to collapse the sense of how we personally arrive at a judgment about a work of literature and how we explain or defend that judgment to others (*co* = "together" and *ducere* = "to lead out"). Criticism is not merely a matter of preference, but an ethical engagement with someone else's representation of the world, and in time that experience may become part of a continuing conversation with other, more or less qualified readers.

Booth models the practice of coduction throughout *The Company We Keep*, rereading familiar works by D. H. Lawrence, Jane Austen, and other writers in light of ethical perspectives he had not really considered before. Indeed, the book opens with the story of one of Booth's colleagues at the University of Chicago, Paul Moses, who scandalized members of humanities departments by announcing that he could no longer teach Mark Twain's *Adventures of Huckleberry Finn* because he found its distorted views of race extremely offensive. In his last chapter, Booth carefully re-examines Twain's portrayal of the escaped slave, Jim, in light of Moses's objections. To his dismay, he finds his faith in Twain's moral vision considerably shaken. A much-loved novel, one Booth taught repeatedly and approvingly for its critique of the destructive morality of slave society, now appears to have deflected his imagination in dangerous ways—by indulging fantasies of Negro gratitude and submissiveness, by caricaturing folly and evil, and by presenting the realities of slavery and the hypocrisy of religion in trite, superficial ways (1988: 476–477). From his conversations with many critics, including Paul Moses (to whom Booth dedicated *The Company We Keep*), Booth's thorough coduction of *Huckleberry Finn* forced him to turn "from untroubled admiration to restless questioning" (1988: 477–478).

This willingness to listen to opposing arguments and to re-examine and revise one's reading in light of other interpretations are important aspects of ethical criticism (indeed, of all criticism). But we can't assess others' readings unless we understand *how* novels and stories assert ethical values. Studying a story's rhetoric and developing a vocabulary to describe narrative techniques and the structure of narratives are ways in which critics determine a text's ethical effects. Terms such as the implied author, autodiegetic narration (when the protagonist tells the story), narratee (the audience directly addressed by the narrator), and unreliable narration are used to make sense of what happens to us cognitively, emotionally, and ethically when we are immersed in a story.[6] Ethical criticism that deploys this kind of terminology is not quite the same as the theory known as narratology, which sets out to determine the fundamental structure of narrative and has its roots in structuralism and semiotics. Ethical critics do not *just* want to describe how a narrative works. They are also committed to staging their own engagement with a text, to coming to terms with its ethical invitations, and to trying publicly to account for what attracts, disgusts, vexes, or consoles them about a particular reading experience. Both a narratologist and an ethical critic, for instance, might dissect the structure and style of Humbert Humbert's first-person narration in *Lolita*, but the ethical critic would not do so without addressing, in some way, his own reactions to Vladimir Nabokov's choice of teller in a story about pedophilia.[7] Looking inward, examining our own ethical responses, is part of the process of ethical critique.

The nature of authorial address—the implied author, the choice of focalization, the narratee, the addressee, and all the questions that arise when we attend to a story's oration—seem to be the crux of the matter to many ethical critics. What is being asked of the reader who fully listens to the narrator of a story or novel? How do we judge a character's motivation, experience, innocence, trustworthiness, and how do we respond to issues about the narrator's judgments, omissions, or selection of details within our own ethical frames of reference? Where is the implied author behind the speaker of the story, and can we comprehend her interests between the layers of its telling? Are we morally bound to our position as witness to the tale? Is resistance to a story a sign of insensitivity or political vigilance? These are essential matters for reading any narrative, and an ethical critic insists that we cannot get to the heart of them through theory alone. We have to focus our attention on the demands of the text through "conscienceful listening"—concentrating on what is being said, by whom, when, and for what purpose, in an attitude of respectful attention (Buell 1999: 12).

Instead of offering a flat account of something like "the morality of fiction," these ethical critics show that an author's rhetorical choices have unavoidable consequences for our involvement in the text. As Phelan puts it, there is a "default ethical relation between implied author and authorial audience" (2008: 53). Our ethical judgments about characters and situations are quite simply tied to the voice of the implied author, a voice we as readers cannot help but listen to.

> If people did not want their stories told, it would be better for them to keep away from me.
>
> (Anderson 1924: 332)

I want now to reproduce in full a short story that I think involves the reader's cognition, emotions, aesthetic response, and ethical judgment. Instead of citing published criticism of the story, I want to offer my own close reading, and extend an invitation to the readers of this book to talk back to me (and the story) from their own knowledge and experience.[8] The story is by the American writer Sherwood Anderson, and was published in *The Triumph of the Egg and Other Stories*, in 1921.

I Want to Know Why

Sherwood Anderson

We got up at four in the morning, that first day in the east. On the evening before we had climbed off a freight train at the edge of town, and with the true instinct of Kentucky boys had found our way across town and to the race track and the stables at once. Then we knew we were all right. Hanley Turner right away found a nigger we knew. It was Bildad Johnson who in the winter works at Ed Becker's livery barn in our home town, Beckersville. Bildad is a good cook as almost all our niggers are and of course he, like everyone in our part of Kentucky who is anyone at all, likes the horses. In the spring Bildad begins to scratch around. A nigger from our country can flatter and wheedle anyone into letting him do most anything he wants. Bildad wheedles the stable men and the trainers from the horse farms in our country around Lexington. The trainers come into town in the evening to stand around and talk and maybe get into a poker game. Bildad gets in with them. He is always doing little favors and telling about things to eat, chicken browned in a pan, and how is the best way to cook sweet potatoes and corn bread. It makes your mouth water to hear him.

When the racing season comes on and the horses go to the races and there is all the talk on the streets in the evenings about the new colts, and everyone says when they are going over to Lexington or to the spring meeting at Churchill Downs or to Latonia, and the horsemen that have been down to New Orleans or maybe at the winter meeting at Havana in Cuba come home to spend a week before they start out again, at such a time when everything talked about in Beckersville is just horses and nothing else and the outfits start out and horse racing is in every breath of air you breathe, Bildad shows up with a job as cook for some outfit. Often when I think about it, his always going all season to the races and working in the livery barn in the winter where horses are and where men like to come and talk about horses, I wish I was a nigger. It's a foolish thing to say, but that's the way I am about being around horses, just crazy. I can't help it.

Well, I must tell you about what we did and let you in on what I'm talking about. Four of us boys from Beckersville, all whites and sons of men who live in Beckersville regular, made up our minds we were going to the races, not just to Lexington or Louisville, I don't mean, but to the big eastern track we were always hearing our Beckersville men talk about, to Saratoga. We were all pretty young then. I was just turned fifteen and I was the oldest of the four. It was my scheme. I admit that and I talked the others into trying it. There was Hanley Turner and Henry Rieback and Tom Tumberton and myself. I had thirty-seven dollars I had earned during the winter working nights and Saturdays in Enoch Myer's grocery. Henry Rieback had eleven dollars and the others, Hanley and Tom had only a dollar or two each. We fixed it all up and laid low until the Kentucky spring meetings were over and some of our men, the sportiest ones, the ones we envied the most, had cut out—then we cut out too.

I won't tell you the trouble we had beating our way on freights and all. We went through Cleveland and Buffalo and other cities and saw Niagara Falls. We bought things there, souvenirs and spoons and cards and shells with pictures of the falls on them for our sisters and mothers, but thought we had better not send any of the things home. We didn't want to put the folks on our trail and maybe be nabbed.

We got into Saratoga as I said at night and went to the track. Bildad fed us up. He showed us a place to sleep in hay over a shed and promised to keep still. Niggers are all right about things like that. They won't squeal on you. Often a white man you might meet, when you had run away from home like that, might appear to be all right and give you a quarter or a half dollar or something, and then go right and give you away. White men will do that, but not a nigger. You can trust them. They are squarer with kids. I don't know why.

At the Saratoga meeting that year there were a lot of men from home. Dave Williams and Arthur Mulford and Jerry Myers and others. Then there was a lot from Louisville and Lexington Henry Rieback knew but I didn't. They were professional gamblers and Henry Rieback's father is one too. He is what is called a sheet writer and goes away most of the year to tracks. In the winter when he is home in Beckersville he don't stay there much but goes away to cities and deals faro. He is a nice man and generous, is always sending Henry presents, a bicycle and a gold watch and a boy scout suit of clothes and things like that.

My own father is a lawyer. He's all right, but don't make much money and can't buy me things and anyway I'm getting so old now I don't expect it. He never said nothing to me against Henry, but Hanley Turner and Tom Tumberton's fathers did. They said to their boys that money so come by is no good and they didn't want their boys brought up to hear gamblers' talk and be thinking about such things and maybe embrace them.

That's all right and I guess the men know what they are talking about, but I don't see what it's got to do with Henry or with horses either. That's what I'm writing this story about. I'm puzzled. I'm getting to be a man and want to think straight and be O.K., and there's something I saw at the race meeting at the eastern track I can't figure out.

I can't help it, I'm crazy about thoroughbred horses. I've always been that way. When I was ten years old and saw I was growing to be big and couldn't be a rider I was so sorry I nearly died. Harry Hellinfinger in Beckersville, whose father is Postmaster, is grown up and too lazy to work, but likes to stand around in the street and get up jokes on boys like sending them to a hardware store for a gimlet to bore square holes and other jokes like that. He played one on me. He told me that if I would eat a half a cigar I would be stunted and not grow any more and maybe could be a rider. I did it. When father wasn't looking I took a cigar out of his pocket and gagged it down some way. It made me awful sick and the doctor had to be sent for, and then it did no good. I kept right on growing. It was a joke. When I told what I had done and why most fathers would have whipped me but mine didn't.

Well, I didn't get stunted and didn't die. It serves Harry Hellinfinger right. Then I made up my mind I would like to be a stable boy, but had to give that up too. Mostly niggers do that work and I knew father wouldn't let me go into it. No use to ask him.

If you've never been crazy about thoroughbreds it's because you've never been around where they are much and don't know any better. They're beautiful. There isn't anything so lovely and clean and full of spunk and honest and everything as some race horses. On the big horse farms that are all around our town Beckersville there are tracks and the horses run in the early morning. More than a thousand times I've got out of bed before daylight and walked two or three miles to the tracks. Mother wouldn't of let me go but father always says, "Let him alone." So I got some bread out of the bread box and some butter and jam, gobbled it and lit out.

At the tracks you sit on the fence with men, whites and niggers, and they chew tobacco and talk, and then the colts are brought out. It's early and the grass is covered with shiny dew and in another field a man is plowing and they are frying things in a shed where the track niggers sleep, and you know how a nigger can giggle and laugh and say things that make you laugh. A white man can't do it and some niggers can't but a track nigger can every time.

And so the colts are brought out and some are just galloped by stable boys, but almost every morning on a big track owned by a rich man who lives maybe in New York, there are always, nearly every morning, a few colts and some of the old race horses and geldings and mares that are cut loose.

It brings a lump up into my throat when a horse runs. I don't mean all horses but some. I can pick them nearly every time. It's in my blood like in the blood of race track niggers and trainers. Even when they just go slop-jogging along with a little nigger on their backs I can tell a winner. If my throat hurts and it's hard for me to swallow, that's him. He'll run like Sam Hill when you let him out. If he don't win every time it'll be a wonder and because they've got him in a pocket behind another or he was pulled or got off bad at the post or something. If I wanted to be a gambler like Henry Rieback's father I could get rich. I know I could and Henry says so too. All I would have to do is to wait 'til that hurt comes when I see a horse and then bet every cent. That's what I would do if I wanted to be a gambler, but I don't.

When you're at the tracks in the morning—not the race tracks but the training tracks around Beckersville—you don't see a horse, the kind I've been talking about, very often, but it's nice anyway. Any thoroughbred, that is sired right and out of a good mare and trained by a man that knows how, can run. If he couldn't what would he be there for and not pulling a plow?

Well, out of the stables they come and the boys are on their backs and it's lovely to be there. You hunch down on top of the fence and itch inside you. Over in the sheds the niggers giggle and sing. Bacon is being fried and coffee made. Everything smells lovely. Nothing smells better than coffee and manure and horses and niggers and bacon frying and pipes being smoked out of doors on a morning like that. It just gets you, that's what it does.

But about Saratoga. We was there six days and not a soul from home seen us and everything came off just as we wanted it to, fine weather and horses and races and all. We beat our way home and Bildad gave us a basket with fried chicken and bread and other eatables in, and I had eighteen dollars when we got back to Beckersville. Mother jawed and cried but Pop didn't say much. I told everything we done except one thing. I did and saw that alone. That's what I'm writing about. It got me upset. I think about it at night. Here it is.

At Saratoga we laid up nights in the hay in the shed Bildad had showed us and ate with the niggers early and at night when the race people had all gone away. The men from home stayed mostly in the grandstand and betting field, and didn't come out around the places where the horses are kept except to the paddocks just before a race when the horses are saddled. At Saratoga they don't have paddocks under an open shed as at Lexington and Churchill Downs and other tracks down in our country, but saddle the horses right out in an open place under trees on a lawn as smooth and nice as Banker Bohon's front yard here in Beckersville. It's lovely. The horses are sweaty and nervous and shine and the men come out and smoke cigars and look at them and the trainers are there and the owners, and your heart thumps so you can hardly breathe.

Then the bugle blows for post and the boys that ride come running out with their silk clothes on and you run to get a place by the fence with the niggers.

I always am wanting to be a trainer or owner, and at the risk of being seen and caught and sent home I went to the paddocks before every race. The other boys didn't but I did.

We got to Saratoga on a Friday and on Wednesday the next week the big Mullford Handicap was to be run. Middlestride was in it and Sunstreak. The weather was fine and the track fast. I couldn't sleep the night before.

What had happened was that both these horses are the kind it makes my throat hurt to see. Middlestride is long and looks awkward and is a gelding. He belongs to Joe Thompson, a little owner from home who only has a half dozen horses. The Mullford Handicap is for a mile and Middlestride can't untrack fast. He goes away slow and is always way back at the half, then he begins to run and if the race is a mile and a quarter he'll just eat up everything and get there.

Sunstreak is different. He is a stallion and nervous and belongs on the biggest farm we've got in our country, the Van Riddle place that belongs to Mr. Van Riddle of New York. Sunstreak is like a girl you think about sometimes but never see. He is hard all over and lovely too. When you look at his head you want to kiss him. He is trained by Jerry Tillford who knows me and has been good to me lots of times, lets me walk into a horse's stall to look at him close and other things. There isn't anything as sweet as that horse. He stands at the post quiet and not letting on, but he is just burning up inside. Then when the barrier goes up he is off like his name, Sunstreak. It makes you ache to see him. It hurts you. He just lays down and runs like a bird dog. There can't be anything I ever see run like him except Middlestride when he gets untracked and stretches himself.

Gee! I ached to see that race and those two horses run, ached and dreaded it too. I didn't want to see either of our horses beaten. We had never sent a pair like that to the races before. Old men in Beckersville said so and the niggers said so. It was a fact.

Before the race I went over to the paddocks to see. I looked a last look at Middlestride, who isn't such a much standing in a paddock that way, then I went to see Sunstreak.

It was his day. I knew when I see him. I forgot all about being seen myself and walked right up. All the men from Beckersville were there and no one noticed me except Jerry Tillford. He saw me and something happened. I'll tell you about that.

I was standing looking at that horse and aching. In some way, I can't tell how, I knew just how Sunstreak felt inside. He was quiet and letting the niggers rub his legs and Mr. Van Riddle himself put the saddle on, but he was just a raging torrent inside. He was like the water in the river at Niagara Falls just before its goes plunk down. That horse wasn't thinking about running. He don't have to think about that. He was just thinking about holding himself back 'til the time for the running came. I knew that. I could just in a way see right inside him. He was going to do some awful running and I knew it. He wasn't bragging or letting on much or prancing or making a fuss, but just waiting. I knew it and Jerry Tillford his trainer knew. I looked up and then that man and I looked into each other's eyes. Something happened to me. I guess I loved the man as much as I did the horse because he knew what I knew. Seemed to me there wasn't anything in the world but that man and the horse and me. I cried and Jerry Tillford had a shine in his eyes. Then I came away to the fence to wait for the race. The horse was better than me, more steadier, and now I know better than Jerry. He was the quietest and he had to do the running.

Sunstreak ran first of course and he busted the world's record for a mile. I've seen that if I never see anything more. Everything came out just as I expected. Middlestride got left at the post and was way back and closed up to be second, just as I knew he would. He'll get a world's record too some day. They can't skin the Beckersville country on horses.

I watched the race calm because I knew what would happen. I was sure. Hanley Turner and Henry Rieback and Tom Tumberton were all more excited than me.

A funny thing had happened to me. I was thinking about Jerry Tillford the trainer and how happy he was all through the race. I liked him that afternoon even more than I ever liked my own father. I almost forgot the horses thinking that way about him. It was because of what I had seen in his eyes as he stood in the paddocks beside Sunstreak before the race started. I knew he had been watching and working with Sunstreak since the horse was a baby colt, had taught him to run and be patient and when to let himself out and not to quit, never. I knew that for him it was like a mother seeing her child do something brave or wonderful. It was the first time I ever felt for a man like that.

After the race that night I cut out from Tom and Hanley and Henry. I wanted to be by myself and I wanted to be near Jerry Tillford if I could work it. Here is what happened.

The track in Saratoga is near the edge of town. It is all polished up and trees around, the evergreen kind, and grass and everything painted and nice. If you go past the track you get to a hard road made of asphalt for automobiles, and if you go along this for a few miles there is a road turns off to a little rummy-looking farm house set in a yard.

That night after the race I went along that road because I had seen Jerry and some other men go that way in an automobile. I didn't expect to find them. I walked for a ways and then sat down by a fence to think. It was the direction they went in. I wanted to be as near Jerry as I could. I felt close to him. Pretty soon I went up the side road—I don't know why—and came to the rummy farm house. I was just lonesome to see Jerry, like wanting to see your father at night when you are a young kid. Just then an automobile came along and turned in. Jerry was in it and Henry Rieback's father, and Arthur Bedford from home, and Dave Williams and two other men I didn't know. They got out of the car and went into the house, all but Henry Rieback's father who quarreled with them and said he wouldn't go. It was only about nine o'clock, but they were all drunk and the rummy looking farm house was a place for bad women to stay in. That's what it was. I crept up along a fence and looked through a window and saw.

It's what give me the fantods. I can't make it out. The women in the house were all ugly mean-looking women, not nice to look at or be near. They were homely too, except one who was tall and looked a little like the gelding Middlestride, but not clean like him, but with a hard ugly mouth. She had red hair. I saw everything plain. I got up by an old rose bush by an open window and looked. The women had on loose dresses and sat around in chairs. The men came in and some sat on the women's laps. The place smelled rotten and there was rotten talk, the kind a kid hears around a livery stable in a town like Beckersville in the winter but don't ever expect to hear talked when there are women around. It was rotten. A nigger wouldn't go into such a place.

I looked at Jerry Tillford. I've told you how I had been feeling about him on account of his knowing what was going on inside of Sunstreak in the minute before he went to the post for the race in which he made a world's record.

Jerry bragged in that bad woman house as I know Sunstreak wouldn't never have bragged. He said that he made that horse, that it was him that won the race and made the record. He lied and bragged like a fool. I never heard such silly talk.

And then, what do you suppose he did! He looked at the woman in there, the one that was lean and hard-mouthed and looked a little like the gelding Middlestride, but not clean like him, and his eyes began to shine just as they did when he looked at me and at Sunstreak in the paddocks at the track in the afternoon. I stood there by the window—gee!—but I wished I hadn't gone away from the tracks, but had stayed with the boys and the niggers and the horses. The tall rotten looking woman was between us just as Sunstreak was in the paddocks in the afternoon.

Then, all of a sudden, I began to hate that man. I wanted to scream and rush in the room and kill him. I never had such a feeling before. I was so mad clean through that I cried and my fists were doubled up so my finger nails cut my hands.

And Jerry's eyes kept shining and he waved back and forth, and then he went and kissed that woman and I crept away and went back to the tracks and to bed and didn't sleep hardly any, and then next day I got the other kids to start home with me and never told them anything I seen.

I been thinking about it ever since. I can't make it out. Spring has come again and I'm nearly sixteen and go to the tracks mornings same as always, and I see Sunstreak and Middlestride and a new colt named Strident I'll bet will lay them all out, but no one thinks so but me and two or three niggers.

But things are different. At the tracks the air don't taste as good or smell as good. It's because a man like Jerry Tillford, who knows what he does, could see a horse like Sunstreak run, and kiss a woman like that the same day. I can't make it out. Darn him, what did he want to do like that for? I keep thinking about it and it spoils looking at horses and smelling things and hearing niggers laugh and everything. Sometimes I'm so mad about it I want to fight someone. It gives me the fantods. What did he do it for? I want to know why.

This story is about the development of a certain kind of ethical awareness and learning the ways of the world. The title and the last line, "I want to know why," bracket Sherwood Anderson's concern to dramatize the disquiet and confusion inscribed by a particular moment in the development of moral understanding—the pain of knowing something subjectively, but not knowing enough theoretically or cognitively to meet the demands of the complex world of adult motives and desires. It is a story that returns us to fundamental questions about subjective and objective forms of knowing, and to the risks and responsibilities of close reading.

The story's ethical *and* aesthetic effectiveness turn on the reader's judgment and interpretation of the narrator, and so almost everything depends on how successful Anderson is in creating a believable idiom and a full sense for the reader of the world of the story—the mores and concrete particulars of early twentieth-century rural America. In my reading, the narrator, like most adolescents, thinks he knows quite a lot of things about his world; he seems intuitive, curious, and observant. What does the narrator know? That "niggers" will "flatter and wheedle," that they're "square with kids" and can be trusted (but white men not always), that "track niggers" can make you laugh every time (but not white men ever), and that certain horses are going to be winners: "If my throat hurts and it's hard for me to swallow, that's him." These remarks reveal the narrowness of the boy's understanding and his moral naïveté (he says "I wish I was a nigger," for instance), and for some readers the casual use of racist epithets may be enough to judge the implied author very negatively. But I want to go along with the character as someone who has a pretty good moral compass, despite the extreme bigotry that saturates his society. Nearly 16, he tells the reader things that show him to be intelligent, emotionally responsive, and a bit high-spirited. It was his scheme to jump the freight trains and go to Saratoga (another reader might see this as stupid or rebellious). He's also a pretty responsible kid who's saved thirty-seven dollars working part-time at a grocery (or irresponsible, because he blows more than half of it). Most of all, I see the narrator as naïve and romantic, sensitive to the beauty of the thoroughbreds and drawn to the exclusively masculine life of the racetrack. "More than a thousand times I've got out of bed before daylight and walked two or three miles to the tracks," he says. "At the tracks you sit on the fence with men, whites and niggers, and they chew tobacco and talk, and then the colts are brought out. It's early and the grass is covered with shiny dew…" Although the racetrack is a hangout for gamblers and ruffians (and he knows that often there's "rotten talk" around the stables), perhaps he is subconsciously attracted to the racetrack on these dewy mornings because it is a peaceful scene of male comradeship, perhaps even of human equality, where "whites and niggers" sit on the fence together and watch the colts.

Anderson conveys the narrator's susceptibility to beauty and his idealistic vision of the horseracing life both in the repetition of certain words ("They're beautiful," "There isn't anything so lovely," "it's lovely to be there," "everything smells lovely," "It's lovely," "hard all over and lovely too") and in the affective, non-cognitive nature of the boy's responses: "your heart thumps so you could hardly breathe," "it just gets you," "It makes you ache," "It hurts you," "I was standing looking at that horse and aching." Although he can't explain some things (he uses the phrase "I don't know why" twice, which is another version of "I want to know why"), and the moral logic of adults is sometimes dark to him ("I guess the men know what they are talking about"), the values of his instinctive life feel indisputable, and so constitute real knowledge about what matters for him. Therefore, the boy's sensitivity and spontaneous affection almost entirely structure his moral judgment: the "niggers" are honorable ("You can *trust* them"), the racehorses are "lovely and *clean* and full of spunk and *honest*," Henry Rieback, the gambler, is "*nice* and *generous*" (and he's the only man who won't go into the farm house). His own father, a lawyer, is not a disciplinarian: he lets him watch the colts in the early morning, he doesn't say much when the narrator returns after his six-day escapade, he doesn't punish him when he eats a cigar to stunt his growth ("most fathers would have whipped me"), and while other fathers say that Henry Rieback's a bad influence, his own father "never said nothing" against him. Is his father uncaring and uninvolved in his son's life, or protectively watchful and nonjudgmental? It's a good question, for there are a lot of fathers and adult men mentioned throughout the story. The boy seems to be searching for a father figure or a role model, someone he can look up to and feel close to. After the race he admits he likes Jerry Tillford "even more than I ever liked my own father," and "I was just lonesome to see Jerry, like wanting to see your father at night when you are a young kid." A psychosocial interpretation along these lines would be compelling, and certainly a major theme is the boy's trauma as he begins to comprehend his complicity in a society where men routinely exploit animals, African Americans, and women for their own pleasure and gain.

I want to dwell, though, on the narrator's solitary labor to comprehend the baffling discrepancy between Jerry Tillford's actions before and after Sunstreak's win and how Anderson involves the reader in his problem—a problem of interpretation, for both narrator and reader. When something disturbs the narrator's moral feeling, he wants to figure it out. He asks why. Not every boy would be like this, but he is. Because he is "getting to be a man," he wants to "think straight and be O.K." This is difficult moral work, and he postpones revealing the purpose of the tale and its central event for most of the narrative—he avoids it rhetorically, and he avoids it emotionally, for almost a year. The rhetorical gesture of postponement is displayed when he lovingly dwells on the details of life at the track, in all the descriptions of people and places that don't seem to advance the tale in any meaningful way, and in his frequent windups to the actual telling, as in, "That's what I'm writing about. It got me upset. I think about it at night. Here it is."

The narrator craves a relationship with an older man who shares his passion and admiration for Sunstreak's power, beauty, and dignity. He wants another person in his life with a deep inner knowledge of these things. His longing is dramatized in the enchanted scene of mutual recognition, where everything drops away but the man, the boy, and the horse, a moment of such intense intimacy and pleasure the boy cries and the man's eyes shine, we presume with a sense of shared companionship and comprehension: "I looked up and then that man and I looked into each other's eyes. Something happened to me. I guess I loved the man as much as I did the horse *because he knew what I knew*." The narrator's love is mixed with his faith that he and Jerry know something that is private, incommunicable, and sacred about Sunstreak's performance in the race that day.

The narrator follows Jerry to the farm house because he wants to sustain the feeling of intimacy: "I wanted to be as near Jerry as I could. I felt close to him." He looks through a window to find Jerry bragging obscenely about Sunstreak, waving his hands around, kissing the "rotten" whore with eyes that "shine just as they did when he looked at me and at Sunstreak in the paddocks at the track in the afternoon." The narrator's response is visceral: "I was so mad clean through that I cried and my fists were doubled up so my finger nails cut my hands." Cognitive understanding of the scene he's witnessed may come later, when he is more mature— his motive for telling the story is even to achieve that kind of clarity. All he knows now, a year or so after the event, is that everything he used to enjoy has been spoiled, tainted, contaminated "because a man like Jerry Tillford, who knows what he does, could see a horse like Sunstreak run, and kiss a woman like that the same day."[9]

If the situation exceeds the narrator's moral knowledge, it's not the same for the reader, who has to explain for herself the meaning of Jerry's behavior. Many times the boy addresses the reader in the second person, as in "Well, I must tell you about what we did and let you in on what I'm talking about," and "I'll tell you about that," or "And then, what do you suppose he did!" This kind of personal address is often designed to engage the reader sympathetically or confidentially, and it does that here. But it also highlights the reader's involvement and responsibility. For how we answer the boy's ultimate question, how we choose to interpret "What did he do it for?" is the ethical crux of the story.

There are a few possible interpretations. Some readers, for instance, might choose to see the story as essentially about a fallen idol and a child's initiation into the crimes and secrets of the adult world. There are many stories on this theme, and it could work. We could see the revelation of Jerry's lust as inevitable, and even view it positively if we disapprove of the narrator's starry-eyed ideas about horses and think he deserves a rude awakening. Yet I don't think that is the essence of Anderson's ethical vision. There are two other possibilities, and they hinge on how we want to interpret the shine in Jerry Tillford's eyes.

The reader knows the boy is an idealistic, naïve person because of the lingering descriptions of the racetrack in the morning, the pleasure he takes in being with men and horses, his naturalness around the black men who work at the tracks. Even the tiny detail that the boys bought souvenirs of Niagara Falls for their sisters and mothers suggests his basic good-heartedness. To me, it seems the implied author advocates the young boy's natural, loving response to the world (though he has a gift for predicting winners, the narrator's not interested in making money from it). The look in Jerry's eyes when he is at the farm house reveals to the narrator something so antithetical to his own feelings of reverence for the thoroughbred that it has confounded his moral world. Is it *the same look* he had when their eyes met across Sunstreak before the race? If it is, then what the narrator understands is that the trainer's response was based on something morally ugly, like pride or greed. He senses the truth that some people treat animals and other human beings like objects for their use, to buy and sell, to own, to brag about. They make a living creature into a commodity.

There's the possibility, though, that Jerry did recognize the magnificence of Sunstreak, as the narrator imagined: "I knew that for him it was like a mother seeing her child do something brave or wonderful." If this is the case, the pang is in the narrator's demand for an explanation for the twisted labyrinth of human motivation, the mixed nature of human desire, the capacity for good and evil. For the experienced reader knows what the young boy does not—that people do, quite easily and consciably, "see a horse like Sunstreak run, and kiss a woman like that the same day." It happens all the time. And yet the pity of this knowledge, shown through the honest and bewildered eyes of a sensitive adolescent, stirs a feeling of heartbreak in the reader—almost of tragedy.

In his frustration, isolation, and need for explanations, the narrator's moral burden is analogous to the reader's, who bears alone the responsibility of listening, knowing, and interpreting the tale. Like the narrator's glimpse into another's private world, the reader has had thrust upon her a new situation, new behaviors which require an ethical response. Listening to the boy's story has changed us, perhaps infected our complacency about the prettiness of things by exposing us to other people's choices, and to the darker possibilities of our own. There are also parallels between narrator and reader in the frame of human communication—just as the boy rhetorically reaches out to the reader to help him make sense of a fallen world and learn how to act within it, the reader may seek other people's opinions about the story.

After Saratoga, the boy knows something's crooked and askew in the moral universe—the things he used to enjoy don't smell and taste the same. But he doesn't know how to explain why it's changed or what it is. More profoundly, he doesn't know *why* it is, and he has no authority figures, books, or religious institutions to help him learn how twisted are the ways of the world. Anderson's story may be an analogue to our own stories about acquiring knowledge, stories that do not start at adolescence and stop at adulthood, but are perpetual as long as we pay attention to who and where we are, as long as we are exposed and hurt by our ignorance. The existentialist philosopher Albert Camus wrote, "Beginning to think is beginning to be undermined" (2001: 4). The boy in Anderson's story, who wants to "think straight and be O.K.," has found his dreams undermined by convoluted truths he doesn't understand. The reader is his co-experiencer in this awakening, for by requiring us to think through the narrator's pain, joy, and anger, the story enjoins us to form a more complicated selfhood, and perhaps want to be the kind of person for whom beauty and honesty matter.

Readers might object to my reading of "I Want to Know Why" as either too ethical or not ethical enough. The narrator's untroubled view of "niggers," for example, could be an extension of the implied author's blindness about the debasing reality of racism. Like Mark Twain, an author he admired, Anderson assumes a white readership, and is not sensitive enough to the ways in which his portrayal of blacks, from the innocent boy's point of view, rests on racist stereotypes.[10] The boy likes the black working men at the racetrack because they seem socially and mentally at his own level, because they let him do what he pleases, because they're more fun than the authoritative white men in his life. The more unpleasant conditions of their life are invisible to him; he's not interested. The ethical movement of the story, some would argue, should have been toward another kind of epiphany, such as the narrator's recognition of the immorality of segregation, or at least some dawning awareness that the black men's labor supports the white men's gain at the track—certainly powerful subtexts.

Women readers, too, might be uncomfortable with my ethical take on the story. Judith Fetterley observes that women appear only twice, and both times negatively. The boy's mother is a stereotypical nag. The African Americans co-opt any positive features associated with female roles, by cooking mouthwatering meals and finding the boys a place to sleep. The men's relation to the whores is thoroughly revolting to the boy. We may argue that Anderson wanted to expose the myth of American masculinity by dramatizing the boy's rage and repulsion at the kinds of relationships a patriarchal society demands. Yet a woman reader "is still faced with a story whose concern is entirely for men and their dilemmas, a story in which what happens to women is of no importance at all" (Fetterley 1978: 21). The story is part of a long line of American fiction in which men's traumatic realizations of "namelessness, self-hatred, and limbo" (1978: 21) are represented as universal human experiences. Women are characterized as scapegoats, fantasies, shrews, or whores against the tragic drama of male self-division.

It's also possible that I have misunderstood the ethical presentation of the narrator as someone whose spontaneity and pleasure in life are endorsed by the implied author. One critic, Donald Ringe, has argued that everything the boy talks about is tinged with "selfish, sensuous gratification," that he's "thoroughly self-centered and apt to judge the value of anything by the pleasantness of the sensations it can give" (1959: 25). His moral judgments are controlled by the enjoyment of what he likes: bacon frying, the smell of coffee, laughter of the "niggers," the dew on the grass, the cleanly trimmed racecourse, the athleticism of the horses. In allowing physical excitement to determine his judgments, he is following the moral path of his idol, Jerry Tillford, and because he does not yet have the framework of sexual desire, this knowledge must be pushed away, postponed. "His moral sense tells him that Jerry must be condemned but he is not yet ready to see his own previous life in similar terms" (1959: 28).

Lionel Trilling has also remarked that Anderson's representation of reality is inadequate—indeed, it is *dangerously* inadequate, an invitation to wistful indulgence, if the reader is an older adult, or in false notions of romantic rebellion against the claims of the modern world, if the reader is still young (1957: 22–23). The very aspects of the narrator's version of things that I responded to positively are for Trilling evidence of the implied author's "standing quarrel with respectable society ... [and] the rational intellect" (1957: 23–24). There is nothing wrong with this moral position, and there are many writers in this tradition, says Trilling. The greatest among them, though, authors such as William Blake and D. H. Lawrence, do more than merely walk away from respectability or denounce the pretensions of rationality. They become agents of a newer, more powerful stream of thought. Sherwood Anderson hasn't this quality of depth and insight. His story is a coming-of-age tale, nothing more.

After reading Trilling's critique, I want to re-examine the roots of my response. Do I prefer stories in which moral values are presented anti-rationally, at a distance from systematic thought? Does this bent of mine point to a lack of ethical rigor? Or perhaps I am stuck inside a memory of my first reading of the story as a young adult, when perhaps I identified with the narrator's confusion and innocence? On the other hand, I can't help thinking there is something wrong in Ringe's interpretation. Surely Anderson regrets that the boy has lost a palpable sense of joy in things, perhaps forever. But it's possible that because I feel mournfully involved in the boy's lost innocence, I've mistaken Anderson's ethical vision in his construction of point of view. And like Booth with *Huckleberry Finn*, I may be accused in my reading of ignoring uncomfortable details about the author's attitude towards race and gender—although attention to those details of the story certainly constitute an ethical critique. A coduction of my reading of "I Want to Know Why" is needed! For if there is something I get about the story, there's also something I can't nail down without the help of other readers, who might notice different items in the formal presentation of the story or offer a different ethical perspective from my own.

From the position of ethical criticism, close reading means dwelling in the author's world for a while, acknowledging the substance of that world, and coming face to face with it. Such a position begins privately and inwardly, as we attempt to figure out where we stand within a text's implied values—the potential benefits or detriments in its offer of friendship. But for ethical criticism, close reading also always constitutes a movement outward, as well. Eventually we will raise our eyes from the book, set it aside, and take our place in the world.

The critic Jane Gallop has argued that if close reading is "learning to hear what's really on the page, listening closely to the other, and being willing to catch what the other actually says," then close reading itself is an ethical practice. "If we can learn to do that with books," she says, "we might learn to do that with people" (2000: 17). Reading literature closely, accommodatingly, may be one means to learn about difference and such difficult virtues as patience, adaptability, self-awareness, and discernment. Close reading, in the sense I have been using it throughout this book, as attending to the use of language, to the occasion of reading, and to our ethical accountability, may be one way people learn to be morally present and to acknowledge other people's reality. It is not the only way, of course. But teaching and encouraging the practice of close literary reading may in the long run help us when we face larger projects and take on other responsibilities—towards tolerance, understanding, and social justice.

Notes

1 For example, Jacques Derrida's *The Gift of Death* (1995) and J. Hillis Miller's *The Ethics of Reading* (1986).

2 A possible factor in the rise of ethical criticism is the posthumous revelation that one of the major deconstructionists at Yale University, Paul de Man, had written pro-Fascist, anti-Semitic articles as a Belgian journalist during World War II. His exacting, brilliant formalism suddenly appeared dangerously removed from the moral concerns of modern people. I think, too, the September 11, 2001 terrorist attacks on the United States made many teachers of literature second-guess the default practice of suspicious, ideological readings, which suddenly seemed "political" only in the insular world of academia. After 9/11, scholars began to argue that criticism should turn toward literature's role in helping people make sense of their lives as political *and* ethical beings.

3 I could also mention the influence of Bernard Williams, Iris Murdoch, Charles Taylor, and Emmanuel Levinas. These philosophers should not be casually bunched together, however. Rorty's anti-foundationalism, for instance, is at the opposite end of the philosophical spectrum from Nussbaum's Platonism. What they have in common is that they belong to the tradition of secular humanism and share a desire to see within philosophy a broader vocabulary for ethics, one that could include narrative, memoir, psychology, and art.

4 For instance, some critics study literary ethics in the context of race, gender, and power; political trauma; democracy and the goals of liberalism; narratology; art and aesthetics; philosophy; and particular social practices and professions, such as medicine, law, and teaching. These approaches are represented in several edited collections, including Davis and Womack (2001); Garber et al. (2000); Adamson et al. (1998); Hadfield et al. (1999); and special issues of *PMLA* 114.1 (1999), *New Literary History* 34.1 (2003), and *Poetics Today* 25.4 (2004).

5 These kinds of friends, admits Booth, have traditionally been hailed as "the classics." Some cultural studies critics object to ethical criticism because its focus is often on works of exceptional literary value. The critics I have been citing have written on the great nineteenth-century novelists (Dickens, Melville, Eliot, Tolstoy), modernists (James, Lawrence, Conrad), and contemporary authors of very high reputation (Toni Morrison, Kazuo Ishiguro, J. M. Coetzee). I personally don't have a problem with this, and agree with David Parker that "canonical" works should not be dismissed on the grounds of their ideological underpinnings:

> It is far easier to sit in political judgment on complex literary works than to elicit from them their ethical inquiries about the difficulties of judging human worth.... There remains the danger that suspicion of the literature of the past will cut us off from significant parts of it, both imprisoning us in the peculiar perspective of the present, and making it necessary, from the ethical point of view, to reinvent the wheel from generation to generation.
>
> (Parker 1994: 196)

6 My examples and definitions are borrowed from James Phelan's short glossary of terms in *Living to Tell About It* (2005: 213–219).

7 An excellent example is Phelan's chapter on *Lolita* in *Living to Tell About It* (2005: 98–131).

8 I also invite readers to sample other critiques, especially Brooks and Warren (1947: 344–350); Trilling (1957: 22–33); Ringe (1959: 24–29); and Fetterley (1978: 12–22).

9 Brooks and Warren single out the phrase "who knows what he does" as especially important: "Man, because he is capable of choice—because he 'knows'
what he does—because he is capable of being better than the brute, becomes,
when he fails to exercise this capacity, something worse than the brute" (1947:
348–349). This reading would be supported by what the narrator says about
the mystical moment before the race: "because he knew what I knew" strongly
implies that Jerry's knowledge, from the boy's perspective, is knowledge that
purity and goodness are real things, and he feels this knowledge unites them.

10 See Smith (1973); Matthews (1982).

References

Adamson, Jane, Richard Freadman and David Parker, eds. (1998) *Renegotiating Ethics in Literature, Philosophy, and Theory*. Cambridge, U.K.: Cambridge University Press.

Altieri, Charles (2001) "Lyrical Ethics and Literary Experience," in *Mapping the Ethical Turn: A Reader in Ethics, Culture, and Literary Theory*, ed. Todd F. Davis and Kenneth Womack. Charlottesville: University Press of Virginia, 30–58.

Anderson, Sherwood (1924) *A Story Teller's Story*. New York: Grove Press.

Anderson, Sherwood [1921] (1988) *The Triumph of the Egg*. New York: Four Walls Eight Windows.

Arnold, Matthew [1880] (1970) "The Study of Poetry," in *Selected Prose*, ed. P. J. Keating. Harmondsworth: Penguin, 340–366.

Booth, Wayne C. (1968) "The Rhetoric of Fiction and the Poetics of Fiction." *Novel: A Forum on Fiction* 1: 105–117.

Booth, Wayne C. (1983) *The Rhetoric of Fiction*. 2nd edition. Chicago: University of Chicago Press.

Booth, Wayne C. (1988) *The Company We Keep: An Ethics of Fiction*. Berkeley: University of California Press.

Brooks, Cleanth (1947) *The Well Wrought Urn: Studies in the Structure of Poetry*. New York: Harcourt Brace.

Brooks, Cleanth and Robert Penn Warren [1943] (1947) *Understanding Fiction*. New York: F. S. Crofts.

Brower, Reuben [1951] (2013) *Fields of Light: An Experiment in Critical Reading*. Philadelphia: Paul Dry Books.

Buell, Lawrence (1999) "In Pursuit of Ethics." *PMLA* 114.1 (January): 7–19.

Burke, Kenneth [1938] (1998) "Literature as Equipment for Living," in *The Critical Tradition: Classic and Contemporary Trends*, ed. David H. Richter. Boston: Bedford Books, 593–598.

Camus, Albert [1955] (1983) *The Myth of Sisyphus and Other Essays*. New York: Knopf.

Davis, Todd F. and Kenneth Womack, eds. (2001) *Mapping the Ethical Turn: A Reader in Ethics, Culture, and Literary Theory*. Charlottesville: University Press of Virginia.

Derrida, Jacques (1995) *The Gift of Death*. Trans. David Wills. Chicago: University of Chicago Press.

Eskin, Michael (2004) "The Double 'Turn' to Ethics and Literature?" *Poetics Today* 25.4: 557–572.

Fetterley, Judith (1978) *The Resisting Reader: Feminist Approaches to American Fiction.* Bloomington: Indiana University Press.

Gallop, Jane (2000) "The Ethics of Reading: Close Encounters." *Journal of Curriculum Theorizing* (Fall): 7–17.

Garber, Marjorie, Beatrice Hanssen, and Rebecca Walkowitz, eds. (2000) *The Turn To Ethics.* London: Routledge.

Gregory, Marshall (2009) *Shaped by Stories: The Ethical Power of Narratives.* South Bend, IN: University of Notre Dame Press.

Hadfield, Andrew, Dominic Rainsford, and Tim Wood, eds. (1999) *The Ethics in Literature.* London: Palgrave Macmillan.

James, Henry (1948) *The Art of Fiction and Other Essays,* ed. Morris Roberts. Oxford: Oxford University Press.

Jameson, Frederic (1981) *The Political Unconscious: Narrative as a Socially Symbolic Act.* Ithaca, NY: Cornell University Press.

Kundera, Milan (1986) *The Art of the Novel.* Trans. Linda Asher. New York: Harper and Rowe.

Matthews, George C. (1982) "Ohio's Beulah Land, or Plantation Blacks in the Fiction of Sherwood Anderson." *College Language Association Journal* 25.4 (June): 405–413.

Miller, J. Hillis (1986) *The Ethics of Reading: Kant, De Man, Eliot, Trollope, James, and Benjamin.* New York: Columbia University Press.

Miller, J. Hillis (2001) "How to Be 'in Tune with the Right' in *The Golden Bowl,*" in *Mapping the Ethical Turn: A Reader in Ethics, Culture, and Literary Theory,* ed. Todd F. Davis and Kenneth Womack. Charlottesville: University Press of Virginia, 271–285.

Newton, Adam Zachary (1995) *Narrative Ethics.* Cambridge, MA: Harvard University Press.

Nussbaum, Martha (1990) *Love's Knowledge: Essays on Philosophy and Literature.* Oxford: Oxford University Press.

Parker, David (1994) *Ethics, Theory and the Novel.* Cambridge, U.K.: Cambridge University Press.

Phelan, James (2005) *Living to Tell About It: A Rhetoric and Ethics of Character Narration.* Ithaca, NY: Cornell University Press.

Phelan, James (2008) *Experiencing Fiction: Judgments, Progressions, and the Rhetorical Theory of Narrative.* Columbus: The Ohio State University Press.

Richards, I. A. (1929) *Practical Criticism.* New York: Harcourt Brace.

Ringe, Donald (1959) "Point of View and Theme in 'I Want to Know Why.'" *Critique* 3.1 (Spring/Fall): 24–29.

Rorty, Richard (1989) "The Barber of Kasbeam: Nabokov on Cruelty," *Contingency, Irony, and Solidarity.* Cambridge, U.K.: Cambridge University Press, 141–168.

Sartre, Jean-Paul [1949] (1988) "Why Write?," in *What Is Literature? and Other Essays.* Cambridge, MA: Harvard University Press, 48–69.

Smith, Anneliese H. (1973)"Part of the Problem: Student Responses to Sherwood Anderson's 'I Want to Know Why.'" *Negro American Literature Forum* 7.1 (Spring): 28–31.

Trilling, Lionel (1957) *The Liberal Imagination: Essays on Literature and Society.* New York: Doubleday.

5　Engaged readings

This chapter offers five models of close reading by contemporary literary critics. As in the previous chapters, the literary work is reprinted in full so we can read it carefully on our own and talk about it with others before jumping to the interpretation that follows.

These are challenging readings. Although the critics do not rely on history or cultural contexts, many of them do fold in allusions to other literary works and to literary history. Their individual voices come through in their tone and mood, and in the specific theoretical or philosophical assumptions that drive their arguments. While respecting the text's autonomy, each critic also reaches for something essential beyond the poem or story—an observation or an insight about the nature of selfhood, pleasure, knowledge, or survival.

Charles Altieri's reading of a poem by the modernist W. B. Yeats asks about the use of abstraction in poetry, leading to a profound meditation on the meaning of self-affirmation. In her interpretation of "The Thread" by Scottish poet Don Paterson, Heather Dubrow weaves a sensitive reading of the poem's prismatic language with reflections on her debt to some of her former teachers, including Rueben Brower, who taught her how to appreciate the nuances of words. Sandra M. Gilbert also honors her former teacher, M. H. Abrams. In her reading of "Edge" by Sylvia Plath, she hopes to release the last poem Plath wrote before she committed suicide from the cultural myths surrounding the poet, and attend to how the sound of certain words communicates meaning. James Phelan, in his rhetorical reading of a short story by the contemporary American writer Tobias Wolff, carefully unbraids the narrative's complex strands and presents his own affective and ethical responses to the story's portrait of a complex and damaged character. Finally, Herbert Tucker applies his mastery of prosody to his reading of a lyric by the elusive Victorian poet Christina Rossetti, leading us to wonder about the formal qualities that make a poem charming, mesmerizing, magical, or seductive.

As we engage these close readings, we might ask how each critic weighs in on the subjective/objective problem, and what strategies and values are detectable in each. Have they illuminated the literary work in interesting ways? Do they explain what they want to find out in their reading? Do they seem personally invested in their analysis of the work? These questions will require us to go back to the poem or story and measure the author's words and our responses against the critic's reading—part of the ongoing conversation that makes up the pleasant and impelling study of literary art.

Reading 1   Charles Altieri

He and She (1935)

William Butler Yeats

> As the moon sidles up
> Must she sidle up,
> As trips the scared moon
> Away must she trip:
> 'His light had struck me blind
> Dared I stop'.
>
> She sings as the moon sings:
> 'I am I, am I;
> The greater grows my light
> The further that I fly'.
> All creation shivers
> With that sweet cry.

There are two traits that I most admire in poetry. The first is the capacity of the poet to make visible a rich imaginative inventiveness, especially in constructing engaging situations in highly condensed form. Imagination is the vehicle by which poetry acknowledges responsibility to the world of fact and ordinary occurrences while dramatizing the writer's control over the specific ways facts make their appearance. And for modernist poetry, imagination is most intensely visible when the world presented is highly concentrated, as if the world were not independent but depended on how the writer acknowledged it. Second, the poet has to make language a vehicle for both embodying and enacting intelligent choices. It is not sufficient to copy or picture or characterize a world. The writer must make language actually perform something in relation to the situation that it composes.

These abstractions are not easy to grasp without examples. So I have chosen a highly condensed lyric, "He and She," written by William Butler Yeats toward the end of his career.

The world in this poem is made up in its details but realistic in its psychology. The poem's twelve lines are divided into two halves. The first half imagines a woman with a fundamentally passive disposition bound to the moon, which in turn is bound to a terror of anything that can shine its own light, like the sun. The second half envisions the woman no longer dependent on the moon but capable of matching the moon when it can sing of freedom. That singing in turn generates an increasing awareness of the fact that she can celebrate her own capacities to give light, and, indeed to become the light that she sings about. The more she identifies her singing with the light, the more she can celebrate herself until the inner celebrating becomes the primary source of outer light.

Yeats chooses a highly symmetrical form because he wants to focus on making present an effective rendering of the differences between two opposed states. Symmetry helps make those contrasts visible. Look, for example, at how the rhymes work. When "she" is afraid in the first six lines the rhymes are an awkward conjunction of repetition ("up," "up") with off rhymes ("trip," "stop"). It is as if the constant motion simply does not allow the mind the concentration on any one thing to perfect something as elemental as rhyme. But the building to "I am I" invites a very different set of quite strong rhymes. This sweet cry is part and parcel of an expression of will that masters the possibilities for rhyme—thus reinforcing the action of setting oneself apart from the world as one's means of lighting one's own way.

More important, the symmetry establishes a powerful contradiction between the psychology of the two states. The last two lines of the first half of the poem present the only words spoken by the passive follower of the moon. Those words deepen the woman's isolation because when she speaks she can only focus on her own terror: for her there is no other world. Her speech in the second part of the poem is also focused on the self. But this is a self in an expansive mode of self-consciousness. Where the moon is the focus of repetition in the first half of the poem, it is "I" that dominates the second half.

In fact the repetition of "am I" becomes the central moment of the poem. For the writing itself realizes that it can produce its own realization of what a full self-consciousness can achieve by stressing this new mode of repetition: in effect the active self-consciousness realizes the full force of what the self is asserting. Think about how rarely we observe the self in a way that enables us to identify completely with what the self is doing, without ironic commentary or doubt or projecting other possibilities. By fully asserting "I am I, am I" the speaker in effect projects aligning the self-reflexive will with the act of self-assertion. In most of our lives we do not will so much as wish we could put together what we observe about ourselves and what we want really to be our nature fully expressed. But in these concluding lines there is no gap between what we see ourselves doing and what we can completely affirm as the self we want to be. There is no gap between willing and observing; there is only union between what is celebrated and what the poem demonstrates as full self-consciousness. We experience the possibility of participating so intensely in a state that there simply becomes no distinction between agent and action: you are for the moment pure lover or sinner or even Kierkegaardian saint.

Perhaps it is no wonder then that the closing lines develop this assertion by producing the strongest contrast in the poem. Remember how "she" is locked into self-doubt, and so she is utterly alone in her being driven to repeat what the authority of the moon requires. "I am I, am I" might seem an even deeper sense of entrapment in the self. But for Yeats self-affirmation is perhaps the only way out of destructive self-consciousness because the joy of affirmation invites a sense of possible sharing. Or, as the poem puts it, self-affirmation makes the best lover because all creation comes to shiver at that sweet cry. How can creation not find intense sexual pleasure in a self that joins creation in its core act of self-affirmation? (If self-affirmation were trapped in fear, there could be no responding "shiver," and no sense of something to be desired intensely.)

But why is the poem so abstract in its celebrating of how affirmation of self joins all creation in a kind of sexual congress? Does not that abstraction having a chilling effect on praise of creation? And can "shiver" effectively stand for the entire demand of sexual pleasure? I think Yeats would say that anything less abstract would be insufficiently concrete—for the "she" who speaks and for the audience who is invited to participate by identifying both with the self-affirmation and with what might make creation shiver. For the ultimate self-affirmation is not of this particular empirical self defined by a specific state of historical contingencies that make us Jews or Arabs or peasants or aristocrats. Ultimate self-affirmation is of the feeling of self abstracted from those contingencies. Ultimate self-affirmation is getting in touch with the intense set of energies that make you feel that what is essential about being you can be contained in one simple cry of complete affirmation. One cannot completely identify with being a peasant or an aristocrat because one cannot completely control the conditions basic to those aspects of self-definition. But everyone can at some moments completely control the feeling of being completely alive and undivided, whatever the condition of the empirical self. Elsewhere Yeats wrote of an ideal state of the mind partaking of "pure activity" as it abstracts from any specific determining contexts.

Abstraction then becomes not a movement away from the real but an engaging of the real within a completely concrete immediacy. And that means the readers also are invited to shed their sense of contingent identities. This is why Yeats could believe that poetry is not the describing of some condition of self-conscious affirmation but is the enacting of that affirmation in a way that is available to an expansive audience if it is willing to abstract way from the empirical conditions that divide us, especially when the poem is so compressed that it forces the kind of concentration that it celebrates. There is a level of experience where readers too can cry "I am I, am I" despite their differences. And then, and perhaps only then, might they experience all creation shivering with that sweet cry.

Reading 2   Heather Dubrow

The Thread (2003)

Don Paterson

>Jamie made his landing in the world
>so hard he ploughed straight back into the earth.
>They caught him by the head of his one breath
>and pulled him up. They don't know how it held.
>And so today thank what higher will
>brought us to here, to you and me and Russ,
>the great twin-engined swaying wingspan of us
>roaring down the back of Kirrie Hill
>
>and your two-year-old lungs somehow out-revving
>every engine in the universe.
>*All that trouble just to turn up the dead*
>was all I thought that long week. Now the thread
>is holding all of us: look at our tiny house,
>son, the white dot of your mother waving.

Threads can bind. And they can wrinkle, unravel, snap. A thread can be fragile as the life of an imperiled newborn or strong as steel. In contrasting the happy family evoked in lines 5 through 14 with earlier threats to his son's survival, Don Paterson's "The Thread" plays those meanings against each other, complicating the simple binaries. In so doing, he explores the threatened but powerful linkages within a family—and gestures as well toward generic and other literary threadings, bindings, and knottings.

Describing the birth of his son as a dangerous "landing" (1), Paterson sets up the contrast with the joyful games at hand. At the same time, the word "ploughed" (2), suggesting as it does both the life-threatening and chaotic arrival of a plane and the steady georgic process of bringing new life to the earth, encapsulates within itself that contrast. And we may be aware from the outset that "thread" rhymes with "dead," creating the pairing that the poem explores in so many ways and incorporates explicitly within its sestet.

The second quatrain evokes—and enacts—the move to the moment when planes represent an energetic force to be imitated rather than a trope for disaster with a whole series of discursive and aural changes: full rhyme replaces off rhyme; the distancing third person of "Jamie" (1) and "They" (3, 4), which mirrors the temporal distance from his birth, becomes "I" (5) and "you and me and Russ" (6), and "us" (6, 7). To put it another way, the repeated third person plural plays the anonymous authority of well-meaning but pessimistic medical authorities against that of a "higher will" (5) described in terms that only glancingly allude to a spiritual dimension and the energy of the current activities. The contrast between the two quatrains is also enacted when past tense declaratives yield to the immediacy of the present participle "roaring" (8) in a quatrain that itself roars with vigor, relief, and joy. Indeed, the recurrence of present participles elsewhere signals the poem's concern with actions and events in the *here and now*.

Yet "here" (6), one of the most intriguing words in the poem, exemplifies the apparent straightforwardness and underlying complexity that often accompany that and other deictics. It is both spatial and temporal, the former reading emphasized by "Kirrie Hill" (8). "Here" (6) surely also refers to the earth of living human beings as opposed to the death that threatened the child. Moreover, "to you and me and Russ" (6) can be read in apposition to "here" (6), thus defining that deictic in terms of the family as its source and symbol.

The opening of the sestet continues the immediacy of "roaring"(8) with "out-revving" (9), playing on repeated –n and –v sounds and even managing to make the sounds of that noisy child charming. Better, better beyond measure, this racket than the eternal silence to which that frail newborn might have been condemned. As the sestet progresses, the distal deictic "that" contributes to the contrast between the *here and now* and the terrifying events following the child's birth: "*All that trouble ... that long week*" (11, 12), *versus* the "Now" (12) that immediately follows those references.

The final three lines make the patterns I have been tracing more explicit. The pronounced medial caesura in line 12 reintroduces the now/then contrasts. Ending on a direct address ("son" [14]) and the injunction to that child of course stresses family ties. Vision is itself a thread that can tie together that family even when one member isn't present. The colon after "all of us" (13) is important: it suggests that the act of looking and waving are part of how the thread works (distance, unlike the distance threatened in the opening of the poem, can be bridged through those actions). And the poem may be suggesting that its own descriptions, the command to "look" (13) that surely extends to the reader as well, help to create and strengthen the thread.

And yet. Contemporary criticism has schooled us to read for gaps and contradictions, for the fraying or lying thread. Surely we also sense some tension between the firm and apparently celebratory declarative, "Now the thread/is holding all of us" (12–13) and the hint of fragility in the size of the house and the reduction of the mother to a dot? Those descriptions may indeed return us to the awareness that threads can be fragile, especially when stretched to extend over a long distance. Close reading requires, I think, an alertness to the fact that if one should not lose sight of the forest for the trees, neither should one risk the opposite.

Why a sonnet? Paterson's edition and commentary on Shakespeare's sonnets as well as his other poems in the genre testify to a deep interest in this form in particular, in this instance offering him the opportunity to map that genre's mined territory of love and loss in terms of familial relationships. Lengths of thread and family trees are also relevant in that Paterson, in exploring his paternal connections, is announcing his filial connections to earlier writers of these fourteen-line poems. Above all, I think, he enjoyed experimenting with the possibilities for playing with sonnet structure, as my point about the different rhyme schemes in the opening quatrains has already suggested and as his frequent experiments with other types of line and other forms confirm. More specifically, in "The Thread" the break between octet and sestet is emphasized by the spacing (a visual analogue to the emphasis on geographical space), yet diminished by the syntax, as well as by the "and" (9) that undercuts the idea of a volta. (In another sonnet in the volume, "The Shut-In," the volta is again emphasized by spacing, but in that case it involves a corresponding shift in focus as well.) Thus the poem itself enacts visually and generically its thematized concern with rupturing and uniting.

Again affiliating itself with and distinguishing itself from other options for the sonnet, especially the Petrarchan and Shakespearean rhyme schemes, this poem has the structure *abbacddc efggfe*. The rhymes of the sestet, one of so many variations that Paterson could have chosen, separate letters only to reunite them, the fundamental pattern of the poem recurring, or to put it another way, it gathers together and encloses its letters, also germane to the gathering in and gathering together of the family.

Implicit in the poem and in my own work in interpreting it is an extension of my opening points about threads. Paterson was surely aware that *fil* is the French word for "thread" and *fils* for "son." And aware as well that although the etymology of "affiliation" involves links with a child, that bilingual wordplay connects threads and affiliations, two concerns that in their biological and literary workings tie together (dare one say) the poem? In any event, writing this essay both activates and complicates my own affiliations and filial loyalties in relation to close reading.

As I have argued at greater length elsewhere, both close reading and New Criticism are often misunderstood or misrepresented, sometimes willfully in a process of dismissal and mockery.[1] Although rebutted in many quarters, these assumptions recur often enough to justify a brief survey here. Yes, New Criticism flourished in the 1950s and 1960s, but alternative approaches such as psychoanalytical criticism and intellectual history were alive and well; and at certain institutions such as Harvard, the New Critics were an embattled minority rather than the only game in town. Moreover, its adherents there and elsewhere were more varied in their assumptions and approaches than we sometimes acknowledge; witness above all the Marxism of William Empson, admittedly an outlier though not unique in his assumption that literary texts interact with a cultural environment. Formalism and close reading should not simply be equated even in the heyday of the latter: some formalists, notably the Chicago School, were not very interested in looking intensively at texts, and some close readers ignored many issues about form. Nor, of course, can we equate close reading and New Criticism, as the often brilliant interpretations of deconstruction demonstrate.

My own education and subsequent responses to it are in some ways a microcosm of the legacies of New Criticism. In my undergraduate days, Harvard relied far too much on large lectures, many of which lacked discussion sections or even paper assignments (even though, as I later learned, funding for that type of learning was available). But the many negative consequences of that system were in significant ways counterbalanced by the opportunity for one-to-one weekly honors tutorials. I was privileged to work in that way with two extraordinary New Critics, David Kalstone and Neil Rudenstine. It is to them I owe becoming a scholar and teacher of early modern literature and a lifelong commitment to reading texts closely. And subsequently the second reader on my dissertation was a dean of New Criticism, Reuben Brower, whose approach was at odds with that of the other reader, an intellectual historian; I was also one of Ben's Teaching Fellows and thus learned his methods of instructing students in close reading—which, memorably, he often preferred to call "slow reading."

In looking back on my training in New Criticism, my overriding response is gratitude to David Kalstone and Neil Rudenstine in particular as well as to Reuben Brower and his whole tribe in general. Sensitivity to the nuances of language has been invaluable to me as a critic and a poet. To be sure, New Criticism and the close reading that often attended it have been rightly faulted for buying into a conception of the well-wrought urn—that is, the unified text, the organic whole—and such assumptions can short-circuit acknowledgment of those textual gaps about which critics in the past thirty years have written so powerfully. Arguably, too, that approach transfers to the text and hence helps to justify and encourage a type of political conservatism and even quietism: societies may be read as well-wrought urns, auspiciously containing rather than cracked by tensions. One can cite significant exceptions, but on the whole neither the texts favored by New Critics nor those critics themselves tend to the practice Melville attributes to Hawthorne: "Say[s] No! in thunder."[2] As I have reported elsewhere, in the late 1960s we graduate students set up a meeting to discuss the Vietnam War with our professors. Reuben Brower remarked that such issues were sometimes very complex (Dubrow 2013: xi–xii). His colleague replied that sometimes they were very simple. Yet I am persuaded that it is possible on the one hand to attack reprehensible social and political values, whether embedded in a text or practiced elsewhere, while on the other hand continuing to respect and delight in formal and other aesthetic achievements. And recognizing aesthetic failures and gaps within a text need not preclude celebrating its often breathtaking triumphs.

Above all, the filial gratitude I feel stems from that legacy of reading slowly. The close reading in which I was trained precludes an assumption no less pernicious than the expectation that a literary text will typically be a harmonious and unified masterpiece—that is, the notion that a quick examination will allow one to extract the "message" from the text (a message often corresponding neatly to one's presuppositions about the author or genre or culture). As a teacher myself, I am committed to passing on the obligations and rewards of lingering and repeated engagements with the text, especially in an era where the social media may encourage rapid perusal of all written matter, and especially in a world where David Kalstone died far too young; my many classes on Sir Philip Sidney over the years have been tributes to him, often silent, sometimes acknowledged.

There were, however, other downsides to the New Critical training I received during those years. Some of its adherents ignored other types of criticism, though most of my own teachers were honorable exceptions. The types of reading in which I was schooled did not emphasize techniques of argumentation enough. Also, in those days Harvard's parochialism was reflected in the fact that exciting theoretical developments (aptly regarded as new critical avenues) were marginalized if not ignored by both the New Critical factions and the practitioners of literary and intellectual history despite—and quite possibly because of—the fact that some of them were taking place just down the road at Yale.

Paterson's poem about gathering and separating, about threads that bind and threads that snap, may also encourage us to relate this personal and professional history from half a century ago to current developments in our own discipline. Countering the distrust that often characterizes encounters between literature professors and their colleagues in creative writing would enable both groups to learn from and with each other when practicing close reading. And the otherwise salutary emphasis on decreasing time to the doctoral degree risks pushing fledgling professors prematurely into a long-term affiliation with a particular critical method as well as with a narrowly conceived specialty. We should indeed be concerned about the recurrence and possible intensification of these and other pressures that discourage a capacious vision of alternative critical approaches and hence preclude toleration and respect for their practitioners roaring down hills not marked on our own maps of methodologies.

Reading 3 Sandra M. Gilbert
Edge (1963)

Sylvia Plath

> The woman is perfected.
> Her dead
>
> Body wears the smile of accomplishment,
> The illusion of a Greek necessity

Flows in the scrolls of her toga,
Her bare

Feet seem to be saying:
We have come so far, it is over.

Each dead child coiled, a white serpent,
One at each little

Pitcher of milk, now empty.
She has folded

Them back into her body as petals
Of a rose close when the garden

Stiffens and odors bleed
From the sweet, deep throats of the night flower.

The moon has nothing to be sad about,
Staring from her hood of bone.

She is used to this sort of thing.
Her blacks crackle and drag.

If there's anyone whose craft and (sometimes) sullen art have been mythol-ogized nearly to death, it's Sylvia Plath. She's been the subject of a novel, a movie, and countless warring memoirs and biographies. She even has a Facebook page (although, to be fair, the last time I looked only two hapless souls had "friended" her). For these reasons, teaching her is incredibly dif-ficult, perhaps especially from a feminist perspective. That old Hollywood magic is riveting, as are the sexual politics of her life: students want to learn more about the soap opera of Ted and Sylvia and Assia and Aurelia, and of course "Daddy," whoever and whatever *he* was. That these figures had been reconstructed in accomplished verse through an extraordinary mastery of the linguistic arts is often hard to explain—even if you tell the class, as I've frequently done, to try to imagine that the poet of *Ariel* is alive and well somewhere in South America.

Inevitably, "Edge," a poem about suicide that Plath produced a few days before her final (and successful) attempt at her own suicide, seems to compel biographical speculation. Never mind critical studies, just look online! The moon is Assia? Aurelia? And the babies—did she really want to kill them too, like a twentieth-century Medea? I had at least one col-league who actually believed that Plath had murdered her children, despite lots of journalistic evidence to the contrary! (And of course Assia Gutmann literalized such a reading of "Edge" when she killed her little girl, Shura, along with herself, a few years after Plath's death.)

But if we *listen* to "Edge," thinking of what M. H. Abrams (2002) calls its sonorous "fourth dimension," we must realize that these incantatory, almost sepulchrally melodious lines were written by a woman in the depths of a dreadful depression, a young mother shaking with grief and rage and fear. And inevitably, they've been read as—and perhaps can be rightly considered—an extraordinary suicide note, a fantasy of the dead body as spectacle, straight out of the tragic histories of Medea (with her dead children) or Cleopatra (suckling a serpent). Originally titled "Nuns in Snow"—perhaps punning on *nones* in snow—"Edge" is one of the few draft manuscripts on which Plath actually wrote her name: "S. Plath" appears in the upper right-hand corner. Perhaps appropriately, considering the final dread it embodied, the poem was scribbled on the verso of a typed copy of the hopeful poem "Wintering."

In addition to its play with Medea and Cleopatra and "Wintering" and convents, the poem had other literary influences. Plath and Hughes were acolytes of Robert Graves's *White Goddess*, whose presence manifests itself here, as the moon stares from her hood of bone, and of William Butler Yeats, whose lunar changes swayed the world. Enriching these parallels, moreover, the poem can be read as a chamber of literary echoes: the sweetly scented "embalmed darkness" of Keats's "Ode to a Nightingale" informs the writer's urge to cease upon the midnight with no pain, Blake's sick rose shapes the closing rose of her imagination, D. H. Lawrence's "Bavarian Gentians," "torch-like, with the smoking blueness of Pluto's gloom," darken the scene, and Wallace Stevens's "Emperor of Ice Cream" helps her remind us "how cold [her subject] is, and dumb" even while she insists that "the lamp affix its beam."

But beyond these and other aesthetic pressures, to tongue the lines and syllables of "Edge" is to inhabit a poem whose artful muscularity reminds us of the ache, the stress, and even, on the edge of death, the joy of language. Sylvia Plath was a superb reader of her own verse, as those who have heard her well-known recordings of "Daddy," "Lady Lazarus," and other poems will know. It's unlikely that she would have ever read "Edge" aloud, except perhaps in her head or in the snow-bitten silence of her last few days. Yet consider how the tolling, tolling bells of its funereal fantasy roll in the mouth. "The woman is *perfected*/Her *dead*/*Body* wears the smile of accomplishment,/The illusion of a Greek necessity/*Flows* in the *scrolls* of her *toga*." When my students want to meditate on the mugs of milk the poet left for her children before she put her head in the oven, I sorrow with them and sympathize, but also point out how remarkably those mugs were transformed into dead breasts metaphorized as elegantly half-rhyming "*little*/*Pitcher*[s] of *milk*." And what Plath herself called the "snow blitz" of that ghastly London winter of 1963 evolved into an extended counter-metaphor of floral maternal reabsorption, in which the dead woman has "*folded*/[her children] back into her body as petals/Of a *rose close* when the garden/Stiffens and *odors bleed*/From the *sweet, deep throats* of the night flower." As a poet myself, I sometimes think I'd almost die to write a line like that—and yet, the "aural actions that body forth" this line, as Abrams writes (2012: 3), are themselves aesthetically life-giving.

What of the mysterious moon that presides over the poem's conclusion? Unlike the moons of Yeats or Graves, this one is colloquial. She has "*nothing* to be sad about" as if she were an indifferent passerby, or as if, as in *Lear*, nothing has come of nothing. "Staring from her hood of bone," she isn't full, she's a crescent with a heart of darkness, so she's "used to this sort of thing"—although her weary sophistication implies power rather than powerlessness, for "Her *blacks crackle and drag*."

Blacks? Crackling and dragging? What can such a scary riddle signify? More than nothing, for sure. We can certainly attempt analyses. The dark of the moon as it wanes or waxes sends out weird electricity, witchlike, and its shadows drag the world for hopeless, helpless souls and bodies, or so we might decide. But whatever we can speculate is eclipsed, after all, by the feeling we have when we *say* the line. "*Her blacks crackle and drag.*" The sound here *is* the meaning and the terror of the meaning. It brings us to the edge of possibility, or, more accurately, the edge of knowledge, at which the poet hovers, imagining "a Greek necessity"—or the illusion of one—and yet resisting it with the bravura tongue of art. Situated on that edge and edgily mythologizing the liminal zone in which, along with the moon, we gaze at death, "Edge" is a final "act of utterance," as Abrams would put it, coming to us from the utter distance to which the blacks of despair *dragged* the poet. Yet unnerving though they are, the risky cadences of this work sing to us still, silencing biographical scandal and reminding us what the muses, even at their most disquieting, can inspire.

For M. H. Abrams, in honor of his 100th birthday, and to celebrate the publication of *The Fourth Dimension of a Poem and Other Essays* (W. W. Norton, 2012).

Reading 4   James Phelan

The Night in Question

Tobias Wolff

Frances had come to her brother's apartment to hold his hand over a disappointment in love, but Frank ate his way through half the cherry pie she'd brought him and barely mentioned the woman. He was in an exalted state over a sermon he'd heard that afternoon. Dr. Violet had outdone himself, Frank said. This was his best; this was the gold standard. Frank wanted to repeat it to Frances, the way he used to act out movie scenes for her when they were young.

"Gotta run, Franky."

"It's not that long," Frank said. "Five minutes. Ten—at the outside."

Three years earlier he had driven Frances' car into a highway abutment and almost died, then almost died again, in detox, of a *grand mal* seizure. Now he wanted to preach sermons at her. She supposed she was grateful. She said she'd give him ten minutes.

It was a muggy night, but as always Frank wore a long-sleeved shirt to hide the weird tattoos he woke up with one morning when he was stationed in Manila. The shirt was white, starched and crisply ironed. The tie he'd worn to church was still cinched up hard under his prominent Adam's apple. A big man in a small room, he paced in front of the couch as he gathered himself to speak. He favored his left leg, whose knee had been shattered in the crash; every time his right foot came down, the dishes clinked in the cupboards.

"Okay, here goes," he said. "I'll have to fill in here and there but I've got most of it." He continued to walk, slowly, deliberately, hands behind his back, head bent at an angle that suggested meditation. "My dear friends," he said, "you may have read in the paper not long ago of a man of our state, a parent like many of yourselves here today ... but a parent with a terrible choice to make. His name is Mike Bolling. He's a railroad man, Mike, a switchman, been with the railroad ever since he finished high school, same as his father and grandfather before him. He and Janice've been married ten years now. They were hoping for a whole houseful of kids, but the Lord decided to give them one instead, a very special one. That was nine years ago. Benny, they named him—after Janice's father. He died when she was just a youngster, but she remembered his big lopsided grin and the way he threw back his head when he laughed, and she was hoping some of her dad's spirit would rub off on his name. Well, it turned out she got all the spirit she could handle, and then some.

"Benny. He came out in high gear and never shifted down. Mike liked to say you could run a train off him, the energy he had. Good student, natural athlete, but his big thing was mechanics. One of those boys, you put him in the same room with a clock and he's got it in pieces before you can turn around. By the time he was in second grade he could put the clocks back together, not to mention the vacuum cleaner and the TV and the engine of Mike's old lawn mower."

This didn't sound like Frank. Frank was plain in his speech, neither formal nor folksy, so spare and sometimes harsh that his jokes sounded like challenges, or insults. Frances was about the only one who got them. This tone was putting her on edge. Something terrible was going to happen in the story, something Frances would regret having heard. She knew that. But she didn't stop him. Frank was her little brother, and she would deny him nothing.

When Frank was still a baby, not even walking yet, Frank Senior, their father, had set out to teach his son the meaning of the word no. At dinner he'd dangle his wristwatch before Frank's eyes, then say *no!* and jerk it back just as Frank grabbed for it. When Frank persisted, Frank Senior would slap his hand until he was howling with fury and desire. This happened night after night. Frank would not take the lesson to heart; as soon as the watch was offered, he snatched at it. Frances followed her mother's example and said nothing. She was eight years old, and while she feared her father's attention she also missed it, and resented Frank's obstinacy and the disturbance it caused. Why couldn't he learn? Then her father slapped Frank's face. This was on New Year's Eve. Frances still remembered the stupid tasselled hats they were all wearing when her father slapped her baby brother. In the void of time after the slap there was no sound but the long rush of air into Frank's lungs as, red-faced, twisting in his chair, he gathered himself to scream. Frank Senior lowered his head. Frances saw that he'd surprised himself and was afraid of what would follow. She looked at her mother, whose eyes were closed. In later years Frances tried to think of a moment when their lives might have turned by even a degree, turned and gone some other way, and she always came back to this instant when her father knew the wrong he had done, was shaken and open to rebuke. What might have happened if her mother had come flying out of her chair and stood over him and told him to stop, now and forever? Or if she had only *looked* at him confirming his shame. But her eyes were closed, and stayed closed until Frank blasted them with his despair and Frank Senior left the room. As Frances knew even then, her mother could not allow herself to see what she had no strength to oppose. Her heart was bad. Three years later she reached for a bottle of ammonia, said "Oh," sat down on the floor and died.

Frances did oppose her father. In defiance of his orders, she brought food to Frank's room when he was banished, stood up for him and told him he was right to stand up for himself. Frank Senior had decided that his son needed to be broken, and Frank would not break. He went after everything his father said no to, with Frances egging him on and mothering him when he got caught. In time their father ceased to give reasons for his displeasure. As his silence grew heavier, so did his hand. One night Frances grabbed her father's belt as he started after Frank, and when he flung her aside Frank head-rammed him in the stomach. Frances jumped on her father's back and the three of them crashed around the room. When it was over Frances was flat on the floor with a split lip and a ringing sound in her eyes, laughing like a madwoman. Frank was crying. That was the first time.

Frank Senior said no to his son in everything, and Frances would say no to him in nothing. Frank was aware of her reluctance and learned to exploit it, most shamelessly in the months before his accident. He'd invaded her home, caused her trouble at work, nearly destroyed her marriage. To this day her husband had not forgiven Frances for what he called her complicity in that nightmare. But her husband had never been thrown across a room, or kicked, or slammed headfirst into a door. No one had ever spoken to him as her father had spoken to Frank. He did not understand what it was to be helpless and alone. No one should be alone in this world. Everyone should have someone who kept faith, no matter what, all the way.

"On the night in question," Frank said, "Mike's foreman called up and asked him to take another fellow's shift at the drawbridge station where he'd been working. A Monday night it was, mid-January, bitter cold. Janice was at a PTA meeting when Mike got the call, so he had no choice but to bring Benny along with him. It was against the rules, strictly speaking, but he needed the overtime and he'd done it before, more than once. Nobody ever said anything. Benny always behaved himself, and it was a good chance for him and Mike to buddy up, batch it a little. They'd talk and kid around, heat up some franks, then Mike would set Benny up with a sleeping bag and air mattress. A regular adventure.

"A bitter night, like I said. There was a furnace at the station, but it wasn't working. The guy Mike relieved had on his parka and a pair of mittens. Mike ribbed him about it, but pretty soon he and Benny put their own hats and gloves back on. Mike brewed up some hot chocolate, and they played gin rummy, or tried to—it's not that easy with gloves on. But they weren't thinking about winning or losing. It was good enough just being together, the two of them, with the cold wind blowing up against the windows. Father and son: what could be better than that? Then Mike had to raise the bridge for a couple of boats, and things got pretty tense because one of them steered too close to the bank and almost ran aground. The skipper had to reverse engines and go back downriver and take another turn at it. The whole business went on a lot longer than it should have, and by the time the second boat got clear Mike was running way behind schedule and under pressure to get the bridge down for the express train out of Portland. That was when he noticed Benny was missing."

Frank stopped by the window and looked out in an unseeing way. He seemed to be contemplating whether to go on. But then he turned away from the window and started in again, and Frances understood that this little moment of reflection was just another part of the sermon.

"Mike calls Benny's name. No answer. He calls him again, and he doesn't spare the volume. You have to understand the position Mike is in. He has to get the bridge down for that train and he's got just about enough time to do it. He doesn't know where Benny is, but he has a pretty good idea. Just where he isn't supposed to be. Down below, in the engine room.

"The engine room. The mill, as Mike and the other operators call it. You can imagine the kind of power that's needed to raise and lower a drawbridge, aside from the engine itself—all the winches and levers, pulleys and axles and wheels and so on. Massive machinery. Gigantic screws turning everywhere, gears with teeth like file cabinets. They've got catwalks and little crawlways through the works for the mechanics, but nobody goes down there unless they know what they're doing. You have to know what you're doing. You have to know exactly where to put your feet, and you've got to keep your hands in close and wear all the right clothes. And even if you know what you're doing, you never go down there when the bridge is being moved. Never. There's just too much going on, too many ways of getting snagged and pulled into the works. Mike has told Benny a hundred times, stay out of the mill. That's the iron rule when Benny comes out to the station. But Mike made the mistake of taking him down for a quick look one day when the engine was being serviced, and he saw how Benny lit up at the sight of all that steel, all that machinery. Benny was just dying to get his hand on those wheels and gears, see how everything fit together. Mike could feel it pulling at Benny like a big magnet. He always kept a close eye on him after that, until this one night, when he got distracted. And now Benny's down in there. Mike knows it as sure as he knows his own name."

Frances said, "I don't want to hear this story?"

Frank gave no sign that he'd heard her. She was going to say something else, but made a sour face and let him go on.

"To get to the engine room, Mike would have to go through the passageway to the back of the station and either wait for the elevator or climb down the emergency ladder. He doesn't have time to do the one or the other. He doesn't have time for anything but lowering the bridge, and just barely enough time for that. He's got to get that bridge down now or the train is going into the river with everyone on board. This is the position he's in; this is the choice he has to make. His son, his Benjamin, or the people on that train.

"Now, let's take a minute to think about the people on that train. Mike's never met any of them, but he's lived long enough to know what they're like. They're like the rest of us. There are some who know the Lord, and love their neighbors, and live in the light. And there are others. On this train are men who whisper over cunning papers and take from the widow even her mean portion. On this train is the man whose factories kill and maim his workers. There are thieves on this train, and liars, and hypocrites. There is the man whose wife is not enough for him, who cannot be happy until he possesses every woman who walks the earth. There is the false witness. There is the bribe-taker. There is the woman who abandons her husband and children for her own pleasure. There is the seller of spoiled goods, the coward, and the usurer, and there is the man who lives for his drug, who will do anything for that false promise—steal from those who give him work, from his friends, his family, yes, even from his own family, scheming for their pity, borrowing in bad faith, breaking into their very homes. All these are on the train, awake and hungry as wolves, and also on the train are the sleepers, the sleepers with open eyes who sleepwalk through their days, neither doing evil nor resisting it, like soldiers who lie down as if dead and will not join the battle, not for their cities and homes, not even for their wives and children. For such people, how can Mike give up his son, his Benjamin, who is guilty of nothing?

"He can't. Of course he can't, not on his own. But Mike isn't on his own. He knows what we all know, even when we try to forget it: we are never alone, ever. We are in our Father's presence in the light of day and in the dark of night, even in that darkness where we run from Him, hiding our faces like fearful children. He will not leave us. No. He will never leave us alone. Though we lock every window and bar every door, still He will enter. Though we empty our hearts and turn them to stone, yet shall He make His home there.

"He will not leave us alone. He is with all of you, as He is with me, He is with Mike, and also with the bribe-taker on the train, and woman who needs her friend's husband, and the man who needs a drink. He knows their needs better than they do. He knows that what they truly need is Him, and though they flee His voice He never stops telling them that He is there. And at this moment, when Mike has nowhere to hide and nothing left to tell himself, then he can hear, and he knows that he is not alone, and he knows what it is that he must do. It has been done before, even by Him who speaks, the Father of All, who gave His own son, His beloved, that others might be saved."

"No!" Frances said.

Frank stopped and looked at Frances as if he couldn't remember who she was.

"That's it," she said. "That's my quota of holiness for the year."

"But there's more."

"I know, I can see it coming. The guy kills his kid, right? I have to tell you, Frank, that's a crummy story. What're we supposed to get from a story like that—we should kill our own kid to save some stranger?"

"There's more to it than that."

"Okay, then, make it a trainload of strangers, make it *ten* trainloads of strangers. I should do this because the so-called Father of All did it? Is that the point? How do people think up stuff like this, anyway? It's an awful story."

"It's true."

"*True?* Franky. Please, you're not a moron."

"Dr. Violet knows a man who was on that train."

"I'll just bet he does. Let me guess." Frances screwed her eyes shut, then popped them open. "The drug addict! Yes, and he reformed afterward and worked with street kids in Brazil and showed everybody that Mike's sacrifice was not in vain. Is that how it goes?"

"You're missing the point, Frances. It isn't about that. Let me finish."

"No. It's a terrible story, Frank. People don't act like that. I sure as hell wouldn't."

"You haven't been asked. He doesn't ask us to do what we can't do."

"I don't care what He asks. Where'd you learn to talk like that, anyway? You don't even sound like yourself."

"I had to change. I had to change the way I thought about things. Maybe I sound a little different too."

"Yeah, well you sounded better when you were drunk."

Frank seemed about to say something, but didn't. He backed up a step and lowered himself into a hideous plaid La-Z-Boy left behind by a previous tenant. It was stuck in the upright position.

"I don't care if the Almighty poked a gun in my ear, I would never do that," Frances said. "Not in a million years. Neither would you. Honest, now, little brother, would you grind me up if I was the one down in the mill, would you push the Francesburger button?"

"It isn't a choice I have to make."

"Yeah, yeah, I know. But say you did."

"I don't. He doesn't hold guns to our heads."

"Oh, really? What about hell, huh? What do you call that? But so what. Screw hell. I don't care about hell. Do I get crunched or not?"

"Don't put me to the test, Frances. It's not your place."

"I'm down in the mill, Frank. I'm stuck in the gears and here comes the train with Mother Teresa and five hundred sinners on board, *whoo whoo, whoo whoo.* Who, Frank, who? Who's it going to be?"

Frances wanted to laugh. Glumly erect in the chair, hands gripping the armrests, Frank looked like he was about to take off into a hurricane. But she kept that little reflection to herself. Frank was thinking, and she had to let him. She knew what his answer would be—in the end there could be no other answer—but he couldn't just say *she's my sister* and let it go at that. No, he'd have to noodle up some righteous, high-sounding reasons for choosing her. And maybe he wouldn't, at first, maybe he'd chicken out and come up with the Bible-school answer. Frances was ready for that, she was up for a fight; she could bring him around. Frances didn't mind a fight, and she especially didn't mind fighting for her brother. For her brother she'd fought neighborhood punks, snotty teachers and unappreciative coaches, loan sharks, landlords, bouncers. From the time she was a scabby-kneed girl she'd taken on her own father, and if push came to shove she'd take on the Father of All, that incomprehensible bully. She was ready. It would be like old times, the two of them waiting in her room upstairs while Frank Senior worked himself into a rage below, muttering, slamming doors, stinking up the house with the cigars he puffed when he was on a tear. She remembered it all—the tremor in her legs, the hammering pulse in her neck as the smell of smoke grew stronger. She could still taste that smoke and hear her father's steps on the stairs, Frank panting beside her, moving closer, his voice whispering her name and her own voice answering as fear gave way to ferocity and unaccountable joy, *It's okay, Franky. I'm here.*

Rhetorical reading seeks to link the act of interpretation to the experience of reading, and it conceives of the literary work as a rhetorical action, a way of doing something with, for, and to an audience. In relation to fictional narrative such as Wolff's story, this conception leads not to a view of the work as a "structure of meaning" or even a combination of story (setting, characters, events) and discourse (narrative techniques) but rather to a view of it as an invitation from an author to an audience to have a multi-layered experience (cognitive, affective, ethical, and more) while engaging with characters in action. This conception underlies my rhetorical definition of narrative: somebody telling somebody else on some occasion and for some purpose(s) that something happened. Furthermore, rhetorical reading sees the audience's multi-layered experiences as closely connected to the author's purpose(s). Purposes range from defamiliarizing the ordinary to inciting readers to act in support of a cause; from encouraging philosophical meditations to evoking laughter, tears, and other emotional responses; from persuading readers of some truths about the world to sharpening their capacity to make nuanced ethical judgments. And of course such purposes often overlap.

In doing interpretation, the rhetorical critic proceeds by attending to the feedback loop among author agency, textual phenomena, and audience response: each affects the other two even as all three are governed by purpose. Thus, the rhetorical critic can begin at any of those three points in the loop, since answering questions about one will inevitably require attention to the other two. With Wolff's story, I start with the textual phenomenon of an ending that initially does not seem to provide the resolution implicitly promised by the story's beginning and middle (note how this formulation already moves toward audience response in its concern with that implicit promise).

In the last paragraph of the story, as Wolff focalizes the narration through his protagonist Frances, he shows her gradually melding her past experiences with and feelings for her troubled younger brother Frank into her present relationship with him. In effect, Wolff ends with a freeze-frame of Frances in the moment when that melding is complete: "*It's okay, Franky. I'm here.*" Before this paragraph, though, Wolff seems to have been constructing "The Night in Question" as a braid of three smaller narratives that will culminate in some kind of change in Frances or in her relationship with Frank: (1) the narrator's story of what happens during Frances's visit to Frank; (2) Frank's story, which he had heard in the form of a sermon by Dr. Violet a few hours before, of what happens to Mike Bolling, the drawbridge operator who must choose between saving the lives of numerous strangers on a train and saving the life of his own son Benny;[3] and (3) the narrator's account, often focalized through Frances, of Frank's childhood battles with his abusive father, battles that Frances joined on Frank's side. Wolff's braiding works well because (a) Frank's story is itself a rhetorical action, and his telling it is the main event in the narrator's story; and (b) the backstory provides valuable context for the audience's understanding of Frances's worried responses to that main event, responses that put her at odds with Frank, who tells the story for the purpose of informing Frances that he has accepted God into his life and thus will be a new and better man.

But Wolff makes two unexpected moves as the story nears its end. First, he does not allow Frank to finish telling his story about Mike and Benny, choosing instead to have Frances break in and predict its ending. Second, Wolff does not allow the narrator to tell how Frank answers the question Frances asks him, a question that the braiding of the two stories seems to have been leading up to: if you and I were in a situation like Mike and Benny's, would you save my life or the lives of "Mother Teresa and five hundred sinners" on the train? Instead Wolff chooses to end by depicting Frances's consciousness as she melds past into present. In this way, Wolff twice disrupts his audience's engagement with the question of "what happens next?" Why would Wolff introduce this double disruption into his narrative?

Consulting my own response and that of many others with whom I have discussed the story, I find that the initial answer is that the disruptions add to the affective and ethical power of Wolff's ending, and, indeed, of "The Night in Question" as a whole. (From here on, I shall use the first person in discussing audience response, but I believe my responses are not idiosyncratic and my goal is to identify their sources in Wolff's shaping of the textual phenomena.) Wolff produces these effects not only through his shaping of that last paragraph but also through his shaping of previous textual phenomena, especially (a) the backstory in the third braid of the narrative, and (b) two key repetitions with a difference.

Wolff uses the backstory to reveal the psychological dynamics of Frank and Frances's underlying sibling bond and some core aspects of Frances's own character. Both she and Frank are survivors of childhood trauma, and their traumatic past greatly influences their present: "Frank Senior said no to his son in everything, and Frances would say no to him in nothing. Frank was aware of her reluctance and learned to exploit it, most shamelessly in the months before his accident." Nevertheless, Frances believes that "No one should be alone in this world. Everyone should have someone who kept faith, no matter what, all the way."

This backstory significantly complicates my understanding of—and affective and ethical responses to—both Frank and Frances. Prior to it, I see them as troubled brother and supportive sister, and am sympathetic to each. The backstory's revelations about their childhood deepen my sympathy, and their resistance to Frank Senior garners my admiration, though Frances's perverse pleasure in it (after one battle she ends up "laughing like a madwoman") leavens that admiration with worry about the effects of this family violence on her. Furthermore, their sibling alliance enhances my sympathy and admiration, even as Frances's greater investment in the alliance points to her vulnerability. But more generally, Wolff guides me to recognize that the dysfunctional—and violent—family dynamics have warped Frances's character. Initially, she both feared and missed her father's attention, but when he never bestowed it, she moved from resenting Frank's obstinacy to supporting and even enabling it. Negative attention seems better to her than no attention, just as resisting her father seems better to her than remaining a passive observer like her mother. In addition, Frances's habit of aligning with Frank has become so entrenched that she is willing to pay a very high price for maintaining it. Although Frank "nearly destroyed her marriage" and "her husband had not forgiven Frances for what he called her complicity in that nightmare [of Frank's drunken behavior]," she cannot do with Frank what she did with her father: resist him. In sum, the backstory shows that Frances is almost as troubled in her own way as Frank is in his—in part because she is so attached to her role as his protector.

Wolff's braiding of his three narrative strands introduces two especially salient repetitions with a difference that further reveal Frances's character: (1) the relationship between Frank Senior and Frank Junior is the negative image of the one between Mike and Benny; (2) the sermon's insistence on the importance of God's constant presence is the sacred version of Frances's secular commitment to always be there for Frank. These repetitions reveal reasons for Frances's negative response to the Mike and Benny story beyond the ones she articulates to Frank. Although Mike is a loving rather than an abusive father, Frances cannot stand to hear Frank tell with so much approval a story in which a father has a hand in his son's death. And she cannot accept Frank's account of being so moved and persuaded by the story, because that account threatens her. If Frank remains a believer in God, then God will replace her as the constant presence in his life. And if Frank replaces her, then she is in danger of losing her own identity.

These points lead to a larger conclusion about Wolff's shaping of "The Night in Question." In standard narrative, we see one or more characters undergo some kind of change, and Wolff's initial braiding of the first two stories indicates that "The Night in Question" will follow that pattern. But Wolff uses the backstory and the repetitions with a difference to reshape the story from one focused on change to one focused on the revelation of character. In other words, Wolff shapes his material so that its narrative elements—those related to our interest in "what happens next?"—become subordinate to its elements of portraiture, elements related to the question "Who is Frances?" "The Night in Question" is thus a portrait narrative, and the last paragraph rounds out that portrait.[4]

In that paragraph Wolff's handling of time is especially noteworthy. He starts in the narrative present with Frances watching Frank as he contemplates her question about whether he would save her. When her reflections get to "Frances didn't mind a fight, and she especially didn't mind fighting for her brother," Wolff takes her thoughts into the past, both distant and recent ("For her brother she'd fought neighborhood punks, snotty teachers and unappreciative coaches, loan sharks, and bouncers"). And then he begins the melding, which reveals the intensity of Frances's own feelings: she feels strong enough to replace her father with "the Father of All" as her opponent. "It would be like old times.... She could still taste that smoke and hear her father's steps on the stairs, Frank panting beside her, moving closer, his voice whispering her name and her own voice answering, as fear gave way to ferocity and unaccountable joy, *It's okay, Franky. I'm here.*" Her being with Frank(y) now in his house becomes for her a replay of her being with him so many times in the past in their father's house, and her mantra applies not just to those past situations but to this one too: "It's okay, Franky, you don't need God; you have me." The "night in question" is not just the night that Mike made his choice about Benny and not just this night when Frank tells her that story but almost every night of Frances's life.

The handling of time and the final freeze-frame show that for Frances her relationship with Frank is all of a piece and the center of her own identity. Her devotion to him is at once understandable, commendable, and scary because, in its "joy and ferocity," it combines love, dependence, dominance, and desperation. As a result, I am immersed in multiple layers of affective and ethical response: Frances's intensity evokes my own intense affective response to being in the presence of her complex character, and my multiple positive and negative ethical judgments lead to a mixture of more specific emotions: sympathy, admiration, disapproval, worry. Frances is both role model and negative exemplar, both responsible for who she is now and in the grip of forces beyond her own ability to control. The more I contemplate her portrait, the more poignant and unsettling, moving and disturbing my experience becomes.

Guiding his audience to such a rich cognitive, affective, and ethical experience is one of Wolff's purposes, and I want to emphasize the value of that experience in and of itself: engaging with a story of this quality is its own reward. But that engagement also encourages the contemplation of multiple thematic extensions of the story, issues that I reflect on as I linger over my experience, and such contemplation is also part of Wolff's purpose. "The Night in Question" readily leads into thoughts about:

- family dynamics and their lasting effects;
- the insidious effects of childhood trauma;
- the role of gender in family dynamics both within and across generations;
- the bases for ethical choices in dilemmas such as the one posed in the story of Mike and Benny and the ones hinted at in Frances's marriage;
- the struggle between religious and secular beliefs;
- the mixed motives behind so many of our own actions;
- the prices we are willing to pay to honor our values, however misguided.

And that's just a partial list.

If I had more space, I'd say more about just everything here, I'd bring in other aspects of the story, especially its beginning, its dialogue, and its depiction of Frank, and I'd link Wolff's handling of time with post-modernism, but I hope what I have done illustrates how rhetorical reading works in the service of its larger purpose: giving us insight into both the nature and quality of the life we live while reading literature.

Reading 5   Herbert Tucker
Echo (1854)

Christina Rossetti

> Come to me in the silence of the night;
>   Come in the speaking silence of a dream;
> Come with soft rounded cheeks and eyes as bright
>   As sunlight on a stream;
>   Come back in tears,
> O memory, hope, love of finished years.
>
> O dream how sweet, too sweet, too bitter sweet,
>   Whose wakening should have been in Paradise,
> Where souls brimfull of love abide and meet;
>   Where thirsting longing eyes
>   Watch the slow door
> That opening, letting in, lets out no more.
>
> Yet come to me in dreams, that I may live
>   My very life again tho' cold in death:
> Come back to me in dreams, that I may give
>   Pulse for pulse, breath for breath:
>   Speak low, lean low,
> As long ago, my love, how long ago.

It's a nice question whether Christina Rossetti's title "Echo" indicates a generic category or identifies a speaker by name; whether it's a title like others the same poet called "A Dirge" and "Sonnet," or whether the poem belongs with dramatic monologues that are spoken, like those Alfred Tennyson titled "Tithonus" and Augusta Webster "Circe," by mythological persons. If the latter, then given the nymph Echo's accursed speech impediment the poem must be a monologue that is interior as well as dramatic. No matter: here is a text that, whether we imagine it meditated in silence or vocally uttered, displays an echolalia that, internally reverberant as a matter of sheer poetic form, also seems right in character for the girl who haplessly gave her heart to a Narcissus who had nothing to give her back. "Come," bids the first word; yet its recurrence five more times in so short a lyric, in the same syntactic sense and the same line position, weakens the imperative grip of its ostensible command. "Come," when it is repeated in this way, becomes not an authoritative order but a solicitous anaphora; it wields, in other words, the different authority of incantation, which in this case is invocation too. And this is just the beginning of a string of verbal iterations, from which the whole poem is woven back and forth: "how sweet, too sweet, too bitter sweet" (7); "letting in, lets out" (12); "Pulse for pulse, breath for breath" (16); "long ago, how long ago" (18).

Rossetti's poem admirably represents a large body of Victorian verse that was in the spellbinding business without advertising the fact. It conjures nothing overtly and names no charm; but for all that it *is* a charm, a plangent performative act wound up in verbal and sonal repetitions that make nothing happen, in W. H. Auden's famous tactical concession about modern poetry, but instead propose themselves as a way of happening, a mouth.[5] Although the charm fails to bring back the beloved whom it recalls—and re-calls, and re-calls—and although its echoing syllables as they pass measure out the very passage of time they undertake to recant, there's still magic in the textual web, which constitutes a peculiarly resilient poetic present out of the absence it constantly acknowledges. Insistent verbal repetition, elaborating a pervasive ambivalence that is introduced early by the oxymoron of a "speaking silence" (2), poises the force of utterance between a yearned-for past and a summons to future return.

Perhaps this attentive double hearkening explains the nonce design of Rossetti's odd six-line stanza, which contrives formally to look in two directions too. By ordinary metrical arithmetic each sixty-syllable sixain would be a cinquain, falling into five equally decasyllabic lines of iambic pentameter, were it not for the impatient glance each stanza's fourth line (4, 10, 16) throws over its pivoting shoulder to lock looks, in rhyme, with the second line above it. This hungry gesture of metrical return in effect orphans the next four syllables to make the best shift they can in a dimeter line whose shortness, whose as-yet-unrhymed isolation, and whose climactic place within the stanza accumulate a tremendous gravitas. Pentameter, then trimeter, then dimeter: Rossetti's stanzaic funnel tapers into an echoic fadeout that scores for special notice those places where the fixedly changing *metrical* pattern differs gradually from itself, stanza by stanza, when it comes to actual *rhythmic* articulation. This occurs most remarkably in those dimeter fifth lines, each one made of monosyllables only. Stanza one fulfills the iambic norm with "Come *back* in *tears*," whose movement stanza two retards, appropriately, in the trochee-spondee pairing "*Watch* the *slow door*," which ushers in stanza three's lingering feast of spondees, "*Speak low, lean low*."

By the time that last heavy-laden dimeter comes around, it is impossible to say who its speaking, leaning agent may be. In the imminence of this spell's suspensive hypothesis, just who is it that is going to "speak low, lean low"? Is it the addressed beloved who has been enjoined from the first to "come," and just two lines previously to "come back"? Or is it the enjoining speaker, who having craved the beloved's return in order "that I may give/Pulse for pulse, breath for breath" may likewise, in the course of so doing, "Speak low, lean low"? To put this syntactic ambiguity another way: there's no knowing whether the verbs in this line are imperative or optative. The confused merger of persons in this penultimate line, or magic spell of reciprocal possession—which also involves by this point, redundantly yet irresistibly, the low-speaking murmurous reader leaning low over the text—animates a correlative ambiguity in the metrically bold, beautifully symmetrical trimeter line above it. Whose "pulse," whose "breath," is whose? In giving "Pulse for pulse, breath for breath," is our speaker just reactively reproductive, giving back verbatim what she hears, with a secondary requital tailored to Echo's ever-diminishing Ovidian terms of endearment? Or is she taking the proactive lead and tasting, at least in fancy, the exquisite gratification of having her own primary initiative requited? Or is the whole set-up, perish the thought, but a scene of invocation as fantastic CPR, in which the only pulse and breath are the speaker's own, in exquisitely deferred recognition that all is for nought, love being, as the rhyming second line of the stanza has already conceded, "cold in death"? The way "As" yields its place to "how" in the final line does seem to give up the ghost—the metaphoric make-believe of a resemblance, between what obtains now and what happened long ago, yielding to the metonymic acknowledgment of an irreversible difference between the one time and the other. And yet the last word standing, the revenant "ago," is just close enough to "Echo" in the title that the poem's looped closure opens out after all, for a fresh reprise of melancholy obsession from the top. A chronic circuit in lyric time, aptly coursed by a poem that keeps starting with "Come" only to keep ending with "go."

Notes

1 For a more detailed discussion of these issues, see Dubrow (2013: especially ix–xiii).
2 Letter to Nathaniel Hawthorne, [April 16?], 1851, www.melville.org/letter2.htm.
3 The story is an adaptation of the "trolley problem" in ethics.
4 For a fuller discussion of portraiture in relation to narrative and to lyric, see Phelan (2008: 22–25, 178–198).
5 See Auden's poem, "In Memory of W. B. Yeats" (1939).

Works cited

Abrams, M. H. (2012) *The Fourth Dimension of a Poem and Other Essays*. New York: W. W. Norton.

Dubrow, Heather (2013) "Foreword," in *New Formalisms and Literary Theory*, ed. Verena Theile and Linda Tredennick. London: Palgrave Macmillan, vii–xviii.

Paterson, Don (2005) "The Thread," *Landing Light*. St. Paul: Graywolf Press, 8.

Phelan, James (2008) *Experiencing Fiction: Judgments, Progressions, and the Rhetorical Theory of Narrative*. Columbus: The Ohio State University Press.

Plath, Sylvia (1992) "Edge," in *The Collected Poems of Sylvia Plath*, ed. Ted Hughes. New York: HarperCollins, 272.

Rossetti, Christina (1979) "Echo," in *The Complete Poems of Christina Rossetti: A Variorum Edition*, Vol. 1, ed. R. W. Crump. Baton Rouge and London: Louisiana State University Press, 46.

Wolff, Tobias (1996) "The Night in Question," in *The Night in Question: Stories*. New York: Knopf, 174–185.

Yeats, William Butler (1957) "He and She," in *The Variorum Edition of the Poems of W. B. Yeats*, ed. Peter Allt and Russell K. Alspach. New York: Macmillan, 559.

A brief glossary

Aesthetic stance   Term used by Louise Rosenblatt (1904–2005) for an orientation to texts that is inward-thinking, non-utilitarian, and attentive to the personal and temporal dimensions of the reading experience; see **efferent stance**.

Affect theory   An emerging field situated at the intersections of neuroscience, sociology, cultural studies, and literature that seeks to investigate theories about human emotion.

Affective fallacy   New Critical term for the error of judging the merit of a literary work based chiefly on the feelings it evokes.

Alterity   Otherness, difference; in ethical criticism, reading is seen as a meeting with otherness, whether the consciousness of the implied author or the linguistic space of the text.

Ambiguity   Having more than one possible meaning; often exploited to enrich a work's imagery, deepen and complicate its significations, and heighten its total effect.

Bibliotherapy   The use of literature and other reading material for therapeutic purposes.

Close reading   Traditionally, a mode of literary engagement that concentrates on the operations of language in a text, to the exclusion of historical or biographical contexts; here, a strategy that emphasizes the point of contact between the reader and the text in order to concentrate on a work's formal elements; on the reader's role in creating meaning; and on the ideas and values implied in the work.

Demystification   In literary criticism, stripping away or exposing the workings of capitalist ideology, patriarchy, and other power structures in a literary work that might otherwise be seen as normative.

Disinterestedness   A critical position of objectivity or unbiased judgment; used by Victorian poet and critic Matthew Arnold (1822–1888) in *Essays in Criticism*.

Efferent stance   Term used by Louise Rosenblatt (1904–2005) for an orientation to reading texts that looks out from the work to what the reader wants to retain or put to use after reading; see **aesthetic stance**.

Ethical criticism   An approach that examines a literary work's involvement in moral and ethical questions, and which requires the critic to explicate a text's implied values and then articulate a response to those values.

Ethical turn   A shift in literary studies that took place in the early 1990s which theorized the various ways literary works communicate moral values and describe ethical situations, and which sought to comprehend the ethical relationship that exists between the reader and the text.

Formalism   An approach to literary works, associated with the **New Critics**, that applies attention to the formal features of a work of literature—its language, structure, rhythm, meter, imagery, metaphors, symbols, point of view, characterization, progression, setting, etc.—without reference to moral content or historical and biographical contexts.

Intentional fallacy   New Critical term for the error of assessing a literary work based on the author's presumed or stated intentions about the work's design, effects, meaning, morality, etc.

Intersubjectivity   In literary studies, the imagined two-way relationship between the reader and the text or the reader and the implied author, and a central concept for reader-response, phenomenology, and ethical criticism.

Intertextuality   The relationship among different literary texts, or the ways in which texts comment on, mold, influence, or reflect one another.

Linguistic turn   In philosophy, the major shift toward theories of language that took place in the mid-twentieth century, i.e., structuralism, post-structuralism, and deconstruction.

Narrative turn   In philosophy, the interest expressed by some prominent philosophers from the early 1990s in the ways literature and stories may contribute to ethical thought and moral knowledge.

New Critics   A group of influential Anglo-American writers in the years before and after World War II who determined that the focus of criticism should be on the words as written in the text itself, rather than on history, the author's biography, or philology.

New Formalism   A movement or tendency among contemporary scholars to revitalize and bring up to date the kind of attentive close reading promoted by the New Critics, usually by focusing on the rhetorical and aesthetic features of a text, mitigating cultural contexts.

New Historicism   Broadly speaking, an approach to literature which assumes that because authors are situated within complex cultural systems their works may replicate the power structures of their historical situations; literary and nonliterary texts must be deciphered as linguistic codes intricately entangled in a set of social and political discourses.

Object-relations theory   In psychoanalysis, analysis of the development of personal autonomy in relation to other people, especially in early childhood; see **transitional object**.

Phenomenology   In philosophy, the study of individual felt experience and human consciousness.

Phenomenology of reading   In literary theory, a focus on the imaginative involvement of the reader in processing language, conjuring images, and making meaning, and on literature's capacity to provoke reflection or reverie.

Reader-response or **reader-oriented theory**   An approach that focuses on the reader's role in literary analysis, either a hypothetical reader created or implied by the text, or real flesh-and-blood readers.

Reparative reading   A term first used in 1997 by Eve Kosofsky Sedgwick (1950–2009) for an alternative critical practice to paranoid or **symptomatic reading** that would take into account the reader's psychological motivations for reading literature, or his or her affective needs and responses.

Surface reading   A term coined by Sharon Marcus and Stephen Best in 1999 to describe an alternative to **symptomatic reading** that would encourage the reader's engagement with what is evident and apprehensible in a text, rather than what is hidden, disguised, or unsaid.

Symptomatic reading   A mode of literary analysis modeled on psychoanalysis that reads against the grain of the text's manifest content or the author's ostensible meaning to excavate its latent cultural and ideological discourses.

Transitional object   In the theory of psychoanalyst D. W. Winnicott (1896–1971), an object, such as a doll or toy, that helps a child psychically differentiate itself from its mother, representing a crucial stage in the development of the self; applied to literary studies, the idea that works of art have the capacity to trigger understanding or permit certain kinds of knowledge about the world to emerge into consciousness.

Index